HEADING AND CANONS

BOOKS
by or edited by
Dr S R Ranganathan

Projected Books

1 Universe of knowledge : Development and structure.
2 Subject heading and chain procedure.
3 Librarian looks back.

New editions in preparation

1 Book selection.
2 Five laws of library science.
3 Library classification : Fundamentals and procedure.
4 Organisation of libraries in India.
5 Prolegomena to library classification.
6 Reference service and bibliography.
7 Theory of library catalogue.

Books available

Hindi

8 Anuvarga-suchi-kalpa, 1952.
9 Grantha adhyanartha hai, 1948.
10 Granthalaya prakriya, 1950.

Copies available with :—
Rajkamal Publications Ltd., 1 Faiz Bazar, Delhi.

English

11 Depth classification, 1953.
12 Documentation problems, 1951.
13 Heading and canons : Comparative study of five catalogue codes, 1955.
14 Library manual, 1950.
15 Library tour, 1948, Europe and America : Impressions and reflections, 1950.
16 Union catalogue of learned periodical publications in South Asia, 1953.

(*Continued on page* 299)

Copies available with :—
1 S. Viswanathan, 11 McNichol Road, Madras-31.
2 G. Blunt and Sons, 100 Great Russel Street, London-W.C. 1.

HEADING AND CANONS

COMPARATIVE STUDY OF
FIVE CATALOGUE CODES

S R RANGANATHAN

S VISWANATHAN, MADRAS
G BLUNT AND SONS, LONDON
1955

Shiyali Ramamrita **Ranganathan** 1892—

Edition 1.   1955

2 : 55,-1, 1
J 5

Printed by S. Viswanathan at the Central Art Press, "Acton Lodge",
11 McNichol Road, Madras 31

To
Sow
SARADA

CONTENTS

8

CHAPTER 0
CONSPECTUS

The following contractions are used throughout this book :

Ala = *Ala cataloguing rules for author and title entries*, prepared by the Division of Cataloguing and Classification of the American Library Association, ed by Clara Beetle, ed 2, 1949. (Ed 1, 1908).

Ccc = *Classified catalogue code* by S. R. Ranganathan, ed 3, 1952. (Ed 1, 1934 ; ed 2, 1945).

Fundamentals = *Library catalogue : Fundamentals and procedure* by S. R. Ranganathan, 1950.

Pin = *Prussian instructions : Rules for the alphabetical catalogues of the Prussian libraries*, tr from ed 2, 1908...... by Andrew D Osborn, 1938. (Ed 1, of the original, 1899).

Rdc = *Rules for a dictionary catalogue* by Charles A Cutter, ed 4, 1904. (Ed 1, 1876 : ed 2, 1889 : ed 3, 1891).

Theory = *Theory of library catalogue* by S. R. Ranganathan, 1938.

Vat = *Rules for the catalogue of printed books*, tr from ed 2, 1939, by Thomas J Shanahan etc., ed by Wyllis E. Wright, 1948. (Ed 1 of the original 1930).

01 Field of Study

The main purpose of this book is a comparative study of the five catalogue codes *Rdc, Pin, Ala, Vat* and *Ccc*. The comparative study is made with the aid of a set of Fundamental Principles and Canons of Cataloguing. These were first formulated in the *Theory*. The study is largely confined to the establishment—*i.e.,* choice and rendering—of heading for author or title entry, main or added. Only a passing account is given of subject heading and series heading.

02 Reason for Restriction

This restriction is for a definite reason. All the five codes do not give rules for subject heading. Moreover, subject heading is largely tied up with classification. It is wasteful to deal with it as a purely cataloguing problem. In dealing with it, it is economical to draw heavily from classification. No code, except *Ccc*, has dealt with subject heading in this way. Thus there is no fair basis for comparative study. The field of subject heading is therefore reserved for another book entitled *Subject heading and chain procedure*.

03 Outcome

The comparative study discloses some hypertrophy in catalogue codes. Naturally, this hypertrophy leads to undue pressure on judgment in practical cataloguing, during the choice and rendering of heading. The root-cause of these ills is outside the strict sphere of cataloguing. A study of the etiology of the ills discloses the root-cause to lie in the author-statement in the title-page of book. Cure should, therefore, be applied to author-statement in title-page. Such a cure will result in considerable economy in cataloguing work. Suggestion of the establishment of an international standard practice for author-statement in title-page is the ultimate outcome of the study contained in this book.

04 Organisation of Chapters

Chapter 1 " **Prologue** " begins with an account of the genesis of this book. Then it gives a rapid history of cataloguing code in general. Then follows an examination of the distinctive contribution of each of the five codes *Rdc*, *Pin*, *Ala*, *Vat* and *Ccc*. It also gives the circumstances leading to the formulation of the Canons of Cataloguing and the other normative principles as a help to the drafting and the comparative study of catalogue codes. Then, it describes " Cycle of scientific method. " Finally, it shows that this cycle has begun in the discipline of cataloguing.

Chapter 2 " **Terminology** " defines important cataloguing terms, such as periodical publication, book, associated book, composite book, author, entry, entry-element and entry-word. This preliminary settling of terminology is found helpful in avoiding the creeping in of fallacy or fault or indefiniteness in the progress of thought in the rest of the book.

Chapter 3 " **Normative Principles** " enunciates general principles governing every discipline, the Five Laws of Library Science forming the principles governing every library technique and practice in the organisation and administration of library, and Canons of Cataloguing governing the technique of cataloguing.

Chapter 4 " **Choice** " makes a rule-by-rule comparative study of the five codes, bearing on the choice of heading—be it name of a personal author or corporate author or collaborator or series or work. It demonstrates a method for the adjudication of the rights of different claimants for the privilege of being chosen as heading. It also brings out the redundance and faults in some of the codes.

Chapter 5 " **Rendering** " deals with the stage after choice. It makes a rule-by-rule comparative study of the five codes, bearing on the rendering of multi-worded names of personal, governmental, institutional, and conference authors, names of series, uniformisation of the name of a sacred book or a classic, and heading for a pseudonymous or an anonymous book.

Chapter 6 " **Added Entry** " is devoted to a brief comparative study of the rules in the five codes, bearing on the choice of headings for book index entry and cross reference index entry. It also touches, without going into details, on the choice of subject heading. Chain procedure is briefly indicated.

Chapter 7 " **Title-Page** " starts with an indication in outline of a draft standard for prel (= preliminary pages of a book). It then gives an indication in outline of a draft standard for the elements to be carried by title-leaves. Lastly, it gives a draft standard for the author-statement in the title-page, its back, and their over-flow.

Chapter 8 " **Inter-National Catalogue Code** " gives the skeleton for an international catalogue code for the books of the past. The sphere of a supplementary national catalogue code is shown to consist of style of writing and printing, and certain essential schedules concerning names of persons, in the cultural groups of the nation. The automatic disappearance of the need for the latter, after the adoption of an international standard practice for author-statement, will simplify the national catalogue codes. It will also simplify the International Catalogue Code. These are indicated.

Chapter 9 " **Epilogue** " makes an appeal to the world of authors, publishers, and printers, of governments now becoming

prolific authors, publishers, and printers all at once, and of classifiers, cataloguers, and documentalists, to adopt international
standards in all matters bearing immediately or remotely on
cataloguing. It appeals for the saving of library man-power for
the essential and humane objective of libraries, *viz.* direct and
personal reference service to each reader. A method of estimate
adopted shows that there will be a saving of 79 per cent in the
technical man-power of a national library system by the adoption
of pre-natal classification and cataloguing of all home-produced
books by the National Central Library of a country. There
will similarly be a saving of 79 per cent in the technical man-power
of each national library system by the exchange of catalogue cards
among the National Central Libraries of the world. A method
is also indicated for an inexpensive, but thorough, method of
continuously building up a National Union Catalogue of home-
produced books and of foreign books coming into the country.
The social benefits likely to accrue by the transfer of 79 per cent
of the technical staff to direct personal service to readers, as a
result of the adoption of centralised national cataloguing and co-
operative international cataloguing, are described. The hope is
expressed of this leading to a contribution by the library profession towards the formation of peaceful co-existence and one-world.

05 Biblio-Ecology

This book happened to take shape in a thin atmosphere of
biblio-ecology even as *Ccc*. It happened to be written out at
Zurich. In that place, there was no access to a familiar collection
of books. Therefore examples could not be picked out for refresh-
ing the memory. This accounts for the absence of examples.
In a sense, perhaps examples are not necessary in this book. At
any rate their omission reduces the cost of physical production.
The codes studied give plenty of examples. And this book has
to be read along with them.

06 Human Ecology

Nor was there access to familiar co-workers and co-thinkers.
Time had to be spent in the isolation of a closed room all through
the two months in writing the book.

07 Acknowledgement

But I was allowed uninturrupted possession, for all the two months, of a copy of each of the under-mentioned books :—

    (1) *Ala* lent by the Bibliothek der Eidgenossische Technische Hochschule, Zurich ;

    (2) *Ccc* lent by the Bibliotheque Nationale Suisse, Bern ;

    (3) *Pin* lent by the Universitato Bibliothek, Basel ;

    (4) *Rdc* lent by the Stadt Bibliothek, Zurich ;

    (5) *Vat* lent by the Bibliothek der Eidgenossische Technische Hochschule, Zurich ;

    (6) *Vat* (Eng tr) lent by the Library of the Library Association, London.

I had to depend solely on these copies as I had not taken any of my books to Switzerland. I express my thanks to the librarians of these libraries for their kindness.

Friday, 27 August 1954.

  248, Hofwiesenstrasse,

      Zurich.

My thanks are also expressed to the following:—

    1. Sri K. Venkataraman, B.A., my cousin, for the willing way in which he prepared the press-copy of the book ; and

    2. Sri S. Viswanathan for the expeditious and participative way in which he printed the book.

Friday, 7 January 1955.

  46, Maurice Nagar,

  University of Delhi,

      Delhi.

CHAPTER 1

PROLOGUE

11 Genesis

It is now twenty years since the idea of a comparative study of catalogue codes occurred to mind. This was after the publication of *Ccc* in 1934. In 1938, Rudolph Gjelsness, Chairman and Editor-in-Chief, Catalogue Code Revision Committee, American Library Association, sent me a copy of the draft of the revision of *Ala* prepared by his Committee. He asked for suggestion. Then, I discovered the handicap due to the absence of a well-defined terminology and of normative principles in cataloguing. The result was the *Theory*. The idea of comparative study was revived by this experience. But other books claimed priority. In 1944, *Fundamentals* was prepared. This led to the discovery of the absence of a code for dictionary catalogue, as full and as rigorous as *Ccc* for classified catalogue. Without it, no fair basis could be found for a comparison of classified and dictionary catalogues. That year had therefore to be turned on the preparation of the *Dictionary catalogue code*. During the next ten years, several other new books had to be given priority. However, comparative study of catalogue codes was continued in teaching the theory of cataloguing. Attempts to find an old student to write out the intended book did not succeed. A kind of forced rest in Zurich during the spring and summer of 1954 gave the opportunity to fulfil the wish formed twenty years earlier. This is the genesis of this book.

12 Pre-Code Period

Catalogue has been as old as book itself. But till about the latter half of the nineteenth century, most catalogues were based on a set of rules framed by individual libraries in a casual way to suit their respective conditions. Such a set of rules was often drafted by the cataloguer of a library on the basis of the tradition, evolved through years and transmitted first orally and later in some written form. Panizzi's 91 rules given in the preface to the *British Museum catalogue* of 1841, embodying the practice of the

14

British Museum Library, is said to have been the most important catalogue code upto that time. This code influenced the cataloguing practice of many libraries with English as the language of the library. Its influence spread also into Latin countries. Other codes of influence in Teutonic countries are said to be the Munich Code of about 1850 and Karl Dziatzko's Code for the University Library at Breslaw. This was prepared in 1874 and published in 1886.

13 Rdc

None of the above drafts set forth cataloguing rules in a systematic or exhaustive way. Nor was there much evidence of their roots stemming from some kind of first principles. Nor again was any of them a general code not particularly conditioned by the practice of a single library. *Rdc* was the first code to reach beyond these limitations.' Its limitation was only in the linguistic context. The library profession has been fortunate in the author of this code. He was a genius. This is seen in the ring of certitude and the profoundness of penetration found in the rules and the commentaries of *Rdc*. They are like the eternal epigrams of a sage. *Rdc* is indeed a classic. It is immortal. Its influence has been overpowering. It inhibits free re-thinking even to-day. It appears to have been the chief source of later codes in the English language. Being a one man's creation, it has been largely apprehended intuitively. It has been later chiselled to a slight degree. That is why *Rdc* is whole as an egg.

14 Pin

Pin may be taken to be the second important code of a non-local nature. It is not, however, the creation of one man largely through intuition. It owed itself to the practical needs of a union catalogue of national coverage. Its foundation is involved. Its starting point was the Munich Code (1850) in manuscript form. With changes, it became Dziatzko's Code (1886). With some more changes, it became the Code of the Royal Library of Berlin (1890). This was expanded in 1892. Prussian government made budget provision for union catalogue in 1896. The catalogue of the Royal Library in Berlin adopted it as the basis. A committee

simplified the Code of the Royal Library to make it better suited
to a library catalogue, by the cutting out of the details prescribed
as for a bibliography. *Pin* resulted in 1899. This committee-
compromise in rehabilitating an existing Code with casual changes
in shape through half a century without guidance by creative
intuition or by normative principles has left its impress on *Pin*.
Still it bears in certain places the impress of Germanic terseness
and thoroughness.

15 Ala

151 Edition 1

Ala may be taken to be the third important catalogue code
of a non-local nature. Avowedly it is a committee-product.
It is probably undirected by consciously applied normative principles. It is largely empirical. It was established by a Committee
of the American Library Association, appointed in 1901. Into
it was drawn the experience of the Library of Congress. It was the
result of reconciling the practices of this national central library
and some scholarly libraries. The Library Association of Great
Britain co-operated with it. But the differences between the two
national library associations could not be reconciled in all cases.
Therefore, the first edition of *Ala* (1908) had alternatives for some
rules. This edition was confined only to author and title entries.
Even within this limited range, it was but a skeleton.

152 Edition 2 (Preliminary)

Committee work was carried to the extreme in preparing the
second edition of *Ala*. The central organisation was the Catalog
Code Revision Committee. Its organs were one Executive Committee, eleven Sub-Committees—for

1 Definitions	7 Capitalisation
2 Documents	8 Incunabula
3 Societies and institutions	9 Maps and atlases
4 Religious entries	10 Music
5 Anonymous classics	11 Index
6 Periodicals	

—, one Advisory Committee, one Committee of the Library Association of Great Britain, one Committee of the Music Library
Association, and one Editorial Sub-Committee. Thus there were

16 organs in all. A preliminary edition was published in 1941.
It was in two parts :—1 Entry and heading ; and 2 Description
of books.

153 CRITICISM

Criticism was invited on this preliminary edition. A committee digested all the criticisms and suggestions offered. Its
report was given in 1944. It was decided to defer further work
on part 2.

154 EDITION 2 (FINAL)

The Catalog Code Revision Committee was discontinued in
1946. An Advisory Board and an editor prepared the final
second edition. Such a labyrinth of committees deliberating
through two decades cannot be expected to produce a natural
whole. The same life-element cannot be expected to breathe
through every rule. Such a code cannot be expected to be an
organic unity with no element of redundancy or inconsistency.
And yet, for a committee-made code not charged with the personality of a single author, *Ala* is a remarkable achievement.

16 Vat

Vat owed itself to a decision of 1927 to prepare a new catalogue
of the printed books in the Vatican Library in Rome. It is interest-
ing to know that the catalogue of the original collection compiled
at the end of the seventeenth century had used forename of author
as entry word. In 1927 the Vatican Library accepted the offer
of help by the Carnegie Endowment for International Peace in
the preparation of the new catalogue. The help was in two forms:
—1 The training of several members of the staff of the Vatican
Library in the library schools of USA ; and 2 Organisation
of the work by a mission of American librarians working in Rome
for a period. The mission consisted of Willim W Bishop, James
C M Hanson and Charles Martel. It was assisted by Milton E
Lord, William M Randoll, also from USA. The mission began
work in February 1928. Later, the Vatican members returning
from USA, after training, were associated with the work of the
mission.

161 DICTIONARY CATALOGUE

The first decision was to choose the dictionary form of the

17

catalogue already popular in USA. The second decision was to evolve a set of catalogue rules on the basis of the Italian *Rules for the compilation of the alphabetical catalogue* (1911) and the *Ala*.

162 FINAL DRAFT

At first the cataloguing was done mainly by the Italian code with amendments made in the light of the *Ala*. But the copies of the Italian code were exhausted. The absence of rules for subject-heading was also giving difficulty from the very beginning. Therefore a complete set of rules had to be worked out. This was done by the Norwegian librarian, John Ansteinsson who started work with the mission but remained till June 1930 to complete the code. Naturally great attention was paid to the cataloguing of Catholic literature. It will be seen later that *Vat* follows the *Ala* very closely. Indeed the foreword to the English translation published by the American Library Association remarks with legitimate pride " The circumstances and the personnel under which they (the rules of *Vat*) were prepared produced the unexpected result that for many years the most complete statement of American cataloguing practice was available only in the Italian language."

17 Ccc

Ccc takes the evolution of catalogue code one step further. The other four codes are all no doubt of a non-local nature. That is, none was a code peculiar to a single library or a small class of libraries and yet, the sphere of application of each is, by implication, restricted to one language. It is taken as if it were natural, without being explicitly pointed out. *Ccc* is the first code to remove this restriction. This it does by means of two concepts :—
1. Language of the library ; and 2. Scale of languages, in which the language of the library comes first and the others come in the descending sequence of favouredness. This concept had been already developed in the *Colon classification* (1933). This concept implies also the concept of " script of the library," and of " favoured script." The use of these concepts bring the *Ccc* nearer to a universal code than the others. And yet, it provides for local variation. A few places where the wording has been faulty in this respect were discovered in the course of writing this book. These faults should be removed in edition 4.

171 GENESIS

Ccc owes itself to the sense of revolt induced in the mind of the author while learning cataloguing in 1924-25, in the School of Librarianship of the University College, London. The first cause of revolt was the method of teaching used. Each rule of the *Ala* was taken by itself as if it were to be put into rote-memory. No attempt at answering the what, the why, or the how of it. No attempt to present the rules as a system. No attempt at studying an alternative code and comparing their relative merits. The second cause was the nature of the code taught. It was the *Ala* of 1908. Its skeleton nature, its mixing up author entry and subject entry, lack of unity in most of the rules—a serious drawback in the drafting of a code—all these added to the result. There was also a third cause. The volumes of the classified catalogue of the Carnegie Library of Pitsburgh and of the Mitchel Library of Glasgow were fascinating. Copies of these were available in the library of the School of Librarianship. But not a word was said in the class either about classified catalogue or about the essential difference between it and dictionary catalogue. A fourth cause came out of the discrepancy between the rules taught in the theory class and those prescribed for adoption in the practical class. Here again, nothing was said or done to satisfy the curiosity of students about this difference. Fifthly, the bibliographical details about format, collation and imprint were over-emphasised in the practical class. The revolt made the author say within himself, " When I go back to Madras,......"

172 FACILITY

On going back to Madras, the author found facility of every kind to re-think cataloguing. In the first place, he had full freedom to do his best in re-organisation—open access, classification, cataloguing, reference service, simplified practice in administration, staff selection, public relation, in fact in every detail in the running of the library and in building it up. Secondly, the annual accession soon rose from 500 to 6,000. This choked, within a year, the pastedown catalogue in use. The necessity to build the catalogue afresh provided the opportunity to change over to card catalogue. This in its turn brought in the opportunity to give up the old method based on the British Museum rules and modified arbitrarily here and there.   The working out of a new code was taken on hand. Thirdly, the author spent much time each day on floor-duty observing the classificatory and cataloguing approach of readers to books.   Their approach had not been coloured at all by any tradition, as most of them tasted library facility—and open access in particular—for the first time in their lives.   This gave as good an approximation as possible to unconventionalised, free, natural mental behaviour.   Fourthly, the author was fortunate in the first two colleagues selected by him—C. Sundaram and K. M. Sivaraman.   Both were young graduates fresh from university.   Both were free from any kind of library tradition in any library technique whatever.   Both had an open mind.   Both had a participating attitude.   Both were devoted to their work.   Both were industrious. All the three were loyal to one another.   In fact, the three worked together in library field, as it were a case of one mind in three bodies. A quantum of intuition was bringing out the Colon Classification and the Classified Catalogue Code.   Intellect was brought into play once a week collectively in all the three to discuss, check up, and polish the product of intuition, in the light of the experience gained by each of the three during hours of floor-duty.   Fifthly, a school of librarianship was established in 1929.   Since then the author had been teaching cataloguing every year.   Sixthly, about 70,000 volumes were classified, catalogued and served during the seven years from 1926 to 1932.   During the last two of these years, the Colon Classification occupied the conscious level.   The Classified Catalogue Code was shaping unexpressed, below the conscious level, except while teaching cataloguing, till 1933, the year of publication of the *Colon classification*.

173 FINAL FORMULATION

After the *Colon classification* came out, the catalogue-valve between the conscious and the subconscious opened out.   The simmering of *Ccc* began within the mind.   The author had to go to Calcutta.   It was a railway journey of 38 hours.   He said to Sivaraman, " Put into my bag plenty of 5 × 3 slips and a few sharpened pencils.   During 24 hours of the forward journey and an equal extent of time in the return journey, the rocking of the train, the utter absence of distraction by any printed stuff, and   the solitude in the railway compartment, helped concentration.   Uninterrupted recording of the flow of the rules of *Ccc* was the result. Some of the rules brought their commentaries in their train. On return to Madras, these were intellectually reviewed by all the three. These were checked up and polished. Examples were provided. The press-copy was typed.

174 FLAWS

The preparation of the second and third editions of *Ccc* provided opportunity for a critical examination of its rules with a fresh intellect unhampered by the memory of their earlier formulation. Moreover, *Ccc* is being used to teach practical cataloguing. Each entry by each student is put " on trial," as in a court of law. The class as a whole critically examines the catalogue cards written in the practical hours. The accuser as well as the accused student should cite the appropriate rule from *Ccc* in support of every statement of his. This method of teaching is putting *Ccc* also " on trial." This has now happened for nearly twenty years. A few trivial flaws thus come to be spotted out from time to time. These are removed in the subsequent edition. This is a continuing process. While writing the present book, flaws in relation to local variation have been spotted out for the first time. These should be set right in edition 4.

175 SANSKRIT VERSION

In 1951, the rules of *Ccc* were rendered into Sanskrit to form the basis for translation into the several languages of India. *Sutra* style (= aphorism) was adopted. This style is the one used for basic codes and texts in Sanskrit tradition. This style is extremely sensitive to the principle of " atomic unit thought " in the construction of a rule. Therefore the rendering into Sanskrit *Sutras* led to the detection of every violation of the severe unitary principle. Drafting in English does not allow such thorough atomisation. Therefore the rectification in the Sanskrit version could not all be incorporated in the English version. However, such as could be, have been noted. The breaking down of some of the rules into more homogeneous units should be carried out in edition 4.

176 RESILIENCE

The rules in the English version too make some approximation to *Sutra* form even as they are in the past and the current editions. This invests the rules with resilience. This proves useful in apply-

ing them to refractory title-pages with the aid of the traditional
Rules of Interpretation. A demonstration of such a procedure
has been given, in the field of classification in the article *Classification
of allusion books* by S. R. Ranganathan and K. M. Sivaraman
published in *South Indian teacher*, 10, 1937, 74-79 and *Modern
librarian* 7, 1937, 127-133. The ruthlessly analytical mesh holding
the rules of *Ccc* invests the code as a whole with a resilience of
another kind. Books appear off and on with cataloguing features
beyond the capacity of the existing rules, even with the prop
provided by the Rules of Interpretation. A few books with
one or other of such new features have come out in recent years.
This will continue for ever. Hitherto, it has been easy to inter-
polate the necessary new rules consistent with the old ones in the
right place in the Code. Three such new rules have been absorbed
by *Ccc* during the last twenty years without any disturbance to the
existing rules. These concern Pseudo-Series, Associated Books,
and Merger Books.

18 Scientific Method

Cataloguing has now emerged from the stage of hand to mouth
existence and rule-of-thumb practice. It has entered the stage
of scientific method. The same is true of the framing of catalogue
code.

181 ENDLESS CYCLE

In scientific method, there is a never-ending succession of
cycles :—

1 from individual experiences, through generalisation, to
     empirical laws derived from them, with the aid of
     normal equations and induction ;

2 through their reduction to a few normative principles,
     with the aid of imagination and/or intuition ;

3 through deductive laws or canons derived from the
     normative principles with the aid of methods o
     inference and semantics ;

5 · through fresh individual experiences not conforming to
     them ;

6 back again through another cycle ; and

7 so on, without end.

182 ESTABLISHMENT OF CYCLE

Such a cycle of development has now been established in cataloguing. Therefore, both the teaching of cataloguing and the framing of catalogue code can have the benefit of normative principles. New types of reading materials apparently transcending the capacity of the existing rules of a catalogue code may be catalogued by a proper interpretation of its rules. If this is not adequate the rules can be amended or extended with the aid, and as a necessary implication, of the normative principles. When the unconcious shift in the social purpose of the library calls for an altogether different kind of library service, organisation and technique, and if the current ones stand abandoned by sheer folk-force, new normative principles should replace the old ones. And the cycle should be started again.

183 CRITICAL STUDY

A critical examination of a catalogue code can be made with the aid of the normative principles. So also can be made a comparative study of several catalogue codes. Lastly, any catalogue code can be rectified in their light.

184 VERBAL APPARATUS

The success of critical or comparative study will depend on the verbal apparatus used to express thought and communicate it. The verbal apparatus should not create " noise " in the process of communication. It should not do so even in self-communication. Grossly disturbing noise is usually caused by the presence of homonyms and synonyms in the verbal apparatus. Even more dangerous and virus-like is the subtle difference in the shade of meaning of a word, due to slight shift of undertones and overtones. To minimise this, we should begin any discipline with the establishment of a special, agreed, dry-as-dust terminology without even the slightest touch of fuzziness. But such a special terminology will have to begin with some undefined terms. These should be clearly stated. Again the meta-language with which we handle the special terminology both at the stage or definition and the later stages of development of thought, should be closely watched, if it is also drawn from the same natural language as the terminology itself. This is so in the discipline of cataloguing to-day. The special terminology should become spontaneous and instantaneous.

Its use should be as much the result of reflex action as that of mother-tongue.   This is an essential factor in scientific method.

185 FIRST APPROXIMATION

The first application of such a scientific method to cataloguing and catalogue code was made in 1938.   Between 1934 and 1938 some of the rules of *Ccc* came up for critical examination from time to time, both in class-room discussion and in staff-meeting to consider problem-books in cataloguing.   On the anvil of such critical discussions, certain normative principles of cataloguing took shape. These were different from the Five Laws of Library Science. Indeed, they were all implications of these laws.   They were also different from the normative principles common to all spheres of human action and thought.   These special normative principles were called Canons of Cataloguing.   These were the product of impersonal intellectual grind during the prolonged earlier stages, and of imagination at the final stage.   The author of *Ccc* had the unusual privilege of continuously subjecting *Ccc* and the other codes to a severe semantic analysis and check-up in the pure intellectual plane—in the class-room and in staff-meetings.   This helped the formulation of the canons ; and it also led to the setting up of the scientific method in the discipline of cataloguing.   The experience of this first attempt was recorded in *Theory*.

186 AT THE NICK OF TIME

It was late in 1937.   The press-copy of *Theory* was lying on the table.   To write or not to write to the Vice-Chancellor for formal permission to print it—that was the question.   A sullen mood for total withdrawal from intellectual work and retirement from office was undermining enthusiasm and zest.   Natesa Ananda, a spiritual friend, called for an all-night vigil.   He counselled persistence in the work on hand.   A new spiritual guide appeared suddenly. He was Purohit Swami.   He had considerable experience both before and after enlightenment.   He had just then returned from Ireland after spending some years with W B Yeats. He administered a genial warning.   He said "Salvation can come only by dogged pursuit of work in society, without either emotional attachment or revulsion."   These correctives had now been working in the mental plane for about twenty-four hours.   There came suddenly, a physical aid in the form of a postal packet.   It contained a mimeographed copy of the draft of the rules for the preliminary second edition of *Ala*. Along with it came also a letter from Rudolph Gjelsness, chairman and editor-in-chief of the Catalogue Revision Committee of the American Library Association. He asked for comments on the draft rules. The next few hours were turned on them. Many inconsistencies were seen. Some faults were detected. But there was no agreed terminology or canons of cataloguing, in terms of which the comments could be put across to a far-off correspondent through a letter. This predicament and the close sequence of it and the advice from spiritual friends at the nick of time led to a decision to publish the *Theory*.

187 SECOND APPROXIMATION

The present book is a second approximation to the application of scientific method to cataloguing. The cycle of scientific method having been formed in this field, this second approximation begins with a chapter on terminology and another on normative principles. Then the several topics in choice and rendering of heading are taken up successively. The corresponding rules in the five chosen codes are examined critically and comparatively. This demonstrates the convenience, if not the need, of having an international standard for the title-page and its overflow, with special reference to author-statement and title. Finally comes a peep into the problems of an international catalogue code. This peep leads to a vision of the library as a social institution to help in the evolution of One-World.

CHAPTER 2

TERMINOLOGY

21 Work

211 **Knowledge-unit.**—Assumed term.

It may extend in print to several volumes at one extreme or only to a single sentence at the other extreme.

212 **Thought.**—Knowledge-unit.

This term is introduced for brevity.

213 **Expressed Thought.**—Thought expressed in language or symbols or in any other mode and thereby made communicable.

214 **Work.**—Expressed thought.

This term is introduced for brevity.

215 **Title.**—Name of work.

216 **Sacred Work.**—Basic work of a religion, generally accepted as such among its followers.

In most schemes of library classification, a sacred work is made a quasi-class *i.e.*, a quasi subject. Each part of it is made a subclass. Chains of the subclasses of a sacred book are usually enumerated in a system of classification.

217 **Classic.**—Work embodied in several versions, adaptations, and translations, attracting other works on itself and coming out in print even long after its origin.

A classic can be made a quasi-class *i.e.*, a quasi-subject in a scheme of classification. It is so made in Colon Classification. Some of these are so made in Universal Decimal Classification also.

218 **Work of Literature.**—Work in the form of poem, drama, fiction, prose, or any other literary form, of which the outstanding qualities are taken to be beauty of form and emotional appeal, and/or which is of intuitive or trans-intellectual origin.

A work of literature can be made a quasi-class *i.e.*, a quasi-subject in a scheme of classification. It is so made in Colon Classification. Some of these are so made in Universal Decimal Classification also.

26

2191 **Quasi-Class.**—Work made into a class in a classification scheme or whose title is used as a subject heading in cataloguing practice.

A quasi-class thus becomes a quasi-subject. In the Colon Classification, a sacred work or a classic or a work of literature is made a quasi-class. In most of the other schemes, a sacred work is made a quasi-class. In most of the cataloguing practices, the name of a sacred work or a classic or a work of literature is made a subject heading.

2192 **Pedestrian Work.**—Work not made into a quasi-class or quasi-subject by the scheme of classification in use or at least the name of which is not made a subject heading in the cataloguing practice in use.

2193 **Micro-thought** and **Macro-thought** are relative terms with meaning loosely fixed by convention. An article in a periodical, or a pamphlet, or a section or a chapter of a book may be said to embody micro-thought. In classificatory language, it forms a class of great intention. Macro-thought forms a class of great extension. It is usually embodied, all by itself, in a book of size greater than a pamphlet.

22 Author and Collaborator

221 **Person.**—An assumed term.

22101 Name of a person is given either by

1 the parents or guardian or other substitute of theirs during childhood ; or

2 the person himself at a later time ; or

3 heraldic convention ; or occasionally

4 a competent authority under a statute or edict.

Name of a person is a proper noun.

222 **Corporate Body.**—A number of persons taken collectively—usually as united, or organised, or coming together informally, in a common cause or for a common action, such as government business, or commercial or industrial or any other business, or deliberation, or collective expression of opinion or statement.

A corporate body may be :—1 a government including a local body ; or 2 an institution ; or 3 a conference including a casual or informal meeting ; or 4 an organ of any of the above.

22201 The name of a corporate body is given to it by either:—
1 itself ; or   2 usage ;   or   3 law ;   or   4 cataloguing convention.

22202 **Distinctive Name** of corporate body.—Name of
corporate body beginning with the name of a person or geographical entity, in noun form, adjectival form, or any other grammatical
form.

2221 **Organ** of a corporate body.—Non-autonomous part
of a corporate body established either by

    1 the constitution of the body ; or

    2 executive or administrative measure for administrative
       work for an indefinite period, within the field of the
       function of the corporate body ; or

    3 legislative or executive or administrative measure for a
       specific work of a limited duration.

2222 **Constitutional Organ.**—Category 1 mentioned in 2221.

2223 **Administrative Organ.**—Category 2 mentioned in
2221.

2224 **Permanent Organ.**—Category 1 or 2 mentioned in
2221.

2225 **Temporary Organ.**—Category 3 mentioned in 2221.

2226 **Organ of First Remove.**—Organ intrinsic to the
constitution of the corporate body.

2227 **Organ of Second Remove.**—Department of any
organ of first remove, non-autonomous and administrative.

2228 **Organ of Third Remove.**—Non-autonomous administrative division of any administrative department.

And so on.

223 **Author of a work.**— 1 person creating the work ; or
                                    2 corporate body owning res-
                                      ponsibility for the thought
                                      and expression constituting
                                      the work.

    1 *Rdc* defines,

author, in the narrower sense, is the person who writes the book ; in a
wider sense, it may be applied to him who is the cause of the book's existence
by putting together the writings of several authors (usually called *the editor*,
more properly to be called the *collector*).

The term "writes" used by *Rdc* is too loose.   It may even include amanuensis.

2 *Pin* does not give a definition of the term " author."   Evidently it takes it as an assumed term.

3 *Ala*, on the other hand, defines author as

writer of a work, as distinguished from the translator, editor, etc.   By extension an artist, composer, photographer, cartographer, etc.

This is rather clumsy.   It is perhaps traceable to not starting the terminology from the very fundamentals.   *Ala* further adds,

in a broader sense the maker of a work, or the person or the body immediately responsible for its existence.   Thus a person who collects and puts together the writings of several authors (compiler or editor) may be said to be the author of a collection.

This is too loose.   The term " maker of a work " may even be misconstrued to include the printer !   Again *Ala* adds,

a corporate body may be considered the author of publications issued in its name or by its authority.

The term " by its authority " is again too loose.   It may open the flood-gates too widely.   As if alarmed by this it makes some amendments in rule 71.   There it says

authors of publications for which they, as corporate bodies, are responsible.

4 *Vat* defines author as

the one responsible for a book ; this may be one or more individuals or a corporate body.

The term, " responsible for a book " in this definition as well as in rule 71 of *Ala* is also vague.   It can mean author, publisher, or even a mere sponsor.

5 *Ccc* avoids all such looseness.   Its definition is equivalent to the one given at the beginning of this section, in this book.

2231 Personal Author.—Person as author, the responsibility for the thought and expression in the work resting solely on his private capacity and not on the capacity of any office he may hold within a corporate body, nor on the corporate body.

2232 Corporate Author.—Corporate body as author, the responsibility for the thought and expression in the work resting solely on it and not on personal author(s).

1 *Rdc's* definition of " author " includes,

" Bodies of men (societies, cities, legislative bodies, countries) are to be considered the authors of their memoirs, transactions, journals, debates, reports, etc.

Rdc 45 repeats the same idea :

bodies of men are to be considered as authors of works published in their name or by their authority.

This is too loose. For example, the title-page of the *Fauna of British India* in several volumes contains the inscription " By the Authority of the Secretary of State for India." Surely, neither the British Government nor the India Office can be taken as author of this set of volumes.

Rdc was however a pioneer in the fight for the establishment of the idea of corporate authorship. Here is a sample of its pleading in the preface to rule 45 and the commentary on it.

Before the *Rdc* were made, catalogues seemed to me to be chaotic collections of empirical entries. I tried to find a few simple principles around which all desirable practices could be grouped. One of these principles is corporate authorship and editorship. I have as yet seen nothing to convince me that it is not a good one, since it corresponds to practice;...... it is convenient in practice.

The chief difficulty with regard to bodies of men is to determine (1) what their names are and (2) whether the name or some other word should be the heading.

2 *Pin* refuses to recognise corporate author in general, as stated in rule 32. It categorically states :—

names of persons, official bodies, corporations, etc., at whose instigation or with whose support the work has originated are disregarded.

However, it admits corporate authorship in the one case covered by rule 60,

sales catalogues, prospectuses, and the like which mention the firm are put under its name.

Its allergy to corporate authorship is shown in the second sentence of rule 60,

if, however, the collector or author is named, they are treated according to rule 59.

This means that he is regarded as the author.

3 *Ala* states,

a corporate body may be considered as the author of publications issued in its name or authority.

Evidently, *Rdc* 45 is the source for this faulty wording. However, it seeks to minimise the danger of the flood-gates being opened in this way by putting a dam in paragraph 2 of rule 71,

monographic works by individual officials, officers, members and employees of corporate bodies, when these works are not clearly administrative or routine in character, are preferably to be entered under personal author, even though issued by the corporate body.

This is a partial and a halty adoption of the specification in *Theory*. The half-hearted nature of its adoption is indicated by *Ala*'s flooding with quite a number of rules to spell out its implications. These rules are 73C ; 75C-D ; 84C-D ; 89C, E, H ; 90A-B and 118A.

Vat defines in page 4,

corporate bodies national and local administrative bodies, ecclesiastical authorities, associations, and institutions are considered the authors of the publications emanating from them or containing acts and documents belonging to them.

The terms " emanating from " and " belonging to " are too vague for consistent application.

5 *Ccc* would use definitions such as those given in sections 2231 and 2232. These are more fully elaborated and explained in chapter 54 of *Theory*. The substance of that chapter is given in the following sections.

224 PERSON *vs.* CORPORATE BODY

2241 If the title-page mentions the name(s) of person(s) only in the place usually giving the name of author and does not indicate the name of any corporate body other than one belonging to the publishing trade mentioned in the imprint, the work in the book is of personal authorship. There is no alternative to be considered.

2242 If the title-page does not mention the name of a person in the place giving name of author but indicates somewhere in itself the name of a corporate body other than a body belonging to the publishing trade mentioned in the imprint, the work in the book is of corporate authorship, provided that even in the latter case it is of corporate authorship, if it is a work by or on the corporate body itself, such as its catalogue, administration report, history, and so on.

2243 If the title-page indicates the name of a corporate body other than a body belonging to the publishing trade mentioned in the imprint, and also the name(s) of person(s) in the place usually giving the name of the author,

1 The work in the book is of corporate authorship, if it is of a deliberative, legislative, directive, judicial,. administrative or routine character limited by the purpose or function or outlook of the corporate body. The mere fact that a book is published, financed, aided, approved, or authorised by a corporate body is

not sufficient reason to deem it to be of corporate authorship, and not to be of personal authorship.

2 The work in the book is of personal authorship, if its primary function is the extension of the boundary of a field of knowledge or its intensification, and the responsibility for the thought and expression in it rests on the person and not on the office held by him in the corporate body, in spite of his being a paid or an honorary employee or a member of the corporate body. The mere mention of the personal name of an official of the corporate body in the place in which author's name is usually mentioned, is not sufficient reason to deem it not to be of corporate authorship, but to be of personal authorship.

225 **Joint Author.**—One sharing responsibility with other(s) for the thought and expression contained in a work, the portion for which each is responsible not being either specified or separable.

1 *Rdc*'s definition is very different. It reads,

joint authorship, writing a book in conjunction, with specification of the part written by each.

2 *Pin* appears to be a mixture of the definition of *Rdc* and the one given in section in 225. This is implied in rules 62 to 68 of chapter 2 under the caption " Joint Authors ". Rule 67 refers to " an individual work that is the common composition of two or three authors ". The other rules fall within the definition of *Rdc*. Curiously *Pin* does not give a definition of joint author explicitly.

3 *Ala*'s definition agrees in substance with the one given in section 225.

4 *Vat*'s definition is,

one who writes a work in collaboration with one or more associates.

This definition is rather vague. For it would bring under joint author a person who is described as merely " directing, or assisting the author ".

5 *Ccc*'s definition agrees in substance with the definition given in section 225.

226 **Collaborator.**—Person or corporate body associated with a work and/or its author in the capacity of director, assistant commentator, illustrator, engraver, translator, reviser, editor, writer of introduction, epitomiser, adapter, libratist, writer of the words in a musical composition, or any other similar secondary capacity not amounting to authorship.

Ccc introduces the generic term collaborator. This is found to be a convenience. This makes the expression of the rules and their discussion less verbose. There is, however, a little confusion caused by its including " Joint author " in the category collaborator. This fault should be rectified in edition 4.

Rdc, *Pin*, *Ala*, and *Vat*, do not use this term to full convenience.

2261 **Compiler.**—One who makes up a work by arranging materials culled from various works.

Perhaps this term also may be included under the generic term " collaborator ".

227 Person *vs.* Person

Several difficulties may arise in deciding the author of a work. The following are elucidations of some difficulties requiring judgment. Other cases will have to be dealt with along analogous lines. The author is indicated in each case.

2271 SPOKEN WORD

The following are works in which the thought expressed in the spoken word is not committed to writing by the author of the spoken word. The writing has to be done by someone else. Nowadays many authors dictate their works ; they do not write them. The writing is done by the steno-typist. And yet there is no doubt that the person who dictates is the author. The steno-typist is not even regarded as a collaborator. However, in the case of the undermentioned forms of spoken word, the words are not published always exactly in the form in which they were spoken. Usually they require editing. The person who collects or notes down the spoken words and gives them the shape of a work should be regarded as collaborator.

No.	Type of Work	Author
1	Arra, table-talk	Talker
2	Dialogue, conversation, debate	Participants
3	Interview	Person(s) interviewed
4	Narration (real and not fictitious)	Narrator
5	Mediumistic communication	Medium(s) and not the disembodied souls.

33

2272 CORRESPONDENCE

In the case of correspondence, the correspondent(s) should be taken as author(s).

2273 MAP AND ATLAS

The cartographer is the author of a map or atlas.

2274 DEPENDENT WORK

There are cases in which one work is got by some modification of another work or by the augmentation of it. Such a work may be called a **Dependent Work**. There are three groups of dependent works. In group one, it is appropriate to take the author of the original as that of the dependent work also. In that case, the author of the dependent work gets the status of collaborator.

In group two, it is appropriate to take the author of the dependent work itself as its author. The author of the original cannot be regarded as a collaborator. There are special rules in cataloguing to associate the author of the original with the author of the dependent work.

In group three, both the original and the dependent work together constitute the work. This group will be dealt with in section 23.

Group 1

Dependent works for which the author of the original should be taken as the author :—

11 Abridgement	13 Paraphrase
12 Adaptation in the same or another language, which has not become a work on its own right	14 Revision
	15 Selection
	16 Translation

Group 2

Dependent works for which the author of the dependent work itself should be taken as the author :—

21 Adaptation in the same or another language, which has become a work on its own right.	27 Index
	28 Libretto
	291 Music-setting
	292 Novelisation
22 Commentary	293 Parody
23 Concordance	294 Sequel
24 Continuation	295 Supplement
25 Dramatisation	296 Versification
26 Imitation	

2275 **Anonymous Work.**—Work of unknown authorship, either personal or corporate.

Many of the sacred books are anonymous. Some of the classics of old are also anonymous. A few pedestran books come out anonymous.

Pin regards a work without personal author as anonymous.

228 **Corporate Body** *vs.* **Corporate Body**

In para 1 of the commentary on section 222, different kinds of corporate bodies were mentioned. Occasionally there is difficulty in deciding between them in regard to the authorship of a work. It will be a convenience in making that decision, to establish a closer meaning of the terms used to denote the different kinds of corporate bodies.

2281 **Government.**—1 Government with full or limited sovereign power. It generally has functions of execution, legislation, judiciary, and administration. Other functions such as defence, taxation, regulation of commerce will vary with the limitation of sovereign power.

2 Local Authority in charge of the regulation, promotion and/or provision of local public services, under power delegated by the government within the territory of which its locality lies, and with defined extent of autonomy ; or

3 organ of 1 or 2 defined above.

1 *Rdc* does not give a definition. But its rules 46–58 imply a definition. These rules mix up definition by implication, and direction for choice and rendering of heading. This is not happy. It would be more helpful to separate the functions of these rules.

2 *Pin* does not recognise government as author. *Rdc* introduced the concept of government authorship. There was then not a little resistance to this new concept. Those, accustomed to the German practice of treating government publications as anonymous, opposed it. The following reply of *Rdc* to such an opposition is of value even to day.

Government publications fall into two classes—onymous and anonymous. As to the first, the Rules (of the *Rdc*) catalogue all works which have an author under this name but the Rules direct that if issued by the government they should also appear either in full or by a reference, according to circumstances, under the department of government which issued them.

As to the second class the anonymous issue, I cannot see the advantage of entering them under the first word. Either (1) they are journals, reports etc., of legislative bodies, of which even my objector allows that the government is the author and puts them (unlike the German) under the country, or (2) they relate to the country, in which case the objector puts them also under the country, but in a subject division and not under the department, or (3) they do not relate to the country. As to (1) we agree ; as to (2) I have no objection whatever to full entry under a country-subject heading alone provided there is entry by reference under the name of the department. When they come on the same page a reference is perhaps unnecessary. The best place for the full entry depends on the object of the catalogue.

There remains only (3) the few anonymous works published by a department which do not relate to the country. Whether or not they ought to be entered under the first word like any other anonymous work, it seems to me that there should be an entry under the department which even more than in the case of works issued with their author's name, must be supposed to adopt the opinions of the work and assume responsibility for it.

3 *Ala* does not give a definition of Government. But its rules 72 to 90 imply a definition. These rules mix up definition by implication, and direction for choice and rendering of heading. This is not happy. It would be more helpful to separate the functions of these rules.

4 *Vat* too only implies the definition in its rules 104 to 125. But it adds to some clarity by putting these rules under the heading " National and Local Government Agencies ".

5 *Ccc* attempts an explicit definition in rule 1203. But it is not properly worded. While teaching, this has been found to prove inadequate for beginners. This is a general symptom of the definition not being precise. Lack of precision bites even a veteran when refractory cases arise challenging judgment.

6 Therefore, it is desirable to provide precise definition in the chapter on terminology, in any code whatever. The definition given in section 2201 is a fair approximation to precision. It may have to be made more precise as and when refractory cases come challenging the adequacy of its precision. This way of clearing up what " government " means even before beginning the rules of cataloguing, is a convenience. Then, the rules on choice and rendering of heading will not become cumbersome as in *Rdc*, *Ala* and *Vat*. The removal of cumbersomeness from the rules reduces the hurdle in the way of beginners. Teaching becomes easier. For veterans too, the mind is kept clear while facing refractory cases.

2282 **Institution.**—1 Independent or autonomous corporate
body other than government. It may be created by a government,
or constituted under a law, or formed voluntarily—either formally
or informally. It should have continued existence and functions
beyond that of merely convening a conference ; or

2 Organ of 1 defined above.

1 *Rdc* does not attempt a definition. But the following specification occurs under rule 61 dealing with corporation and quasi-
corporations :—

This includes associations, societies, clubs, guilds, business firms, institutes,
private schools, colleges and universities, libraries, galleries, museums,
ecclesiastical organisations, churches, convents, monasteries, and all similar
bodies provided they have an individual name.

By ' individual name ' of a corporate body is meant ' distinctive
name of corporate body ' as defined in section 2202.

2 *Pin* does not recognise institution as author. *Rdc* introduced
the concept of institutional authorship. There was then not a
little resistance to this new concept. Those accustomed to the
German practices of treating a publication of an institution as
anonymous opposed it. The following reply in *Rdc*'s commentary
on Rule 44 to such an opposition is of value even to day :—

I think the American practice of regarding bodies of men as the authors of
their own journals, proceedings, etc., and as collecting-editors for the collections
issued by them is preferable to the German practice of dispersing these works
throughout the alphabet under the noun which happens to be first in the title.

The American way is preferable for two reasons : first, because as a matter
of fact these bodies *are* the authors not only of their own proceedings but also of
their collections regarded as a whole ; secondly, because as a matter of convenience,
both in the enlargement of the library and in the serving of the public it is better
that all the books connected with the name of a society...... should be brought
together in one place. It is true that in a dictionary catalogue this may be accom-
plished more or less inappropriately by entry under the name of the society as a
subject ; but in an author catalogue it does not come about at all. If you want
to find in Kayser's list of the books published in Germany in the last five years
all the publications of a German learned body you must look under Abhandlungen,
Almanach, Annalen, Arbeiten, Archive, Aufsatze, Beitrage, Bericht, Bibliothek,
Bulletin, Centralblatt, Corresondenzblatt, Ephemeriden, Erlauterungen, Jahr-
buch, Jahresbericht, Journal, Kalender, Magazin, Memoiren, Mittheilungen,
Monatsblatt, Nachrichten, Preisschrift, Programm, Publicationen, Repertorium,
Resultate, Sammlung, Schriften, Sitzungsberichta, Studien,Tageblatt, Tagebuch,
Uebersicht, Verzeichniss, Versammlungen, Viertaljahrschrift, Vorlesungen, and
Zeipchrift, because the works may be under any one of these ; and if by racking

your brain you remember all of them and have patience to look them all up, yet are not sure that there is not something important hidden away under some other word which you may think of when it is too late—Verhandlungen, for instance.

3 *Ala* gives the following definitions and specifications in the preface to its Rules 91 to 130 :—

A society is an organisation of persons associated together for the promotion of common purposes or objects, such as research, business, recreation etc.,......
academies (learned societies), associations, and societies of all kinds, scientific, technical, educational, benevolent, moral, etc., even strictly local or names from a country, state, province, or city ; also clubs, gilds, orders of knighthood, secret societies, Greek letter fraternities, Young Mens' and Young Women's Christian Associations, affiliated societies, political parties, religious sects, etc., as distinguish-ed from institutions (establishments).

Institutions (establishments) are entities whose functions require a plant with buildings, apparatus, etc., as distinguished from bodies, organised group of persons such as societies, associations,etc., whose duties may be performed equal-ly in one place or another—colleges, universities, schools, libraries, museums, galleries, radio stations, observatories, laboratories, churches, monasteries, convents, hospitals, asylums, prisons, theatres, buildings, etc.

In a sense, societies are entities distinguished from institutions and institutions are entities distinguished from societies. The cirle of mutual dependence of the definitions of these two terms is inno-cently complete. *Ala* seems to recognise the null-content of these two definitions. But it seeks to throw the blame on other languages. For it adds :—

The designations academy, athenaeum, college, institute, lyceum, museum, etc., and similar terms in other languages are used interchangeably for cultural associations and educational institutions ; these are to be entered as societies or as institutions according to the nature of their organisation.

Ala tries to cut the circle by another criterion :—

The necessity of having a permanent material equipment tends to identify an institution with a locality.

What about the Royal Society ? Has it no necessity of a permanent equipment ? The simple matter is that the overlap between society and institution is far too great to justify their being distinguished in so far as corporate authorship is concerned.

The implications of *Rdc* Rules 59 to 89 appear to have been the basis of such a distinction between society and institution. Chapter 5 " Rendering " shows the complications created by this distinc-tion. This appears to be a case of acceptance, without question, of certain rules handed down by tradition, and devising a defini-tion to suit them, rather than settling the terminology in the ideal plane independently and then making the rules to suit it. This unconscious submission to tradition has occurred in spite of the following warning of *Rdc* given in the commentary on its rule 45 :—

In regard to (2) (whether the name of some other word shall be the heading), the catalogue hitherto published may be regarded as a series of experiments. No satisfactory usage has as yet been established.

4 *Vat* follows *Ala* in substance.

5 *Ccc* has abolished the distinction between society and institution. It is based on further experiments. It is also based on the normative principles given in chapter three and their implications.

2283 **Conference.**—1 Meeting for deliberation, or formulation and expression of opinion or sentiments, not convened by any single government or to form a government, or by any single institution or to form an institution ; or jointly by more than one of them and not confined to the members of such corporate bodies, but convened and conducted either spontaneously or by a body which has no existence beyond the conference convened and held by it or whose primary function is only that of convening or holding such conferences at intervals ; or

2 Organ of 1 defined above.

2284 Conference *vs.* Person

Conference is deemed author only of its agenda, minutes, resolutions, report of proceedings, and similar collectively created thought. But a collection of learned papers or memoranda presented by person(s) or body(ies) is deemed to have the respective person(s) or body(ies) as author(s).

2285 Government *vs.* Institution

Several institutions are government-owned or nearly so. Some of these are autonomous. Some are managed directly by government as if they were departments or other organs. There are all possible grades of transition from an unmistakable organ of government to an independent institution. Now and again, there is also shift of the same institution in course of time from the status of independent institution to any status short of an unmistakable organ. A useful test is this :—

Organ of first remove is usually mentioned in a modern written constitution. On the analogy of this, organ of first remove of a nation with unwritten constitution may be recognised.

6285 Heading and Canons

Another fact has to be remembered. There is tendency for the state to take up more and more functions, beyond the traditional and primary ones of government, execution, legislation, defence, judiciary and administration. It takes up many service functions, such as

1 construction and maintenance of high-ways, bridges, harbours, air-ports and such other essentials of transport ;

2 Astronomical and meteorological observations through its own observatories ;

3 Communication systems such as railways, tramways, bus system and air ways, postal, telegraph, telephone, wireless and radio services ;

4 healing the sick and wounded through its own hospitals and its own sanatoria ;

5 Teaching through its own schools, colleges and universities ; and

6 Banking service through its own banks ; etc.

Except perhaps the first mentioned above, the others are not included among primary functions.

For works bearing on the discharge of primary functions—administration reports, reports of deliberation, direction, and so on and in general for thought created and expressed by an organ of government of first remove, second remove etc. as defined in sections 2221 to 2228, the government or its appropriate organ, as the case may be, should be taken as its author.

Any autonomous or non-autonomous organisation, engaged in the work of research, production, commerce, and supply of commodities and services to the public, is deemed to be the author, as an institution, for all works containing thought and expression created by it. It is so even if the institution is owned and managed by the government.

But for such a convention, most institutions will come into the category of governmental body, as the state progresses along lines of socialisation. In a truly totalitarian state, there can be no corporate body other than governmental one. To break up this octopus-type of governmental authorship, cataloguing convention distinguishes between an organ of government and an institution along lines mentioned above.

The above-mentioned criterion to distinguish between governmental and institutional authorship will be sufficient in most cases. But there will occasionally be refractory cases baffling this criterion. No help except the personal judgment of the cataloguer will be of avail in such cases. By a periodical review of such elusive cases, the criterion can be made progressively sharper.

2286 Ecclesiastical Polity

Ecclesiastical polity has features similar to those of a government. There are organs of different removes from the central authority. There are also autonomous institutions. The criterion to distinguish between an organ and an institution is to be applied to a religious body as to a governmental body.

2287 Institution *vs.* Institution

The choice between a parent institution or one of its organs on the one side, and an autonomous affiliated institution on the other, in the claim to be deemed as author of a work, should be decided along lines analogous to the choice between the claims of government and institution, set forth in section 2285.

2288 Synopsis

This section gives, for ready reference, a synopsis of the cataloguing conventions more or less stabilised at present, in deciding the nature of the corporate body to be deemed the author of a work—Parent Body or an organ of it on the one side, and a dependent or affiliated institution on the other side.

Group 1

Each of the following institutions should be taken as author of its works, as if it were independent of the parent body if any exists, be it government or institution :—

Abbey	College	Park	School
Bank	Convent	Political party	Stock Exchange
Board of Trade	Endowment	Post office	Telegraph office
Cathedral	Firm	Produce Exchange	Telephone exchange
Cemetery	Foundation	Religious order	Temple
Chamber of Commerce	Guild		University
Church (place of worship)	Masonic Body		
	Monastery		
	Mosque		
	Mutt		

3

41

Group 2

Each of the following institutions should be taken as author of its works as if it were independent of the parent body, if any exists, be it government or institution, *provided it has a distinctive name* :—

Botanical garden	Festival	Museum
Chapel	Hospital	Observatory
Experimental Station	Laboratory	Shop
Exhibition	Library	Zoological garden

If any of the institutions has no distinctive name, it should be treated as an organ of its parent body.

Group 3

Any formal or informal group of the members of a parent body formed for recreative, ameliorative or any other economical or social purposes other than any forming a distinctive purpose of the parent body, should be treated as an organ of the parent body even if it has a distinctive name.

Group 4

Each section or branch of an institution should be taken as author of its work, provided it has a distinctive name not involving the name of the parent body.

If a section or a branch does not have a distinctive name not involving the name of the parent body it should be treated as an organ of the parent body.

Group 5

Each international institution or conference—isolated or continuing,—of private persons, non-governmental institutions or national governments should be taken as author of works produced as a result of its deliberations.

23 Document

231 Embodied Thought.—Record of work on paper or other material, fit for physical handling, transport across space, and preservation through time.

Recording may be done by hand or printing process, or by near-printing process or by type-writing, or by any kindred process, or by sound-recording machinery or by any other means. Record also denotes a record reproduced by photographic or other processes from a record already made. The material on which recording is done may be paper or any substitute for it, or gramophone plate, or sensitive paper used for photographic reproduction, or any other material suitable for the recording process used.

232 **Document.**—Embodied thought.

This term is introduced for brevity. It was brought into use a few decades ago to emphasise embodied micro-thought. It is now used to include any embodied thought, micro or macro.

233 **Title-Statement.**—Record, in a document, of the title of its work.

234 **Author-Statement.**—Record, in a document, of the name of author(s) and collaborator(s) of its work, if any.

2341 **Supplement to Author-Statement.**—Statement of the year of birth (and also of the year of death in the case of a deceased person), and of the alternative name(s), if any, of each person mentioned in author-statement.

225 **Imprint.**—Record in a document of name(s) of publisher(s) and of place(s) of publication, and year of publication, of the document.

226 **Volume.**—Several leaves of paper or other material used for recording on, forming the whole or part of a document, fastened together so as to be opened at any particular place.

227 **Title-Page.**—Page of a volume containing title-statement. Usually it also contains the author-statement and the imprint.

2271 **Over-flow of Title-Page.**—Page(s) immediately succeeding or preceding title-page and containing part of the information usually given on title-page.

228 **Thought-Content.**—Expressed thought embodied within a document, or a volume of it, is its thought-content.

23 Types of Document

231 **Periodical publication.**—Document with the following attributes :—

1 A volume or a small group of volumes of it intended to be published or completed normally once in a year (or at other regular intervals), though irregularity in interval is not ruled out ;

2 Each successive volume or periodical group of volumes is usually distinguished by the year of publication and/or by a number belonging to a system of simple or complex ordinal numbers. Such a number is usually called a volume number ;

3 The intention had been to continue the publication of the volume for ever though not actually carried out ;

4 The intention had been to continue the same title in all the volumes, though not actually carried out ; and

5 *Either* 51 Each volume is made up of distinct and independent contributions, not forming a continuous exposition, normally by two or more personal authors and normally the specific subjects and authors of the contributions in successive volumes also being in general different, but all the subjects falling within one and the same region of knowledge, contemplated to be brought within its purview ;

Or 52 Each volume or each periodical group of volumes embodies more or less similar information mainly relating to its year (or other period) of coverage.

The term " periodical publication " is also used to denote any volume of a periodical publication as defined above.

2311 Periodical.—Periodical publication with attribute 51 mentioned in 231, or any volume of it.

2312 Serial.—Periodical publication with attribute 52 mentioned in 231, or any volume of it.

232 Book.—Document other than a periodical publication. That is, it has been completed or had been intended to be completed in a finite number of volumes. It is generally in one-volume. Some are in many volumes.

2321 Anonymous Book.—Book whose title-page or its overflow does not give an author-statement or indicate corporate authorship.

233 Composite Book.—Book with two or more contributions, each with its own title, distinct and independent, not forming a continuous exposition, and often, though not necessarily, by different authors.

2331 Ordinary Composite Book.—Composite book provided with a single, generic title to denote all the contributions collectively.

Anthology of several authors, christomathy, hymn-book, prayer-book, song-book, symposium, and similar compilations come under this category.

2332 **Contribution.**—Work forming a part of a composite book or a periodical or a serial.

23321 **Article.**—Contribution in a periodical.

2333 **Artificial Composite Book.**—Composite book which is not ordinary, *i.e.*, without a generic title to denote all the contributions collectively.

234 **Simple Book.**—Book which is not composite, *i.e.*, which embodies continuous exposition usually either by a single author, or by two or more joint authors ; but it may also be anonymous.

235 **Multi-volumed Book.**—Book in two or more volumes, giving a continuous exposition of a subject, and, for this or for any reason in the distribution of thought among the volumes, compelling all the volumes to be treated as an inseparable set, *i.e.*, as if they take the place of a single volume.

236 **Edition.**—*Either*, 1 One of the different forms in which one and the same work is published and each form has a distinctive name such as " Arden Edition ", " Variarum Edition ", " Standard Edition ", " Ananda Asrama Edition ", " Memorial Edition ", " Loeb Classics " and so on ;

Or, 2 One of the different printings or reproductions of a document with or without slight change in thought-content, and each being distinguished from others either numerically or by other equivalent term such as " New ", " Revised ", " Enlarged ", and so on.

237 **Related Book.**—See section 3338.

24 Series

241 **Series.**—Set of books not constituting a multi-volumed book with the following attributes :—

1 The books are issued successively by one publisher or by one corporate body, usually in a uniform style and having some similarity of subject, standard, or purpose ;

2 Each book has normally a distinct and independent title of its own ;

3 There is a collective name to denote the set. This is called the **name of the series.** It is given in all or at least in one of the volumes of the set ; and

4 Each volume is or can be assigned a distinct number belonging to a system of simple or complex ordinal numbers,

such as 1, 2, 3 etc. ; or 3·1, 3·2, 3·3 etc. ; or 1955·1, 1955·2, 1955·3 etc.

242 **Pseudo-Series.**—Set of books not constituting a multi-volumed book and with the following attributes :—

Either

1 All the books have a common author ; and

11 *Either*, all the books or volumes have a common generic title ;

12 *Or*, all the books or volumes belong to the same edition having a distinctive name other than numerical or equivalent ones ; and

13 The name of the author taken along with the generic title or the name of the edition is suitable to be used as if it were the name of a series.

Or

2 All the books have a common author or not ; but

21 The titles of the various books have a common part capable of being used as their common generic title, suitable to be used as the name of the pseudo-series ;

22 The title of each book has, in addition to the generic part, a distinctive part ;

23 Each book is brought out in different numerically denoted editions independently of the other books ; and

24 Each volume is or can be assigned a number belonging to a system of simple or complex ordinal numbers.

25 Sponsor

25 **Sponsor.**—Corporate body under whose auspices or with whose authority or goodwill or with whose finance a periodical publication is published, though the responsibility for the thought and expression does not rest on it but rests on the respective personal authors of the contributions contained in it.

A sponsor is not an author. But a periodical publication is often traced by a reader through the name of its sponsor.

1 *Rdc*'s definition makes a society the author of its memoirs, transactions and journals as seen in section 2332. Moreover in the preamble to the commentary on its rule 133, *Rdc* makes the following statement :—

Memoirs or other papers given in addition to ' proceedings ' proper may be considered as the work of the society acting through its members ; the society therefore, is the author.

Rdc is, however, in divided mind. For it adds in the next sentence,

There are, however, some ' journals ' published by or ' under the auspices of ' societies which are really periodicals......The society being not the author but the editor. Again, there are works which occupy a border land between the two classes in regard to which the puzzled cataloguer should remember that it is not of much importance which way he decides, provided he is careful to make all necessary references.

2 *Pin* has no problem in this case as it does not recognise corporate author.

3 *Ala* has prescribed a definite procedure in the following rules :—

71 (paragraph 3). Periodicals are entered according to the general rule (5 C) even though issued by governments, societies, institutions.

5 C (A) (paragraph 2). A periodical issued by a society, institution, or government body is ordinarily to be entered under its title...... with added entry for the issuing body.

The spell caused by *Rdc* is, however, still there. There is nothing explicit in the rules about ' memoirs ', ' proceedings and journals '. But the definition of ' periodicals ' excludes them. It has therefore to be treated as if the society were the author and not merely sponsor. This will be definitely wrong in the following cases and many others :—

1 *Memoirs* of the Madras Library Association.

2 *Journal* of the Indian Mathematical Society.

3 *Proceedings* of the London Mathematical Society.

4 *Vat*'s prescriptions are similar to those of *Ala*.

5 *Ccc* had deemed a sponsor as author even in its third edition. But this mistake was set right in the amendment to *Ccc* worked for the *Union catalogue of periodical publications of South Asia* (1953) by S. R. Ranganathan and others. The amendment is also stated in that catalogue.

26 Catalogue and Entry

261 **Catalogue.**—List of the documents in a library, or in a collection forming its portion.

2611 **Documentation List.**—List of documents listed together for some purpose. The purpose is usually bringing to reader an exhaustive or select list of documents relevant to the pursuit of his enquiry or study. This term is used to emphasise the inclusion of micro documents.

2612 **Bibliography.**—Older name for documentation list. Originally it was mostly a list of macro documents. Subsequently, it has begun to include also micro documents.

262 **Entry.**—Record in a catalogue or documentation list, forming an ultimate unit-record.

2621 **Specific Entry.**—Entry mentioning a specific document.

2622 **General Entry.**—Entry not mentioning specific document.

2623 **Consolidated Entry.**—Two or more entries consolidated into a single entry.

2624 **Consolidated Specific Entry.**—Entry mentioning two or more specific documents.

2625 **Consolidated General Entry.**—Two or more general entries consolidated into a general entry.

2626 **Word Entry.**—Entry beginning with a word, or in rare cases, with a symbol given in the author statement of a document as a substitute for name of author.

2627 **Number Entry.**—Entry beginning with a call number or class number.

2631 **Dictionary Catalogue.**—Catalogue in which all the entries are word-entries. This is of one part only. In it, entries are arranged alphabetically.

2632 **Classified Catalogue.**—Catalogue in which some entries are number-entries and some are word-entries. This is of two parts. The part consisting of number-entries is classified part. The part consisting of word-entries is the alphabetical part. In the classified part, entries are arranged by class numbers and call numbers. In the alphabetical part, entries are arranged alphabetically.

264 **Main Entry.**—Specific entry giving maximum information about a whole document. All other entries, specific or general, relating to the document in question, are derived from the main entry.

2641 In a dictionary catalogue, main entry begins with the name of the author of the book or a substitute for it, or the title in the case of an anonymous book and periodical publication. In other words, it is a word-entry.

2642 In a classified catalogue, main entry begins with call number in the case of a book, and a class number in the case of a periodical publication.

265 **Added Entry.**—Entry other than main entry.

266 **Specific Added Entry** is briefer than main entry in multiple card system or book form of catalogue. It differs from the main entry in its heading only in unit card system. It does not draw any information from outside main entry.

2661 **Cross Reference Entry.**—Specific added number-entry in a classified catalogue. It refers from the class number of a specific subject forming a portion of a document to the host document. It also gives the place of occurrence in the latter.

267 **General Added Entry** may be one of three kinds. It is a word-entry both in dictionary catalogue and classified catalogue.

2671 **Cross Reference Index Entry.**—General added entry referring from one word or set of words to another word or set of words. The former word or set of words usually forms a name of a person, a geographical entity, a series, or a book. Cross reference index entry occurs both in dictionary catalogue and classified catalogue. This is the only class of entry transferable between dictionary catalogue and classified catalogue. It is quite alike in both kinds of catalogues.

2672 Cross Reference Index Entry may draw information from outside the document.

2673 *See also* **Subject Entry.**—General added entry referring from the name of one subject to that of another. This occurs only in dictionary catalogue. It is derived from the class number of the document or of any portion of the document for which a specific added subject entry is made. It runs parallel to the class index entry of classified catalogue.

2674 **Class Index Entry.**—General added entry referring from the name of a class to its class number. This occurs only in classified catalogue. It is derived from the class number of the main entry or cross reference entry of a document. It runs parallel to the *see also* subject entry of dictionary catalogue.

268 **Chain Procedure.**—Procedure for deriving *see also*

subject entry or class index entry from class number, in a more or less machanical way.

27 Section of Entry

271 In dictionary catalogue, Main Entry of a non-anonymous book or a periodical publication consists of the following successive sections :—

2711 **Leading Section.**—The first section of entry. It is author section. It contains statement of the name(s) of author(s) or collaborator(s) used as substitute(s). It may also contain connecting words, words descriptive of the role of a person whose name is mentioned and/or other terms to distinguish two or more persons or corporate bodies having the same name.

2712 **Title Section.**—It contains statement of the title of the document and of collaborator(s), if any, made readable as a continuous whole. It may mention name of edition.

2713 **Note Section.**—It contains a statement of

1 Name of series including pseudo-series ; and/or

2 Information about the relation of the document to another related document.

2714 **Collation and Imprint.**—It contains information about format, number of pages, and statement of imprint of the document. This is necessary in a documentation list or bibliography. But it is optional in a catalogue. When the entry is of a portion of a document, this section should give information about the host document and the exact position of the portion containing it. This section is then called **Location Section.**

2715 Call number.

2716 Accession number.

272 In dictionary catalogue, the author section of main entry is absent in the case of an anonymous book and a periodical publication. The title section becomes the leading section.

273 In classified catalogue, main entry of a non-anonymous book or a periodical publication consists of the same sections as in dictionary catalogue. But the call number is put in the leading section. And the other sections are slided down as a consequence.

2741 A Specific Added Word Entry consists of the following successive sections :—

1 Leading section.—This consists of a statement of name of

author or collaborate or title or series or a derivative from relation-note ;

2 Intermediate item.—This consists of a statement about the document depending on the nature of the leading section ; and

3 Index number.—It may be call number or class number.

2742 A Cross Preference Entry of classified catalogue consists of the following successive sections :—

1 Leading section.—This consists of the Class Number of the referred-from subject ;

2 Directing section.—This consists of the term " *See also* " ; and

3 Referred-to section.—This consists of Call Number, heading, short title of the host document, and details of location, such as page number, parts etc.

2743 In unit-card-system of catalogue, a specific added entry of a document differs from its main entry only in the occupant of the leading section.

275 A Cross Reference Index Entry consists of the following successive sections :—

1 Leading section.—This consists of a statement of the referred-from item ;

2 Directing section.—This consists of the term "*See also*"; and

3 Referred-to section.—This contains a statement of the referred-to item. This is the alternative name of the referred-from item, that has been used in the leading section of a specific word-entry.

276 A *See also* Subject Entry of dictionary catalogue consists of the following successive sections :—

1 Leading section.—This consists of the name of referred-from subject ;

2 Directing section.—This consists of the term " *See also* " ; and

3 Referred-to section.—This consists of the name of the referred-to subject used in the leading section of a specific subject entry.

277 A Class Index Entry of classified catalogue consists of the following successive sections :—

1 Leading section.—This consists of the name of class ;

2 Directing section.—This consists of words directing attention to the next section ; and

3 Referred-to section.—Class number.

28 Heading

281 **Heading.**—Any one of the following sections :—

1 Leading section of any word-entry, that is of

11 any entry of dictionary catalogue ; and

12 any word-entry of classified catalogue ;

2 Second section of a main entry of classified catalogue ; or

3 Third or referred-to section of

31 a *see-also* subject entry of dictionary catalogue ; and

32 a cross reference index entry of dictionary catalogue
or classified catalogue.

2811 **Heading.**—Also the occupant of the heading-section, *i.e.*,
of " heading " in the first sense.

2812 A heading, in the second sense, is the name of

1 a person ;

2 a geographical entity ;

3 a corporate body ;

4 a book, *i.e.*, title ;

5 a series ;

6 a subject ; or

7 a language.

2813 A person or a corporate body whose name is used as
heading may be

1 author ;

2 joint author ;

3 collaborator ;

4 joint-collaborator ; or

5 subject of document.

2814 A collaborator may have any one of the capacities
mentioned in section 226.

282 An entry may be named after the occupant of the leading
section.

Example Call number entry ; Author entry ; Joint-author
entry ; Collaborator entry ; Joint collaborator entry ; Commentator entry ; Editor entry ; Translator entry ; Personal name

entry ; Corporate name entry ; Title entry ; Series entry ; Pseudo-series entry ; Subject entry ; Alternative name entry ; and so on.

283 Homonym.—One and the same name denoting different entities, say 1 person(s) ; 2 geographical entity(ies) ; 3 Corporate body(ies) ; 4 book(s) ; 5 series ; 6 subject(s) ; and 7 even entities belonging to different categories enumerated above.

2831 Homonymous Heading.—A heading which is a homonym.

284 Individualising Element.—Term(s) added to a name in a heading to resolve a homonym so as to individualise the entity intended to be denoted.

285 Descriptive Term.—Term added after the name of a person or corporate body, inclusive of individualising term, to denote the role played, other than author, such as *Jt auth, Comm, Ed, Tr, Illsutr,* and so on.

286 Entry Element.—Word(s) at the beginning of a heading forming a unit-block and usually entered in the most dominant style in the heading, or at least so as to be easily distinguished from the other word(s) in the heading.

2861 Entry Word.—First word of entry element—and, therefore, also of heading.

287 Secondary Element.—Word(s) added after the entry element and usually entered in ordinary style less dominant than that of the entry element.

288 A personal heading may consist successively of :—

1 Entry element ;
2 Secondary element ;
3 Individualising element ; and
4 Descriptive element.

2881 The structure of a corporate name heading will be given in section 54 and its sub-divisions. It may be stated here that a corporate-body-heading may consist of two or more headings distinguished as main heading, first sub-heading, second sub-heading and so on.

2882 The structure of title heading will be given in section 57 and its sub-sections.

2883 The structure of series heading will be given in section 58 and its sub-sections.

2884 The structure of subject heading will be given in section 593 and its sub-divisions. It may be stated here that like corporate name heading, subject heading may consist of two or more headings, called respectively first sub-heading, second sub-heading and so on.

CHAPTER 3
NORMATIVE PRINCIPLES
30 Four Classes

There are three classes of normative principles for cataloguing :—

1 General laws ;

2 Laws of library science ;

3 Canons of cataloguing derived from the laws of library science for immediate application ; and

4 Principle of Local Variation.

31 General Laws
311 LAW OF PARSIMONY

Law of Parsimony.—Between two or more possible alternative rules bearing on a particular phenomenon, the one leading to over-all economy of man-power, materials, money, and time considered together with proper weightage, is to be preferred. This is illustrated at several places in this book. Here are a few instances. Cross reference index entry is the outcome of a compromise between the Law of Parsimony and Canon of Sought-Heading. The distinction made in *Rdc* between " full " and " short " style in cataloguing is a contribution of the Law of Parsimony. The distinction between " bibliographical " and " library " catalogues made in *Ccc* and *Theory* is a joint contribution of the Law of Parsimony and the Canon of Context. The Law of Parsimony would make a fundamental difference in the rules about specific added entries, according as the catalogue card is printed or typed (or hand-written). In the former case, it would recommend the unit-card system. In this a copy of the main entry card itself would be used as specific added entry card, by merely inserting in the leading section the heading of the added entry. For this purpose, the first line of the printed card should be left vacant. This is provided for in rule 33 *et seq* of *Ccc*. On the other hand, if the catalogue card is typed or hand-written, the Law of Parsimony would recommend a multiple card system. In this, each added entry is made briefer than the main entry. The words used in each added entry would be the minimum necessary to satisfy the Canon of Relevance. To achieve this, the Law of Parsimony would allow a number of additional rules in the catalogue code, to take care of different kinds of added entries. Such additional rules for specific added entries would prescribe omission of series note and accession number, shortening of title, and shortening of every other category not acting as a link between main entry and specific added entry. For example, in the classified catalogue, rule would provide for the omission of forenames in author's name occurring in the second section of an entry.

312 Law of Impartiality

Law of Impartiality.—Between two or more claimants, say for use as heading, the preference of any one should be made only on sufficient grounds, and not arbitrarily. For example, in the case of joint authorship, the Law of Impartiality would recommend equal right to the names of all the authors for choice as heading.

313 Laws of Interpretation

Laws of Interpretation.—There are well known principles of interpretation. 1,008 principles of interpretation have been listed in *Nyaya kosa*. These principles have been evolved to a remarkable extent by the philosophers of the *Purva-Mimamsa* and *Nyaya* schools of Indian philosophy. In law too, such principles are applied necessarily. A catalogue code is like a legal document. Any rule in it should be interpreted like a legal text. For example, there may be conflict between one rule and another. In actual application, the conflict should be resolved with the aid of the Laws of Interpretation. Periodically, the rules should be amended in the light of experience, so as to remove conflicts or at least to reduce them to a minimum, if they could not be totally removed. It is the application of the Laws of Interpretation that led to revision of the definition of composite book and to the concept of pseudo-series. One of the Laws of Interpretation is called " Lost-horse, Burnt-chariot " Principle. Its application in the field of classification occurs in the article *Classification of allusion books* referred to in section 176.

There is often conflict between Law of Parsimony, Laws of Library Science and Canons of Cataloguing. The conflict has to be removed quite often with the aid of the Laws of Interpretation. One of the Laws of Interpretation, for example, is this :—The claim of the normative principles special to the business on hand— Cataloguing, in this case—should be given priority over a normative principle of general application—say, Law of Parsimony or Law of Impartiality or occasionally even a Law of Library Science. Conflict may arise between one Law of Library Science and another in framing a particular rule in catalogue code. The Fifth Law— Library is a growing organism—often sides the Law of Parsimony and gets into conflict with the other Laws of Library Science. In such a case, the Principle of " the later the law, the greater its weightage " is applied. If possible, a compromise has to be arrived at in every case of conflict. It has been an unfulfilled ambition to scrutinise the entire *Ccc* from the angle of the Laws of Interpretation. Mahamahopadhyaya S. Kuppuswamy Sastry was a specialist in the subject. He and the author had intended to take up such a scrutiny of the *Ccc* after both would retire from the salary-earning stage of life. But, alas, he died before the author retired. He then sought to do the work in collaboration with a student of his; but it did not mature. The application of the Laws of Interpre- tation to *Ccc* will be an eminent subject for investigation by an aspirant to a doctorate in library science.

32 Laws of Library Science

The Laws of Library Science were first formulated in 1928. They are the following :—

1 Books are for use ;

2 Every reader his book ;

3 Every book its reader ;

4 Save the time of the reader ; and

5 Library is a growing organism.

In these laws, " Book " should be interpreted to include any macro and micro document. " Time " should be interpreted to include objective and subjective time. " Growth " should be interpreted to include child-growth by addition and adult-growth by replace- ment. The application of these laws to problems in cataloguing is illustrated in Ranganathan's *Five laws of library science* (1931) and his books on cataloguing.

33 Canons of Cataloguing
331 Canon of Ascertainability

331 **Canon of Ascertainability.**—The choice and render- ing of main entry and specific added entry, and the heading and every other element in either entry should be determiṇed by the information found in the title-page of the document and its over- flow pages ; in extreme cases the information may be taken from the other pages of prel ; but it is not desirable to go beyond the prel.

3311 For the name of series, the half-title-page may be used as a supplementary source.

3312 In the case of an ordinary composite book, the generic contents-page may be used as a supplementary source.

3313 In the case of an artificial composite book, the title- page of each constituent document may be used as a supplementary source.

3314 A plea of this book is that the back of the title-page should give also all the alternative names of an author or collaborator. Then the application of the Canon of Ascertainability can be extended even to cross reference index entry.

3315 Another plea is for pre-natal classification of each book. Then the back of the title-page will give the call number of the book.   It can also give the class numbers of the subject-analyticals needed.   When these suggestions are implemented by the publish- ing trade in co-operation with the National Central Library, the chain procedure will bring even the class index entry of classified catalogue and the specific subject entry and the *see also* subject entry of the dictionary catalogue, within the perview of the Canon of Ascertainability.

Many of the internal inconsistencies of existing catalogue codes are traceable to their stepping out of the title-page and prel and going into the market place so to speak, in search of data for choice and rendering of headings of entries. *Rdc* itself started this practice.   The authority often quoted by it for doing so is " usage among readers."   But it has to be remembered that " usage of readers " and " cataloguing rules " often stand in the relation of " hen first or egg first." This vicious circle should be avoided. A safer course is to base catalogue rules on what is ascertainable about the cataloguing elements of a document within the document itself. During the last one or two centuries, sheer folk-force has led the title-page and its back to evolve towards being a complete repository of the cataloguing elements of a document. Its evolution has been described in detail in *Social bibliography : Physical bibliography for librarians* (1952) by Ranganathan. The title-page is a gift of the early printers. It has been exploited in succession by patrons, publishers and authors. It is open to cataloguers too to exploit it. Exploitation here means not only using the information given in title-page, but also endeavouring to make the back of the title-page and its over-flow carry all such information as the cataloguer needs but is not at present given in them. In other words, the influence between the title-page and cataloguing profession should be reciprocal. Each should enrich and help the other. To make this possible, the title-leaf in the material plane and the Canon of Ascertainability in the idea plane—*i.e.*, the plane of normative principles should be made the sheet-anchor of catalogue code. The details of this reciprocal relation will get developed in the course of the later chapters. Till the title-page and its over-flow including its back begin to carry all the data needed for cataloguing by the adoption of an international standard on the subject, any heading fished out from the market place, or from any other document by the same author or even from outside the prel though within the document itself, should be accommodated only in the leading section of a cross reference index entry and the back of the main card. But such an exotic heading should never be allowed to aspire to become the leading section of main entry or of a specific added entry.

332 Canon of Prepotence

Canon of Prepotence.—The potency to decide the position of an entry among the various entries in a catalogue should, if possible, be concentrated totally in the leading section ; and even there, it should be concentrated, as much as possible, in the entry element. If total concentration in the leading section is not possible, the minimum possible potency should be allowed to flow beyond it, to later sections ; and even this should be distributed in the later sections in decreasing order of intensity.

3321 DISTRIBUTION OF POTENCY

The essence of library catalogue is arrangement of entries. The entries get sorted letter by letter or digit by digit, beginning with the very first of these found in an entry. The potency goes on decreasing downwards from the first letter or digit. Any mistake in the first letter or the digit will therefore be fatal. The entry will be virtually lost in some far-off region of the catalogue. The range within which the entry may get lost goes on decreasing, as we move on from the first letter or digit to the last. The range is reduced to a reasonably small one, only by the time we reach beyond the end of the entry word, or of the entry element, or of the class number. Therefore, any casual error, allowed to creep into these, carries a high penalty.

3322 SWEEP OF THE EYE

Moreover, the prepotent elements of as many consecutive entries as possible should be made to lie within a single sweep of the eye if the catalogue is in book-form. To facilitate this, the most dominant type-face is prescribed for the entry element—say bold face. This enables the eye to overlook the impotent part of the entries, in the first round of search. This enables concentration on the entry element or the call number as the case may be.

3323 CLASSIFIED CATALOGUE

Again in classified catalogue in book-form alphabetical index entries are made short. They are reduced to a line an entry type, if possible. They are further printed solid in small points, such as eight points. This is done in order to bring as many of the entry elements as possible within a single sweep of the eye. This is greatly facilitated because the necessarily fuller and swollen main entries get separated out into a separate sequence on account of their being number-entries. A reader normally begins with the alphabetical index. He is thus helped in his first round of search to catch a great many entries within a single sweep of the eye. This is an advantage of classified catalogue. Dictionary catalogue does not have this advantage ; because it mixes massive main entries and slim added entries.

3324 First Enunciation

The Principle of Sweep of the Eye is an important corollary of the Canon of Prepotence. It was enunciated for the first time in the *Union catalogue of periodical publications* of S. R. Ranganathan published in the *Annals* part of the *Abgila*, 1, 1950, 177-189. This principle has been consciously applied in designing the *Union catalogue of learned periodical publications in South Asia* by S. R. Ranganathan and others.

3325 Dictionary Catalogue

In Dictionary Catalogue, it is not possible to exhaust the potency in the leading section *i.e.*, heading of the main entry ; because an author may write many books. But in classified catalogue, it is possible to exhaust the potency in the leading section or the call number of the main entry, if the scheme of classification used individualises a book as the Colon Classification does. This can be achieved even in schemes whose class may not be co-extensive with the thought-content of document, provided a suitable book number is improvised for the scheme.

3326 Language of Catalogue Heading

The potency of an entry should seldom go beyond the first one or two words in the second section. It is for this reason that most of the catalogue codes recommend the omission of the initial articles, honorifics and other puffs in the title. Some codes ask for the retention of initial articles, if grammatical elegance requires it ; at the same time they prescribe ignoring them while arranging. This is a fault. This imports the niceties of spoken language and literary prose into the catalogue. Catalogue-language is a jargon. It is an artificial language. It is different from natural language. This is lost sight of an account of the illusion caused by the use in catalogue heading of the words of natural language. This illusion should be constantly lifted away while drafting a catalogue code. The artificiality is caused by the syntax of the catalogue-language. This is totally different from that of the natural language. The catalogue-heading-language has therefore freedom from the niceties of natural language. This was first pointed out in *Fundamentals*, section 824 and its subdivisions.

3327 Statistical Approach

Canon of Prepotence yields an important deduced principle

applicable to the choice of entry element in a multi-worded heading —*i.e.*, in the rendering of a multi-worded term chosen for use as heading. That principle is a statistical one. " The entry element should be chosen from among that class of words, occurring in the multi-worded term chosen for use as heading, which is more numerous than the other classes of words occurring in it." For, the probability for the same word to be used as entry element in several headings decreases with the numerousness of the class from which the word is chosen ; and the greater this probability, the greater will be the concentration of potency in the entry element. This statistical principle is responsible—unconscious though it might have been—for the choice of the family name as the entry element in rendering a Western personal name for use as heading. It is the overlooking of this statistical principle that has vitiated *Ala's* prescription of place-name as entry element for institution-heading, in spite of its having accepted the place-name as the entry element in the name of Government improvised by cataloguing convention. This statistical principle plays some part, though again unconsciously, in the choice of entry element in the real title for title heading, as prescribed in *Pin*. This statistical principle should be exploited fully in the framing of a cataloguer code. Its use will be demonstrated in Chapter 5 " Rendering."

3328 GOVERNMENTAL AND UNIVERSITY SERIES

Here is an example of the application of this principle to series-heading. Many universities and governments have established their own series. They are generally given common names, such as Publication series, Library science series, English series, Hindi series, Historical series, Economic series, Pamphlet series and so on. These names do not have sufficient potency. They often become homonyms. To resolve the homonym and to increase the potency, the name of the university or the government or even a department of either may have to be added. If the purpose be merely individualisation, the name can be added at the end. But if the purpose is increasing the potency of the heading, the name should be added at the front. While drafting *Ccc* in 1933, the author had not enunciated the Canons of Cataloguing. These had not come up in the conscious level. He was therefore unable to decide the issue on proper grounds. Much indeterminacy or inconsistency was the result. It is only now, sixteen years after the Canons of Cataloguing were enunciated, that he is able to see this difficult issue lighted up by the Canon of Prepotency.

333 Canon of Sought-Heading or Canon of Relevance

Canon of Sought-Heading or **Canon of Relevance.**—
The decision whether an entry

> with a particular type of heading, or
> with a particular choice for that heading, or
> with a particular rendering of that choice, or
> with a particular added entry arising out of it,

should be based on the answer to the question ; " Is reader or library staff likely to look for a book under the particular type or choice or rendering of heading ? "

3331 JUDGMENT

The answer to this question is a matter of judgment. The judgment should be based on experience in reference service—
i.e., in eliciting from readers their requirements. Induction should be applied to the words usually brought up by readers in looking into the catalogue to choose their reading materials. The judgment should also be based on experience in book-selection. Induction should be applied to the types of heading found necessary to help either in filling up gaps in the library collection or in avoiding un-intended duplication. It has also to be based on the obligation of the reference-section to give a reader alternatives to a document, when the one actually sought is not actually in at the moment. The alternative may be essentially the same as the one sought. For, the same book might have appeared with a different title. Or, it might have been merged into another book. Or, it might be an extract from some other book. Reference-section will also have the obligation to produce to a reader all the documents associated with another document mentioned by him.

3332 CLAIMANT TO STATUS OF HEADING

There are several elements on the title-page. The Canon of Ascertainability is indifferent as to which element the claim to become heading is allowed. All that it is concerned with is that no element outside the title-page should be allowed to become heading of a main entry or any other specific book-entry. It is the business of the Canon of Sought-Heading to admit or reject the claim of any element in the title-page to become heading. A trivial case of rejection is the claim of the year or the place of publication or the name of publisher. Author heading and subject heading are the most popular among sought-headings. Collaborator heading comes next in popularity. Title heading is taken to be a sought-heading in some catalogue codes without any discrimination. But the Canon of Sought-Heading does not admit the claim of every kind of title. In the majority of documents, the title is expressive ; i.e., it is indicative of the subject of the document. Here we have to remember the Law of Parsimony. But so far as the Law of Parsimony is concerned, it is indifferent whether the subject heading is dropped out or the title-heading is dropped out. It leave it entirely to the discretion to the Canon of Sought-heading. The latter would like to respect the Canon of Consistency in the exercise of its discretion. For that purpose it argues within itself as follows :—In an expressive title, the first word occurring in title-statement in the title-page is often as blurb, such as Elementary, Advanced, Comprehensive, Primer, Treatise, Text-book, etc. This is impotent. Further, it is not always brought up by readers. It is uncertain which word in the title the reader brings up. There are also several other difficulties in the choice of entry element in a multiworded expressive title,— such as, title in sentence form, morphological variants of entry element, abbreviations or signs as entry element, and different titles for the same document appearing in different translations and even in different editions in the original language. This question has been elaborately gone into by *Pin*. Its rules 181 to 238—i.e., 58 out of its 241 rules—are turned on this problem. They are put into a separate chapter marked part three and entitled " Real Titles." In the light of these factors, according to the Canon of Sought-Heading, it is doubtful wisdom to give title entries to expressive titles. The subject entries will serve the needs of one seeking a document with an expressive title through its title. On the other hand, there are titles that are not expressive of the thought-content of documents. Such a title is often " fanciful, " as *Ccc* puts it. It is usually crisp. It almost amounts to a proper name. At any rate, typographical featuring on the title page usually helps the picking out of the crisp part of the title, which alone often sticks to reader's mind. Whatever be the variation of the title in different editions, the crisp part persists; it serves as a " uniformised title ; " it becomes a sought-heading. The Canon of Sought-Heading admits the claim of such a crisp non-expressive fanciful title to be used as heading. A discussion of the claims of the various elements in title-page to be used as heading will be found in part one of *Fundamentals*.

3333 CROSS REFERENCE INDEX ENTRY

The institution of the majority of cross reference index entries had its origin in the Canon of Sought-Heading. A reader might remember an author or collaborator who might have used alternative names or variant forms of one and the same name in different documents. Some of these may be real and some pseudonymous. This makes no difference in the problem being considered. Whatever be the name sought by the reader, the catalogue should inform him of all the documents written by him under other names too. The Canon of Sought-Heading recognises this fact. All such names are proper names. Only a few persons indulge in such alternative names. The claim of each name to be used as heading may be admitted. Such is the verdict of the Canon of Sought-Heading. But its verdict is different in regard to alternative names of subjects. They are to be treated proper names. Practically every subject admits of alternative names. Therefore, the Canon of Sought-Heading discretely gives way absolutely to the Law of Parsimony in the case of subject headings. No cross reference index entry for subject name headings. But in the case of other name headings, the Canon of Sought-Heading arrives at a compromise with the Law of Parsimony. The result is cross reference index entry for the alternatives. This account of the genesis of cross reference index entry explains the denial of alternative name entry to subject headings and its prescription for any other name heading.

3334 PSEUDO-SERIES

The concept of pseudo-series owes its origin practically to the Canon of Sought-Heading. The question " What are the plays of Shakespeare with Variorum editions? " was asked by a scholar. The catalogue based on the 1934 edition of *Ccc* or any other then prevalent code, could not give an immediate answer to this question. Similar experiences accumulated through years, while doing reference service. This led to the concept of pseudo-series. A tentative definition and set of rules were incorporated in the 1945 edition of *Ccc*. It is now being made more precise than before. *Ala* also has recognised the problem, though it has not used the term " pseudo-series."

3335 Extract

A reader may ask for a document. It may have gone out on loan. But an extract from it may be there, as a separate document. There is some probability for this extract to satisfy his want. But he will not be able to look for it under its own heading. Because he may not know of its very existence. Therefore, when he looks for the original book under its own heading which he knows, he will be helped if there is a note in its entry with the information " *a portion printed as* " followed by the heading etc. of each of the extracts from it, owned by the library. There should also be a note in the main entry of the extract stating that it is an extract from such and such a book. *Vice versa*, the reader may know only of the extract. A note in its entry saying " Extract from ...... " will help him to think of the original. It may be of use to him. His seeking for it might have been unexpected. But this note will make him seek it. This service should be done by the catalogue.

Rdc does not appear to have provided any rule to carry out this indication of the Canon of Sought-Heading.

Pin has sensed this in the rule :

26 (2). Reprints with a title-page are entered according to general rule... the statement of origin is placed at the end of the entry in the shortest forms.

But, it has failed to provide for an entry beginning with the heading and title of the original, which is what is essential to satisfy the Canon of Sought-Heading.

Ala rule 22C deals only with selections from a book and an anthology of an author. Its rule 5C (4) deals similarly with selections from a periodical. *Ala* does not deal with the problem of a single portion of a book published as a separate document and needing to be linked up with its original to satisfy the Canon of Sought-Heading.

Vat Rule 12 corresponds to *Ala* rule 22C. Its Rule 245 corresponds to *Ala* rule 5C (4). But its rule 246 deals with a single extract. However, its prescription is only similar to that of *Pin*. Thus *Vat* also fails to carry out the indication of the Canon of Sought-Heading.

Ccc has conformed to the Canon of Sought-Heading in regard to extract even in its edition 1 (1934). Its prescription is contained in the following rules :—

Rule for Main Entry

14 The note, if any, is to be written as a single paragraph made up of one or more of the following parts, in order, in so far as they are applicable to the book :—

   3 Extract note.

143 An extract Note is to consist successively of

   1 The connecting words " Extract from ; " and

   2 The specification of the work from which it is an extract.

Rule for Added Entry

321 A Book Index Entry is to be given using as heading each of such of the following as the book admits of :—

   6 The heading of the work mentioned in the Extract Note.

3216 If the heading is of the sixth kind enumerated in Rule 321 it is to be the same as that of the work mentioned in the Extract Note.

3226 If the Heading is of the Sixth kind enumerated in Rule 321, the Intermediate Item is to consist, in order of,

   1 the title of the work mentioned in the Extract Note ;

   2 a full stop ;

   3 the descriptive words like " *a portion printed as* " or " *a portion bound as* ; "

   4 the Heading in the Main Entry of the Extract with the provision that, in the case of personal names it is sufficient if the surname alone is written and that, if a name is in two or more sentences, the full stops are to be replaced by commas ;

   5 a colon ; and

   6 the short title of the Extract

   provided that, if the Heading is First Word of Title, (4) and (5) are to be omitted.

3336 ASSOCIATED BOOK

Another cataloguing problem arising out of the application of the Canon of Sought-Heading to related books was first sensed in 1935. While giving a course of lectures on school library work, use of books for collateral study by pupils came to be discussed. In tracing many such books, the tracing could be done with the help of class numbers. Then came books for collateral study by teachers themselves. Here a basic book was found to have given rise to another book going into an altogether different chain of classes. To put it more clearly, the two books did not fall into one and same chain ; in other words, their main classes were themselves different. At the same time, one book was not found caught within another ; in other words, it was not a case for cross reference entry or subject analytical. None of these known cataloguing devices could meet the situation created by this class of related books. Here is an example : Anderson and Marsdon's *Short history of the British Empire* (1934) and Wren's *Teacher's handbook to Anderson and Marsdon's Short history of the British Empire* (1935). These two books went into the two different main classes History and Education respectively. The basic book is not a classic. To put it in classificatory language, the work contained in that book is not made into a quasi class. There is therefore no means of the two books being brought to light in a single chain of classes. Therefore classification cannot be of help in bringing out the fact of these two books being related. The problem was therefore passed on to the care of cataloguing. But *Ccc* was not then equipped with the rules necessary to handle this problem. Similar experiences had been accumulating for nearly fifteen years. Even pupil's books are found related similarly, *e.g.*, a book on practical physics is associated with a particular book on theory. The increasing pressure of this problem led to a solution in 1948. This was published in *Catalogue of associated books* by P. K. Garde and S. Parthasarathy appearing in the *Annals* part of the *Abgila*, 1, 1950, 64 to 68. Definite rules on Associated Book Note were incorporated in the third edition of *Ccc* in 1952.

3337 MERGER BOOK

In 1953, K. D. Puranik brought the two following books to notice :—

1 **Boek** (J H). Economics and economic policy of dual societies as exemplified by Indonesia. 1953.

"Revised and Enlarged version of the author's two earlier studies published separately......under the titles :

Structure of the Netherlands Indian economy, 1942 ; and

Solutions of the Netherlands Indies economy, 1946 "

2 **Kalaecki** (M). Theory of economic dynamics, an essay on cyclical and long-range changes in capitalistic economy. 1953.

" Published in lieu of the second editions of :
Essays in the theory of economic fluctuations ; and
Studies in economic dynamics."

The application of the Canon of Sought-Heading to these two sets, each of three books, led to the concept of " Merger Note ". Rules to meet the cataloguing problems of merger books were framed for incorporation in the fourth edition of *Ccc*. Puranik's paper on the subject entitled '*Cataloguing of merger book* ' has been published in the new quarterly " *Annals of library science*," 1, 1954, 112 to 115.

3338 RELATED BOOKS

It has now become possible to handle extracts, associated books and merger books—all by a single rule on " Related Books."

Two or more books are said to be related books if the following conditions are satisfied :—

1 None of the books is a classic. That is, in classificatory language the work contained in none of the books is converted by the scheme of classification into a quasi-class ; and

2 The classes to which the books belong do not occur in one and the same chain of classes. Here we assume a chain to begin from a main class of the scheme.

3 It is possible to recognise one of the books of the set as the basic book. It is also possible to coin a term to denote the relation of the basic book to the other related books and also the relation of any of the other books to its basic book.

The fourth edition of *Ccc* should include this definition. It should also provide a single rule for all kinds of related books.

3391 Subject-Heading, Chain Procedure

When the Rules of Chain Procedure were formulated for the first time in 1938 in *Theory*, chapter 11, the rules were too crude. For, every link in the chain was given the right to ask for a class index entry of its own. For example, in the chain of the class number L183, the link 3 gave the class index heading "Ear. Medicine." The link 8 was also allowed the class index heading " Head. Medicine." Again, the link 1 was also allowed to give the class index heading " Regional organ. Medicine." Lastly, the link L was allowed to give the class index heading " Medicine." This ruthlessly mechanical way of deriving class index entries from the chain of links in class number, led to a plethora of class index entries. Some of these were irritating the mind vaguely. The Law of Parsimony too protested. But there was no way of removing the irritation and satisfying the Law of Parsimony.

In 1952, the Canon of Sought-Heading took shape. It ruled out as unsought the two headings " Head. Medicine " and " Regional organ. Medicine ". Similar weeding out of unsought headings was indicated in every class. The rules of chain procedure were themselves re-enunciated in the third edition of *Ccc*.

3392 DICTIONARY CATALOGUE

During the visit to London in June 1954 for consultation with colleagues in the profession, A.J. Wells, editor of the *British national bibliography* brought an important experience to notice. While the subject heading got by the Rules of Chain Procedure did its work well in classified catalogue, it did not produce the desired result in dictionary catalogue. The discussion of this subject took a fruitful turn as soon as the Canon of Sought-Heading was consciously taken as guide. It was seen that the Rules of Chain Procedure for dictionary catalogue should be different from those for classified catalogue. Wells, Coates (also of B N B) and the author discussed the lines along which the rules should be enunciated for dictionary catalogue. The problem is set forth in *Chain procedure and dictionary catalogue* by S. R. Ranganathan published in the *Annals of library science*, 1, 1954, 216 to 221.

3393 PRUNING BY LAW OF PARSIMONY

The alternative-name entries, the special notes and their associated added entries, the subject analyticals and the *see also* subject entries in dictionary catalogue, and the class index entries in classified catalogue, promoted by the Canon of Sought-Heading may swell to disproportionate dimensions, unless the answer to the question, " Is it truely a Sought-Entry ? " is considered with great care. The Law of Parsimony would ask for considerable pruning. Pruning can be done to an appreciable extent with the aid of the Canon of Context explained in section 334.

334 Canon of Context

Canon of Context.—The rule in a catalogue code should be determined in the context of :—

> the nature of the cataloguing features of a book, prevalent in the mode of book production ;
> the nature of the organisation of libraries prevalent in regard to mode and quality of library service ; and

the coming into existence of published bibliographies, and particularly bibliographical periodicals.

The rules should also be changed from time to time to keep steps with changes in context.

• 3341 WEIGHTAGE TO PHYSICAL ATTRIBUTES

When manuscripts were loosely assembled sheets, not firmly bound, a detailed description of size, collation, and even of leaves perhaps was necessary in catalogue entry. To add to this, each copy of a book was virtually unique. It was often a rarity. It was property. Each entry in a catalogue was therefore over-weighted with details of physical bibliography. This is true as much with manuscript as with incunabula. They are of immense help in historical bibliography. For a long time after the invention of printing—even long after the incunabula period—these conditions prevailed in some measure. The mental set of cataloguers of pre-printing days and incunabula days continued for long after the context had changed. *Rdc* saw the continuance of this mental set even down to the last quarter of the nineteenth century. It therefore called it " full " cataloguing. It recommended " short " cataloguing for service libraries. This recommendation was opportune ; and it was readily accepted by the progressive members of the profession. Because the great increase in the annual output of printed books and even in the annual accession in a library made " full " too costly for practice. The Canon of Context gave weight to this change in context. It supported the Law of Parsimony. And cataloguing code was modified. The jurisdiction of the old code was confined to bibliographical description.

3342 BACK-LOG

However, the back-log of the mental set led to the retention of collation, name of publisher, name of place of publication, and price in library catalogue. So long as library organisation put a physical barrier between reader and library collection, collation served a useful purpose. For reader naturally wanted to know the number of pages of a book before applying for it. Canon of Relevance voted for its retention. Publisher's name too was somewhat helpful in evaluating a book without seeing it. But the place of publication and price were hardly relevant to the needs of either the reader or the staff. Publisher's catalogue gave this information. The staff had an additional source in the accession register. These details are necessary in catalogues of publishers and book-sellers, the accession register and certain other forms of bibliography. But they were not necessary in a library catalogue. In spite of this, the back-log of an earlier context is still persisting in practice unmindful of the Canon of Context. This back-log should not be allowed today to enter the catalogue of any service-library. The catalogue of the National Central Library serving also as the National Bibliography is the only library catalogue where such details should be allowed to continue.

3343 OPEN ACCESS

A further change has now occurred in the context. This change lies in the domain of organisation of a library. It is the introduction of open access system. Now the barrier between the reader and book collection has been removed except in the case of pamphlets, weekly-built books, and rare or costly books. These form only a fraction of the collection of a service-library. A book within direct access to reader does not need the mention of its format, collation etc. in its catalogue entry. The Canon of Context recommends that the catalogue should indicate a pamphlet by a simple device, like underlining the book number ; it may indicate an over-size book by over-lining the book number and so on. This problem is fully discussed in *Theory*, part 1. The indication of the Canon of Context is that, in all books other than to which open access cannot be given, all items, other than name(s) of author(s), title with puff omitted, note giving series or certain other peculiarities prescribed by the Canon of Sought-Heading, call number and accession number, should be omitted from the main entry of the catalogue of a service-library. *Ccc* was one of the first codes to cut out items other than the above quite ruthlessly in a library catalogue. It may however be added that if centrally printed catalogue card is used, the unit card system may come into force and the main entry will be allowed to have all the bibliographical details needed in National Bibliography. For, it is cheaper to use the same card both for the National Central Library and a service-library.

3344 EXPECTATION OF LIFE OF BOOK

To-day the demand for simplification is reinforced by another factor in the context. Books are plentiful and cheap. Only a small percentage have permanent value. Thus, the preciousness of books as permanent possession has diminished considerably. Further, Democracy passes the library copy of a book to many hands. Therefore, books perish rapidly by legitimate use. We have begun to realise that a book is a mortal, though the work embodied in it may be immortal. Except in a comparatively small percentage of books which form the classics of permanent value, even the thought-content of a work is soon out-moded. And in the case of some works, the thought-content even becomes quite wrong in course of time. A copy of a book embodying such out-moded and wrong thought-content may be necessary in a few libraries, in order to serve the interest of historical and antiquarian research. Perhaps, it should be sufficient to have copies of such out-moded works in one dormitary library in each country or in each constituent state, or in a few regions of each country. In a service-library, such books are not only a burden, but they may even be a social danger. Because, the lower intellectual strata in a democracy may not be able to sense the erroneousness of the information or knowledge given in such books. I usually high-light this new element in the context by the provocative statement :

The expectation of life of a modern book is only ten years. A service-library hoarding books over ten years old is punishable for one or other of two reasons. Either it has neglected to circulate the book properly as is evident from its being not worn out sufficiently and reduced to pulp to make its being weeded out a necessity ; or it is retaining a book embodying out-of-date knowledge and exposing them to use by the public. Either of these is a social danger. If the work as well as the book embodying it are of fleeting value, there is no harm in weeding the book out in ten years. If the work is immortal and its body perishes by actual use, one will have to withdraw it in ten years ; moreover its very value will enable it to come again in a new embodiment.

We can generally grant that the span of life of a book of to-day is limited, even though the work embodied in it may have unlimited span of life. This context makes one scrutinise severely the cost of cataloguing. It calls for simplification of catalogue entry. A revision of catalogue code becomes necessary.

3345 New Demand

Intensification and extention of research activity in the community creates new demands on the catalogue. Over-all economy in man-power of a nation calls for a new division of labour. In this new division of labour, the library profession should relieve the other professions of the task of search for literature. The librarian has become a partner in every research organisation. Moreover, the tremendous turbulance in the universe of knowledge of to-day throws a heavy burden on the library profession engaged in search for literature. The search, moreover, has to be expeditious. To discharge this new function, the library profession has to throw a new burden on library catalogue. Subject analyticals have to be multiplied, in order to bring to the notice of the reader even micro thought embodied in articles in periodicals and in portions of books. Many libraries have begun to practise this—particularly research, industrial, commercial, governmental and even public libraries. *Ccc* has provided detailed rules for this.

3346 International Bibliography

Another change has come in the context. It has been brought about by the pressure of the economics of cataloguing service. There is much unfavourable disproportion between the cost of subject analyticals and the extent of their use. However, the social value of even limited use is immense. A reconciliation of these two conflicting findings should be found. It has been found. It is the publication of subject bibliographies as an international project. This change in the context does make the catalogue code add a section that subject analyticals should not be attempted by a library catalogue in the fields of knowledge provided with international bibliographies.

3347 National Documentation

But there is an unavoidable time-lag, between the appearance of a document and its mention in international bibliography. This is unavoidable on account of the problems created by the space to be covered and by the needs of processing. During the interval of this time-lag, a service-library cannot fail in its search for literature. The failure here is particularly anti-social, because, it is nascent thought that counts in research. Here again, the pressure of the economics of cataloguing comes into play. This pressure too has been removed by a new development coming into vogue just at this time. A temporary " documentation list " is being published by a nation. For this purpose, nation after nation has begun to establish a National Documentation Centre. It scans all the periodicals produced in the country or taken into the country. It classifies the articles. It publishes a classified list of them week by week. The context changes with its establishment. The Canon of Context is sensitive to this change. It tells individual service libraries " Don't attempt subject analyticals in duplication of entries in national documentation lists." It also tells the National Documentation Centres, " Remember that your documentation list is only for temporary use. It will soon be replaced by the fully comprehensive international bibliographies in the diverse subjects. Don't waste your resources in making your documentation list exhaustive. Know what work is in progress in your country. Include in your document list, only the titles justified by this context."

3348 OTHER CHANGES IN CONTEXT

The world of books is not static. The context is ever-changing. Nature of book changes. Make up of title-page changes. Nature of readers changes. Out-look of library service changes. Degree of national and international co-operation changes. The Canon of Context demands that cataloguing practice should also change. For this purpose, it demands that catalogue code should change too in consonance with the change in the other factors. If the international standard for title-page and its back conforms to the recommendations in chapter 7 " Title-page," many of the rules in the current catalogue codes will have to be omitted. Several others will have to be changed. New ones will have to be added.

The refrain of the Canon of Context in its application to library catalogue and to library catalogue code is :

Ever becoming, Ever new.

। नवो नबो भवति जायमान : ।

335 Canon of Permanence

Canon of Permanence.—No element in an entry, and the heading in particular, should be subjected to change by the rules of a catalogue code, except when the rules themselves are changed, in response to the Canon of Context.

The Canon of Permanence is backed by the Canon of Ascertainability. This Canon is often violated by *Ala*. Its rules prescribe the choice of the latest name of a personal author or corporate author, for heading. Therefore, whenever an author changes name, a library has to change all the entries under earlier names. It must be remembered that this is forcibly felt in the entries of periodical publications. It goes without saying that such a change automatically violates also the Canon of Ascertainability in regard to the earlier documents.

Ccc's rules respect the Canon of Permanence. This is an automatic result of its respecting the Canon of Ascertainability. Moreover, its rules for the cataloguing of periodical publications require only the addition of a new section in the main entry, whenever there is change of name, without any disturbance to what is already there in the entry.

336 Canon of Currency

Canon of Currency.—The term used to denote a subject in a subject heading of dictionary catalogue and of a class index entry of classified catalogue should be one in current usage.

3361 CONFLICT OF CANONS

Name of a subject keeps changing with time. Unless the current name is used in the heading readers cannot benefit by it. To satisfy this Canon the headings of subject entries and class index entries should be changed as and when a new name stabilises itself. This leads inevitably to a violation of the Canon of Permanence. This conflict between two Canons is resolved by a partition of the field of sway. Canon of Currency has sway only over subject heading in dictionary catalogue and class index heading in classified catalogue. The Canon of Permanence has sway only over name-heading other than subject heading. It has sway only in heading made of name of person, geographical entity or corporate body.

3362 DILEMMA

The Canon of Currency has to face a dilemma. The question is, " Current among whom ? " For two different terms are current at the same time among specialists and non-specialists, to denote one and the same subject. The first belongs to special terminology built up by the specialists themselves. The second belongs to the natural language spoken by the common man. The general tendency is to prefer the term in natural language. This preference often leads to a multi-worded term in natural language in preference to a single-worded term in specialist language, *e.g.*, " Child Medicine " in preference to " Pediatrics ". In spite of the increase in the number of words to be used, natural language is preferred. This is due to the pressure of the Second Law of Library Science. According to it, a specialist reader knows the common name as well as the technical name of a subject. The non-specialist reader knows only the common name ; he does not know the technical name. Moreover, the specialist is a highly organised personality ; he has greater intellectual awareness and agility. It is not so with the common reader. Therefore, to serve every reader without exception, common name should be preferred to special terminology, in subject heading. This is the joint finding of the Canon of Currency and the Second Law of Library Science as a helpful way of getting out of the dilemma.

337 Canon of Consistence

Canon of Consistence.—The rules of a catalogue code should provide for all the added entries of a document to be consistent with its main entry. Also the main entries of all documents should be consistent with one another in certain essentials, such as choice of heading.

Rules such as " Do this in one way for American books and in another way for Italian books, or German books and so on " should not find a place in an International Catalogue Code. Such rules can appear only in a National Catalogue Code.

The Canon of Consistence does not insist that all books in a particular library should be catalogued ; nor does it insist that all books in a library should be catalogued to the same degree of fulness. These issues are left to the care of the Laws of Library Science and the Law of Parsimony. The Principle of Local Variation, described in the next section, goes into the details of these problems.

The Canon of Consistence does insist that the main entry of all documents should be of the same species. For example, in dictionary catalogue the main entry is author entry. No main entry should be other than author entry, except in the case of an anonymous book which has no author. *Ala* makes subject entry the main entry when the author is a government, in some of the cases, such as documents embodying the laws or constitution of a country. This will be gone into in greater detail in chapter 4.

338 Canon of Purity

Canon of Purity.—The rules of a catalogue code should not make one type of entry serve the purpose of another.

Ala prescribes subject heading in the place of author heading for the main entry, in several of its rules for corporate author headings. This will be shown in detail in section 432 of chapter 4 " Choice ".

34 Principle of Local Variation

Principle of Local Variation.—The International Catalogue Code should mark out the factors to be left to the care of National Catalogue Code. A National Catalogue Code should similarly mark out the factors to be left to the care of the supplementary code of individual libraries.

341 Inherence

Catalogue is a tool for a reader to find out his requirement in the library. It is an important tool in library service. Intimacy characterises service. Intimacy underlines the individuating particularities in the reader-library setting. The catalogue is a medium of communication in this intimate setting. Thus, local colour should be inherent in library catalogue. A library catalogue does have to conform to a pattern conceivable in abstract. The pattern should also be prescribed in abstract. But to invest it with the intimacy inherent in service, it should be impressed with essential local colour. This is the message of the Principle of Local Variation. This local colour is to be assumed by the library catalogue in successive stages. Three stages are unmistakable. Corresponding to each stage there should be a different catalogue code. The International Catalogue Code gives only a general blue print, as it were.

342 Script and Style

The style of writing or printing the elements in a catalogue entry depends on the script and the type-faces available for the script. For example, Roman character admits of upper case, lower case and italics. It admits also of antique face. Even when written by hand, it is possible to have corresponding varieties. But many of the Indian characters do not admit of all of them. As it is to-day we have to have recourse only to white and black, and variation of *matra* (size). The International Catalogue Code should therefore deal with style, only in general terms—of dominance, subordination, and the like. The actual method of implementing these prescriptions will have to be stated only in National Catalogue Code. In this sense, it has to fill up some details in the blue print sketched by the International Catalogue Code.

3421 TRANSLITERATION

Headings in many catalogue entries are proper names. They are names of persons, geographical entities and corporate bodies. They do not admit of translation. For they are terms of extension. They are not expressive terms. Whatever be the script used in a catalogue entry, the heading should represent the proper name phonetically. This indicates transliteration. The letters of one script do not have phonetic equivalents in another script. Therefore, transliteration is not a simple affair. Till now, the Roman script has been largely playing the part of the host-script. This has been due to historical circumstances. The renascence phase of the present cultural cycle appeared in areas of Roman script, a few centuries earlier than in areas of any other script. Therefore, during the last few centuries, transliteration had virtually meant transliteration into Roman script. This has become such a rigid part of the mental part of the West that the reverse movement of transliteration seems to have very little chance to be recognised, even at international level. This is again due to the same historical factor. International bodies have been all along effectively confined to the membership of the West. Therefore, the idea produced by reflex action, on hearing the term transliteration, is that of the Roman script as the host-script. Therefore, the so-called International Catalogue Codes provide only for one-way transliteration. This is a violence to the Principle of Local Variation. The newly awakening countries have much to do to remove this violence. In my recent experience with the UNESCO Project on the Rendering of Asian Names, I have found this mental set in the people of the West too rigid to be broken. They cannot even dissociate transliteration from rendering. Nor do they see the reciprocal feature of transliteration. For them, Rendering of Asian Names is mostly transliteration in Roman script. This is a vexatious barrier I have met with in many international meetings. The West should become a little more aware of the " whole problem ".

343 Personal Name

At present, certain National Catalogue Codes claiming international status presume competence to prescribe rules for the rendering in heading of a personal name of any culture whatever. This is attempting the impossible. Considerable research awaits to be done to delimit the boundary of the International Catalogue Code in this respect. The first step in this direction was taken by UNESCO through its International Advisory Committee on Bibliography in 1952. In 1951, the Indian Library Association and the Indian National Commission for Cooperation with UNESCO accepted a resolution of the author to request UNESCO to make the rendering of Asian names the subject of one of its bibliographical projects. This was done. The task was in the end entrusted to the author himself. This gave an opportunity to face the problem squarely. Meetings with several cultural groups slowly allowed some awareness to dawn on the problem. Some streak of light has fallen on the problem.

3431 ENTRY ELEMENT

It was the Canon of Prepotence that let the light in. A modern personal name has many words. The potency from the angle of arrangement is not equally incident on all the words. In many names, it is greatest on one word. Generally speaking, a prepotent word in the name can be found. But in an appreciable number of cases, potency is concentrated most, not on one word, but on a doublet—that is on two words. Sometimes it is spread on three words. Whether a single word is prepotent or a double or a treble word is prepotent, is obvious only to a native of the country to which the name belongs. An alien cataloguer cannot acquire sufficient competence in this matter. Even if a persevering cataloguer is enterprising enough to master alien names, it is doubtful if he can do it for all the foreign cultural groups. If he attempts to do, he will become a specialist in cultural sociology at the cost of his loyalty and duty to the library profession in general and cataloguing profession in particular. Our experience with such cultural-cum-linguistic specialists functioning as cataloguers, confirms this fear. For, by the sheer impossibility of doing two things at one time, they are found to be naturally un-informed about current progress in the discipline of cataloguing and about the great changes coming over library service in our own days. They even show a tendency towards bigotry which denies even the very existence of library science and the discipline of cataloguing. A step in the right direction appears to be to entrust the problem of " single-worded or multi-worded entry element " to the care of the respective National Catalogue Codes. It is the duty of each National Catalogue Code to devise a method by which the singleness or multipleness of the entry element could be mechanically found out by a cataloguer of an alien culture. The most obvious method will be to append to the National Catalogue Code schedules of multi-worded entry elements, assuming that these are fewer in the cultural group concerned than the single-worded entry elements. There may be less cumbersome methods available in certain cultural groups. For example, while discussing this problem with Sinhalese scholars in Ceylon, the concept of " Starter Word " emerged. By a " starter word " is meant a word which is the first of a multi-worded entry element. The other words are found to be consecutive to the starter in the way in which the full name is uttered or printed on title-page. Perhaps a reprint of such a national schedule may be separately issued for use by other national groups.

3432 Place *vs* Function

Another problem calling for local variation in names of persons is the spotting out of the entry element. In the catalogue codes of the West the Family Name is prescribed as the entry element. In the names of Western cultural groups the Family Name usually occurs last in the whole name. This fortuitous coincidence of the positional and functional attributes of the entry element has led to the habit of equating the last word in a name with the family name and vice versa. This equation is applied, by habit, to names in foreign cultural groups also. The result is

quite wrong in many cases. Realisation of this mistake drives
the cataloguer to another extreme. A rule is improvised making
the first word the entry element. The position of the entry element—which carries the greatest concentration of potency—refuses
to be so easily tied down by a simple formula. Further complications arise by inclusions of removable impotent elements and also
irremovable impotent elements anywhere amidst the words in a
name. This again high-lights the necessity for the catalogue code
to submit itself to the Principle of Local Variation. In this
context, " local " is equivalent to cultural. A tentative formula
has been proposed in Ranganathan's *Report to UNESCO on the
rendering of South East Asian names* (1953). It only sets a possible
line of investigation and a probable pattern for a code of rules
on the rendering of names. The problem requires arduous pursuit
in every cultural group of the world.

3433 DELIMITATION OF PROVINCE

Each National Catalogue Code should give its definitive rules
on the subject in a form admitting of machanical application by
foreign cataloguers. The province of the International Catalogue
Code should be merely to indicate model patterns out of which
each national code may choose whatever suits it best.

344 Analytical Entry

The extent of subject and author analyticals is subject to
local variation of a narrower variety. This is bound to vary
from library to library. Therefore a National or an International Catalogue Code should make the rules on such entries
permissive, and not compulsory. The supplementary Catalogue
Code of a library should have a rule defining their permissible
extent in more rigid terms. For example, a library in India need
not give analytical entries for essays in English as there is the
Essay index of Wilson and Co. But it should give analytical entries
for essays in Indian Languages, until an *Essay index* comes to be
published.

345 Fleeting Material

In a governmental library and in a library of a business body
or academic institution, a large and even exhaustive collection
may have to be made from time to time, in connection with a
particular problem engaging attention at the moment. After the

problem is disposed of, the collection may, not have use in the
library. A few years ago, the Library of the United Nations had
to amass considerable material on the Palestine Problem. After
the settlement of the problem, that library could not afford to
keep on the entire load on its shelves. Such materials have only
a limited period of use. We shall therefore denote them by the
term " Fleeting Material ". The duration of the accession as well
as of the use of fleeting material may be too small to complete
their cataloguing except by putting an enormous strength of temporary staff on it. And yet, it will all amount to a waste after a
short while. The Canon of Local Variation would allow such
fleeting materials to be merely shelf-listed ; perhaps even this
would be too much in some cases. It will be sufficient merely to
arrange them on the shelves and deem them to stand " self-cata-
logued" so to speak. This was, for example, enunciated as follows
by the United Nations International Committee of Library Experts
which went into " the kinds of library service required by the
United Nations and the methods by which such service can be
most effectively provided " during its meeting from 2 to 9 August
1950. The author was a member of that committee. And he
had to stress this point hard. This was because he had seen
mad proposals of librarians that every scrap of printed paper
coming into the library has a claim to a share of the cataloguing
time of the library. Lay-managements were misguided by this
absurd insistence. The document *Library services of the United
Nations* (1950) gives on page 11 the recommendation of the International Committee in the following terms,

" No attempt should be made to build up the collections for purposes of
general historical research beyond the needs of the United Nations...... The
library should be free to provide more summary treatment for much of its
material and in some categories may omit cataloguing altogether."

346 Selective Cataloguing

Even in other kinds of libraries, the Principle of Local Variation
will prescribe selective cataloguing. Materials used only occasionally may have to stand on the shelves or in vertical files, " self-
catalogued ". Ignorance of this has led to havoc being played in
certain places.

Another application of the Principle of Local Variation is the freedom given to an individual of library to cut down details rigorously for entries of certain kinds of materials. *Pin* devotes its Rule 23 to an enumeration of the various groups of documents to which simplified cataloguing may be allowed in public reference libraries. Here are some illustrative groups :—

1 Manuals for schools or self-education ;
2 Guides for elementary knowledge including books on sports ;
3 Materials on domestic economy lacking scientific interest ;
4 Popular informative books, especially in science, medicine and law;
5 Instructions for non-commissioned officers and privates ;
6 Books of superstitious and occult content (!) ;
7 Light reading materials and songs for social purposes ;
8 Juvenile and picture books ;
9 Prayer and devotional books ;
10 Minor works of local interest such as reports on festivities, exhibition catalogues, etc. ;

For these books added entries are almost omitted, various editions are combined on the same card and various other simplifications are made.

Again, cataloguing may have to be done to different degrees of fulness for different categories of materials. Mere shelf-listing may be sufficient for some. At the other extreme, for incunabula, for instance, detailed bibliographical cataloguing is necessary. The Principle of Local Variation will call for all degrees of play of selective cataloguing.

347 Change of Catalogue Code
3471 Capitulation to Dead Past

The Canon of Context will bring about changes in the rules of catalogue code. At present this change is met in one of two ways in cataloguing practice. According to one, the entire collection of a library is re-catalogued. The cost of this is enormous. Often to find the necessary money, active service is starved ; reference service is cut out ; book-fund is depleted. All this amounts nearly to criminal waste of library fund. Law of Parsimony is therefore chagrined. In the second way of practice, eyes are closed to the change in the catalogue code in the ostrich way. The obsolete code is perpetuated in defiance of the Canon of Context and the Laws of Library Science, and to the neglect of readers' unexpressed needs. This way amounts to tying the future up, to the dead past. This capitulation to the dead past is fatal to any social institution ; and library is a social institution.

3472 LIVING THE PRESENT

The right way shown by the Canon of Context is to live the present. We should neither waste the resources nor do disservice to readers. The Principle of Local Variation helps us to chalk out the right way. According to it, the documents of a library fall into three groups :—

1 New documents ;

2 Documents of recent past continuing to be in active use ; and

3 Old documents rarely, or only occasionally, in use.

When the Catalogue Code has to be changed, the three groups should be treated differently.

3473 NEW DOCUMENT

From the date of change over, all the new documents should be catalogued by the New Code. These should be kept as " New Collection ". Their catalogue cards also should be kept as a " New Collection ", according to the Principle of Parallel Movement enunciated in chapter 8 of Ranganathan's *Library administration* (1935) and *Library manual* (1951). This does not mean any extra cost.

3474 RECENT DOCUMENTS IN ACTIVE USE

Within a short period after the date of change over to the new code, or even in anticipation of it, the active documents of the recent past should be rapidly re-catalogued. In most cases, no serious change will be necessary. The only work to be done will be to pick out their cards from the old collection, and insert them in the new collection. The documents themselves should be similarly transferred from the old to the new collection, as and when the cards are transferred, according to the Principle of Parallel Movement. A suitable mark should be put above the class number on the tag in the back and in the back of title page to indicate the absorption of the document in the New Collection. In some cases, slight changes in the existing cards may prove sufficient. Only in a few cases, total re-cataloguing may become necessary. In all cases, the routine of absorption should be completed for each quantum of documents as if it were a single indivisible job ; otherwise, chaos will result. The quantity of man-hour needed for this routine of absorption will depend upon the number of documents to be so absorbed within the short time. In a service-library, eighty percent of use is estimated to be confined to the accessions of the last five years. Even this eighty percent is likely to be distributed as follows :—50 per cent of the current year, 25 per cent of the past year, 12 per cent of the second last year, and so on in diminishing order. One method of systematically picking up the documents in active use is to register for the Catalogue Revision Section all the documents of the " Old Collection " going out on loan. When they are returned by readers, the documents will automatically go to the Catalogue Revision Section. Their catalogue cards should be checked up and the routine of their absorption into the new collection should be completed. The pressure of this work will be high only for about three months in most libraries. Thereafter, it will decrease progressively. This way of absorption of old documents in current use will require additional staff only for a short period. The number of volumes to be so treated may not exceed 10,000. The extent of extra work to be done on this kind of absorption in a National Central Library can be worked out from experience. Even there, the proportion of special staff, needed, to the permanent staff and the duration for which the special staff will be needed will not be different from that of a service library.

3475 METHOD OF OSMOSIS

After the first few months of high-pressure absorption, the daily quota will become small. It will go on thinning almost to a vanishing point in about five years. By that time, all the " live books " would have been transferred by the " Osmotic Pressure of Use " from the Old Collection to the New Collection. The " dead books " will for ever remain in the Old Collection, without any harm to any reader. This is the Method of Osmosis. It is available both for change of catalogue code and for change of classification scheme, at the least cost. This is a contribution of the Principle of Local Variation applied in one of its extreme spheres of jurisdiction. This Method of Osmosis suggested itself to the author while visiting many aged libraries during his tour of Europe and America in 1948. The pathetic book of the younger members of the cataloguing sections of big libraries caught his eye. They were internally revolting against having to use catalogue codes of earlier centuries. But their chiefs, who had given up active cata-loguing and active reference service and had become mere adminis-trators and committee-men, did not have the time or the willingness to understand the urge of the juniors to change over, in order to make library service real. Or, cataloguing was, in some places, done by the old guards in whom mental fibrosis had set in and who did cataloguing without any awareness of the latest thought on library service or sensitiveness to the social changes since the time their codes were framed. When their thought was disturbed, they immediately struck the disturber, crying, "Theory, theory, all theory !" This made the author think out the deeper reason for such wide-spread resistance to any change in cataloguing and classification. It was found to be the cost of the re-cataloguing of the whole of a large collection. This simmered in the mind for some time. The Method of Osmosis came forth as a possible solution.

CHAPTER 4

CHOICE

In this chapter, we shall consider the choice of heading for main entry.

40 Simple Book

Rdc. Rule 1   Make the author-entry under (A) the name of the author whether personal or corporate, or (B) some substitute for it.

Pin. Rule 30   The name of the author is decisive for the arrangement of works ; if one is neither named nor ascertained, the real title is decisive.

Ala. Rule 1   Enter a work under the name of its author whether personal or corporate...... When authorship is undeterminable, entry is made under a heading substituted for an author's name (as a pseudonym) or under title.

Vat. Rule 1   A book is entered under the name of its author, whether individual or corporate.   The name of the author is usually taken from the title-page.   Sometimes, however, it is not given on the title-page, and must be sought elsewhere ; at the beginning or end of the text ; or in the dedication, preface, license, privilege, etc ; or else it is taken from other editions of the same work, or from various bibliographical sources.

Ccc. Rule 12   The heading is to consist of the earliest of the following which the book admits of :

1 The name of a Personal Author ;
2 The names of two Joint Personal Authors ;
3 The names of a Corporate Author ;
4 The names of two Joint Corporate Authors ;
5 A pseudonym or two pseudonyms ;
6 The name of a person other than the author, *i.e.*, of a Collaborator ;
7 The names of two persons other than authors, *i.e.*, of two Collaborators ;
and 8 The First Word of the Title, not an article or an honorific word.

The classified catalogue based on an individualising scheme of classification came into vogue only during the present generation. A catalogue had therefore been commonly taken to be alphabetical. Even arrangement of books on shelves had to be alphabetical till about three generations ago.   The framing of a catalogue code of general application began about three generations ago.   It had therefore to pay much attention to the heading and, particularly to its entry word, in the main entry.   One consequence of this was that a main entry should have a definite and easily ascertainable heading.   The name of the author was, in most cases, more precise than the title.   Its dominant word was more easily and consistently

determined than that of the title. It stuck to the mind more
commonly than the title. There was no other element with at
least an equal claim for use as heading. The subject matter was
no doubt more relevant, in most cases than the name of the author
or the title. But then, it was not always stated in the title-page.
Much work was needed to determine it. Even when determined,
it cannot be named precisely and consistently by a definite word.
For, a subject had no proper name as an author. Classification
technique had to make much progress before the subject matter
of a document could be determined more or less uniquely. Even
then, classification had had to improvise an artificial language of
ordinal numbers to name the subject. Thus, its name could not
be precisely and consistently stated in a natural language. Part 1
of *Fundamentals* elaborates the reason for the preference of author
heading for main entry. Thus three generations ago even the
arrangement of books on the shelf had to be by name of author.
In the event of author's name being not known, title was used for
arrangement. Of course, this was prevalent where the primitive
method of arranging in accession order or the newly talked-of
method of compact shelving was not preferred. In the catalogue
itself, arrangement of cards by author heading was followed
only where the irrelevance of the sequence of catalogue cards
came to be insisted upon by the recently evolving mechanical
method of search. Thus generally speaking, search in a catalogue
has to depend mostly on the author heading of main entry. Therefore, if author's name could not be found out, it was natural to
look for " substitute " for " author's name."

1 *Rdc* reflects this conclusion. For, having stated the preference for " name of author," it directs the use of some " substitute,"
for a book without a stated author. Its rules 7 to 20 and 96
to 109 are devoted to prescription of substitutes.

2 *Pin* states a simple dichotomy. It prescribes " name of
author " for a book with a stated personal author, and " title "
for one without it. In other words, it recognises the claim of no
other element for the heading. Evidently it does not want to introduce into the very first rule on heading a vague undefined term,
such as " substitute." In fact, the rules on substitutes constitute
a separate chapter in *Pin* under the heading " Extention and Res-

triction of Author Concept." This is at best a camouflage to hide *Rdc*'s " substitutes."

3 *Ala* admits of " substitutes." But it excludes " title " from the meaning of " substitute." On the other hand it recog- nises " title " only as a revertioner, so to speak, *i.e.*, as claimant on its own right whose claim would become operative only in the absence of the first claimant or its substitute or nominee.

Ala further takes away a little of the vagueness of " substitute " by giving one illustration for it *viz.*, " pseudonym." Notwith- standing this illustration its first rule does introduce an undefined term. To know the possible substitutes, one has to search through the whole code. By such a search we get the following list of substi- tutes. The rules mentioning them are given within brackets.

1 Compiler [5E(2), 5E(4), 6C, 8B, 9A(4) 9A(5), 12E, 21C, 88C, 89E, 117A(5)].
2 Editor [5A(1), 5A1C, 6C, 7A(4), 8A, 8B, 9A(4), 9A(5), 12E, 14C, 21C, 29C, 84C, 89E].
3 Publisher [10, 10A, 12F].
4 Source [54].
5 Subject [87, 90B, 90C, 90D, 90E, 90F].
6 Translator [21B].
7 Vessel [7A(5)].

4 *Vat* makes a regression from *Ala*. For its Rule 1 is worded as if every book should have an author. But in actuality some of the Rules 3 to 37 prescribe the use of a " substitute " as heading, though this term is avoided. Rule 1 is inoperative in many cases. And yet it produces a wrong impression as if it were operative in all cases.

5 *Ccc* avoids the vague term " substitute." It enumerates in Rule 12 all the possible claimants to be chosen as heading. It arranges them in order of preference. This explicit enumera- tion of the claimants for use as heading is a help. It also adds to the elegance of a code of rules. There is, however, room for improvement. The phrase " which the book admits of " is vague. It can be replaced by the more precise phrase " which the title- page of the book indicates." Secondly, the eighth category may be " Title " instead of " First word of the title." It has been found from experience that the use of the first word alone in the heading is clumsy. It does not carry any advantage with it. The

implication of Rule 12 of *Ccc* is loyalty to the Canon of Ascertain-ability. It does not direct the cataloguer to seek the name of the author elsewhere, if it is not given in the title-page.

401 CLASSIFIED CATALOGUE

Ccc. Rule 1 The Main Entry is to consist of the following sections in the order given :—

1 Call Number (Leading Section) ;

2 Heading ; etc., etc.

The above rule shows that the leading section in the main entry in Classified Catalogue is call-number. In arrangement of documents on shelf or in other receptacles and in arrangement of main entries, the call number is prepotent. All the potency is exhausted in it, if the scheme of classification individualises a document as the Colon Classification does. The heading occupies only the second section. It is absolutely impotent.

402 IMPORTANCE OF HEADING

And yet *Ccc* cares as much for the heading of the main entry as *Rdc*, *Pin*, *Ala*, *Vat* and the *Dictionary catalogue code* of Ranganathan which are all codes for Dictionary Catalogue. Why does it do so ? It is because, as stated in section 265, all the added entries of a document are derived from the main entry ; and all of them, except cross reference entry, are name-entries, in the alphabetical part of the catalogue. They have to be arranged alphabetically In this, the heading and its entry-word have great potency. There-fore, the heading of the main entry which is the source of the heading of the added entries has to be constructed with care.

403 CLASSIFIED POCKET

However, *Ccc* is able to take freedom to determine the heading of main entry in strict accordance with the definition of author, collaborator, etc., and the Canon of Ascertainability. But *Rdc*, *Pin* and *Vat* capitulate in certain cases to the inherent and inexo-rable urge in man for classified arrangement. Consequently they unconsciously prescribe rules leading to the formation of classified pockets in the arrangement of main entries. Occasionally, they even prescribe subject heading for the main entry. This is done in the name of author heading ! This fault was pointed out to the Catalogue Revision Committee of the American Library Association even when the second edition of *Ala* was in the draft stage. It was further explained in *Theory* which came out in 1938. And yet the inexorability of classified pockets is such that *Ala* could not be dissuaded from drifting into a mood for prescribing rules for their creation—among its rules for author heading.

404 JUSTIFICATION

It may be possible to justify that the subject heading is sought in preference to author heading. If it be so, the correct course should be to prescribe that the author heading should be omitted in such cases. The rules for establishing subject heading for main entry should be transferred to the part of the code dealing with subject headings. But the *Ala* does not do so. Perhaps it may be argued that these rules are retained in the part on author headings since the part on subject headings is not yet published. But the *Vat*, which has included the part on subject headings has inserted similar rules—its rule 115 for example in the chapter on " Corporate Bodies as Authors." And *Vat* professes—in the preface to the Italian edition and the foreword to the American translation— that it is at-one with *Ala*.

405 FREEDOM

Classified Catalogue has freedom to by-pass the urge for classified pockets while choosing the heading of the main entry. For the leading section propitiates fully the urge for classified arrangement. The class index entries in the alphabetical part provide the alphabetical key to be used by the reader to enter the catalogue just at the point where he finds the class number to enter the correct region of the classified part. In this region, the heading can conform to the mandates of the Canon of Ascertainability unreservedly, in choice and rendering. It can be strict in prescribing author heading when the name of author, personal or corporate, is found or is indicated on the title-page.

41 Personal Author Heading

Rdc. Rule 2. Anonymus books are to be entered under the name of the author whenever it is known.

Pin. Rule 30 implies that the name of author should be used as heading even if it is not found on the title-page provided of course it can be ascertained.

Ala. Rule 2. Enter a work under the name of its author, when known, whether or not his name appears in the publication.

Vat. Rule 1 prescribes similarly.

Ccc. Rule 121. If the title-page contains the name of one and only one personal author that name should be used as the heading.

The prescription of *Ccc* is in strict conformity to the Canon of Ascertainability. The other four codes do not respect that Canon fully. The usefulness of the Canon can be upheld as follows in the case of books whose title-page fails to mention the name of the author though it is knowable :—A main purpose of a modern library catalogue is to help a reader to find his book—to help the fulfilment of the Second Law of Library Science. When the title-page of a book does not mention the name of its author, a reader who had seen it once will ask for it only by its title. Even a reader who had been told about it by somebody else is likely to have heard the title only. Therefore it is the title-heading that will answer the needs of such readers. To satisfy their needs, title-entry of the book is necessary.

On the other hand, scholars may ask for the book by the name of the author in case it has been found by research. To satisfy their needs, author entry is necessary.

This means that the book should be given both title-entry and author-entry. The question is : Which of these should be the main entry and which an added entry ? The Canon of Ascertainability would decide this issue with what is ascertainable from title-page, rather than from outside it.

This makes the establishment of the main entry and the release of the book for public use possible without any time-lag, which the finding of name of author from external sources would cause. This would also finalise the main entry. Whenever the name of the author comes to be known by research, an author-entry can be made as an added entry. It may be asked :—Why should we not use the name of author as heading when it is well-known, even if it is not found in the title-page ? In answering this question, the Canon of Consistency would put its weight on the side of the Canon of Ascertainability.

But why do the other codes make the author-entry the main entry and the title-entry an added entry ? Because, they are guided by the requirement that the main heading had, in the days past, to fix the position of the books on the shelf. Perhaps a second reason is that the drafting of these codes had been severely empirical as based on tradition without guidance from any normative principle or Canon of Cataloguing.

But then, even *Ccc* had no canons to guide it while being drafted. For, it came out four years before the Canons of Cataloguing were enunciated for the first time. It is true. But *Ccc* had the benefit of being guided by the normative principles which had been enunciated as the Five Laws of Library Science six years earlier. Moreover, it should have followed the spirit of the unstated canons unconsciously. This could have been possible.

1 For, it presupposed classified arrangement of books on the shelf.

2 It did not have the obligation to help in bringing together, on the shelf, all the books by one author.

3 Its presumption of the use of an individualising classification scheme made prepotent the call number in the leading section of the main entry. In other words, the heading, which occurred only in the second section, was impotent in regard to arrangement of entries. In fact *Ccc* could make any author-entry—even of an author mentioned on the title-page—a mere added entry to help those making author approach.

411 REDUNDANT RULES

The following rules are redundant :—

4111 *Rdc*

9 (Artist, Cartographer, Architect)	14, 15 (Commentary)	19 (Selection)
	16 (Continuation, index)	20 (Concordance)
11 (Music)	17 (Abridgment)	21 (Translation)
12, 13 (Catalogue)	18 (Revision)	22 (Ana, Table-talk).

4112 *Pin*

37 (Abridgment)	44, 45 (Revision)	52, 55 (Thesis and Dissertation)
38 (Correspondence)	48 (Work of Art)	
42 (Editor's work is principal matter)	50, 51 (Music)	59 (Catalogue).

4113 *Ala*

3E (Narrator)	11 (Medium)	18 (Heraldic visitation)
4B (Spoken words)	12 (Music)	19 (Work or Art)
6 (Correspondence)	13 (Catalogue)	20 (Revision)
7 (Expedition)	14 (Radio-script)	21 (Translation)
8A (Inscription)	16 (Ship's log)	22 (Abridgment, Adaptation, Paraphrase, Selection)
9 (Manuscript)	17, 17E (Thesis and Dissertation)	
10 (Map)		

23 (Dramatisation, Novelisation)	25 (Supplement and Continuation)	27 (Index)
		28 (Concordance)
24 (Pardy and Imitation)	26 (Sequel)	29 (Commentary).

4114 *Vat*

The rules corresponding to the above mentioned rules of *Ala*.

4115 *Ccc*

1263 (Commentary)	1291 (Ana)
12971 (Correspondence)	1298 (Revision).

Each rule in each of the above groups merely amounts to an elucidation of the definition of " author." Either, it should be left to the care of the section on terminology as shown in sections 223 and 227 and its subsections in chapter 2 ; or it may be mentioned in a commentary on the basic rule for choice of personal author, reproduced at the beginning of section 40 of this chapter. To swell the total number of rules by inclusion of redundant rules is not good drafting. The resulting hyper-trophy bewilders a beginner. It may confuse even a veteran on occasions.

412 FAULTY RULES

The following rules are faulty :—

4121 *Rdc*

Rule 129.   A single inscription by an unknown author needs no title-entry; but should have subject entry under the subject of which it treats, or the name of the place where it is found, or both.

An inscription is generally named after the place where found, if there is no author. The name of the place can therefore be a helpful substitute for the name of author. It is not right to make the name of subject a substitute for name of author. This would violate the Canon of Purity.

4122 *Pin*

Rule 47.   Independently published indexes, repertories, and the like are put under the title of the work to which they relate. Reference is made from the indexes.

This violates the Canons of Consistency and Purity. This is discussed in detail under rules 27A and D of *Ala* in section 4123.

Rule 57.   Personal publications (felicitations, addresses, journals, sermons etc. without author-statement are put under the name of the person to whom they relate.)

This violates the Canon of Purity. For, the "person" is only the subject of the publication. This heading cannot arise out of " extension of author concept " as the heading of the chapter, in which this rule occurs puts it.

Rule 58 Laws, patents, certificates, bulls, pastoral letters and other official publications are put under the originator if he is named in the title.

This is the result of the denial of the concept of " corporate author " by *Pin*. Surely, the rule itself states that these works are not produced in the private capacity of the originator but in his individual capacity. If at all, *Pin* should make its main entry a title-entry. Because it does so with all other works of corporate authorship. Its making it an author-entry in this case is a violation of the Canon of Consistency.

4123   *Ala*

Rule 27A. Enter a separately published index to a single work of an author with the work, making added entry for the compiler.

This implies that the author heading will be the name of the author of the original. Surely, this is faulty. For the author of the index is the compiler ; it is not the author of the original. This violates the Canon of Consistency. What should have been the motive behind this inconsistency ? Obviously, the motive is to bring the index close to the original. This is no doubt a legitimate motive. But to acheive this end by abusing the term " author " is certainly wrong. It produces a classified-pocket within alphabetical arrangement by name of author. Classified catalogue does not land itself in this predicament ; because, it achieves the end with the aid of a separate classified part made of number-entries. The correct method for dictionary catalogue is to achieve the end through specific subject entries.

Rule 27D. Enter a combined index to several publications of one society or institution, under the name of the body, with added entry under the compiler, and several serials indexed, giving heading, brief title, and the word " index " in parentheses.

Most of the remarks on the preceding Rule 27A apply to this Rule also. A combined index should be treated as a composite book, of an extremely complicated nature. Several works (indexes) have got telescoped into another. The composite work has got an author, *viz*., compiler. His name alone can be author heading. The result of telescoping is that the index is multifocal. Classified catalogue would enter the work as for one of the foci and record it under the class number for it. It will give added entries—cross-reference entries—to the other foci. If dictionary catalogue is true to its preferred alphabetical arrangement, it too should make the main entry carry the name of the compiler as heading. The urge towards classified-pocket should be satisfied only by subject analytical entries for each index under the name of its own original as heading with the word " index " in parentheses.

Rule 27G. Enter indexes of laws which do not index a particular work under the name of the country or other jurisdiction, with form subdivision " Laws, statutes, etc. (Indexes)."

This is again a violation of the Canon of Purity. The compiler who is the author is relegated to added entry. And the subject entry is pushed up as main entry.

Rule 27H. Enter an index to a particular code...... under the name of the jurisdiction with form subdivision "Laws, statutes, etc, the name of the code, and form subdivision, (Indexes)."

This carries the violation of the Canon of Purity a step further.

4124 *Vat*

Vat's rules have the same faults as *Ala's* rules. The following are the corresponding rules :—

Vat 13 = *Ala* 27A ; *Vat* = *Ala* 27D ; *Vat* 15(a) = *Ala* 27E

414 DOUBTFUL VALIDITY

The following rules are of doubtful validity :—

4141 *Rdc*

Rule 10. The photographer need not in general have an entry, even in a special catalogue of photographs.

Rdc would treat a photographer only as a collaborator not deserving even an added entry. In a photographic reproduction of a work of art, the photographer may perhaps be given the same status as the printer of a book. He may then be overlooked in catalogue entry. But photography itself can be the art in some pictures, albums and books. Indeed, the ' subject ' of the photograph may not have primary or even real interest. The only point of the interest can be the art exhibited by the photographer, even as it is in painting. It is doubtful if it is proper to overlook the name of the photographer in a case like this.

42 Joint Personal Authors' Heading

Rdc Rule 3. Enter works written conjointly by several authors under the name of the one first mentioned on the title-page, with references from the others.

Pin Rule 67. An individual work that is the common composition of two or three authors is put under the author first named ; references are made from the others.

Ala Rule 3A.   Enter under the first author mentioned on the title-page of a work produced jointly by two or more authors in which the contribution of each is not a separate and distinct part of the whole.   Make added entry with designation "joint author" for any author after the first whose name is included in transcribing the title.

3B.   In a work of joint-authorship in which the chief responsibility rests with one author, but the title-page reads "with the collaboration of......" or words to that effect, the making of added entries for the collaborators will depend on (1) the nature of the work ;   (2) the number of collaborators and the importance of their contribution.

Vat Rule 2.   Works written by two or three authors in collaboration, without indication of the parts and sections written by each, are entered under the name of the first one mentioned ; added entries are made under the names of the authors with the abbreviation for the words " joint author " (collab) added to the heading.

Ccc Rule 122.   If the title-page contains the names of two and only two Joint Personal Authors, both the names are to be used as the heading with the conjunction ' and ' connecting them.

Rule 1222.   If there are three or more Joint Personal Authors, the name of the first mentioned author alone is to be used as the Heading and the word ' etc.' is to be added thereafter.

Rdc started the tradition of choosing the name of the first author alone for heading.   This is a violation of the Law of Impartiality.   This is continued in all later codes except *Ccc*.   *Ccc* prescribes the choice of the names of both the authors if there are only two authors.   This is at once in conformity with the Canon of Ascertainability and the Law of Impartiality.

But, *Ccc* too violates the Law of Impartiality when the number of authors is three or more.   Its defence of this violation is as follows :—

The special treatment given to the number 'two' and denied to the number ' three ' and the greater numbers is purely out of deference to the habit of readers. It is found from experience that books by two authors are usually referred to by the names of both the authors, as ' Harkness and Morley,' ' Beaumont and Fletcher,' ' Jathar and Beri, ' and so on.   But such a practice does not obtain when the number of authors is greater than two.

Thus, it is a case of conflict between the Canon of Sought-Heading on one side, and the Canon of Consistency and the Law of Impartiality on the other.   *Ccc* upholds the former.   Incidentally it also satisfies the Law of Parsimony ; but this has not been the intention ; nor has it weighed with the *Ccc* in this context.

There is an unfortunate implication of Rule 1222 of *Ccc*. As a result of the omission of the names of the second and later authors in the main entry, none of these names gets a joint author entry in the alphabetical part. This is too bad. The rule in question should be amended to remove this fault. The correct procedure will be to mention all the names on the back of the main entry. This implies an amendment to Rule 321, category (2). It should be amended so as to read as follows :—

The name of the second and later Authors, or Collaborators, in case the Heading of the above mentioned first kind indicates joint authorship or joint collaboratorship.

Pin and *Vat* make no provision for a book of three or more authors.

43 Corporate Author Heading

Pin Rule 60. Sales catalogues, prospectuses and the like which mentioned the firm are put under its name (if the collector or the author is not named).

Ccc Rule 123. If Corporate Authorship is indicated by the title-page, the name of the Corporate Author is to be used as heading.

Ccc states its rule in terms of the Canon of Ascertainability— *i.e.*, in terms of what is indicated by the title-page. *Pin* also does similarly for the very narrow limit to which it has reduced corporate authorship. The other three codes do not have a corresponding rule. Their rules, intended to correspond to the above mentioned rules of *Pin* and *Ccc*, merely define terminology. These rules are *Rdc* 45, *Ala* 71, and *Vat* 104-105.

The problem of corporate authorship is a difficult one calling for much judgment, even when the title-page is relied on. The following five difficult issues arise :—

1 Corporate Body *versus* Person ;
2 Conference *versus* Person ;
3 Government *versus* Institution ;
4 Institution *versus* Institution ; and
5 Parent Body *versus* Organ.

These difficult issues should be fought out, as a preliminary step, at the level of terminology. This has been done in sections 221 to 223, 2231, 2232, 224 and its subdivisions. It is also further discussed and clarified in sections 228 and its subdivisions. Section 2288 gives a synopsis covering some of the most difficult problems. The rules of *Ccc* are based on such clarification of terminology.

Therefore, it is able to deal with the choice of corporate author heading by a single simple rule. *Pin* escapes the problem by denying corporate authorship except in a trivial case. But the other codes make their rules on corporate authorship swell into great numbers because they mix up in the same rule the definition, the choice, and the rendering of corporate author and of its name. This is not good drafting. The resulting hypertrophy bewilders a beginner. It may confuse even a veteran on occasions.

430 Parent body *vs* Organ

The problem of Parent Body *vs* Organ needs a little more discussion than the one implied in sections 2221 to 2228. A difficult matter often turning up for judgment in the choice of corporate author is :—

    1 Is it the parent body as a whole ? or
    2 Is it an organ of it, of the first remove ? or
    3 Is it an organ of a later remove ?

In most cases, the title page—*i.e.*, the Canon of Ascertainability—will decide the issue.

But the title-page might have been carelessly drafted. Only an organ of an earlier remove, than the strict organ-author, might have been mentioned. In most of these cases, a persual of the introduction, preamble, letter of transmittal or in rare cases, a glance through the whole document may decide the issue. This would involve of course a considerable wastage of man-power. This is avoidable. The means to avoid it is to set up a standard for the title-page and its overflow for works of governmental, institutional and conference authorship. Works of governmental authorship are in the hands of a paid staff of high calibre. They are also becoming numerous. Conformity to standard may not be as difficult in their case, as in the case of the other two kinds of corporate authorship. Standardisation of title-page will give great relief. Its example will make the other types to fall in line. In the interest of over-all national and international economy, the International Standards Organisation and the various National Standards Bodies should establish a standard for the author-statement in the title-page of documents of corporate authorship.

4301 Legal Publications

Legal publications raise certain issues of their own, in regard to authorship. For example, a bill is usually by the work of a Ministry. Its modification is the work of Select Committee. The Act, before the assent of the Head of the State, is the work of Legislature. These cases give no difficulty. But the final Act is the work of Legislature and the Head of State. Constitutionally, the work of each is of equal weight. Quantitatively they are quite unequal. Further, most Acts provide only a skeleton. The details have to be filled up by the Executive or even by a Department. For these reasons, the whole Government should be taken as the author of an Act, or a collection of Acts.

Another difficulty may arise. Editions of an Act may be brought by a person, with notes, commentaries and case-laws in various degrees of proportion. Perhaps here a convention may be adopted :—

It should be treated as a composite book, as if the person is the author of the notes etc. and the Government as the author of the text itself.

431 Redundant Rules

The following rules are redundant :—

4311 *Rdc*

49 (Report by a subordinate office)	52 (Calendar of Papers)
50 (Digest of laws)	55 (Non-official's report).

4313 *Ala*

73C	(Address by Head of State, other than prescribed by constitution)	89I	(Court rules)
		89J	(Grand jury)
75	(Executive departments)	90A	(Single plea)
84D	(Digest of laws)	90C	(Contested election)
89C-D	(Decisions of single Court)	90H	(Collected trials)
89H	(Digest of decisions)	96	(Political party).

4314 *Vat*

114 (Legislative documents)		121 (*c*)	(Court proceedings etc)
121 (Court)		121 (*d*)	(Defence record).
121 (*b*) (Digest of decisions)			

The choice prescribed in the above-mentioned rules is in accordance with the accepted definition. In most cases, the rule merely elucidates the difference between personal authorship and corporate authorship. *Rdc* merely emphasises the right corporate author. The proper place for such elucidation is not the body of rules on choice of heading. The proper place for it is in the chapter on Terminology. If necessary, it may be reinforced in a commentary on the basic rule for the choice of the corporate body, whose name should be used as author heading. There is nothing gained by increasing the number of rules in order to accommodate such an elucidation of the terms used in cataloguing convention. It is bad drafting. It bewilders beginners. *Ccc* has separated terminology from rules for choice of heading.

432 Faulty Rules

The following rules are faulty :—

4323 *Ala*

Ala Rule 79. **Delegation.** Enter a delegation, delegates or delegate officially representing a country at a conference or congress, under the name of the conference or congress with a sub-heading for the delegation. The sub-heading will consist of the phrase " Delegation from (country)."

Delegation to conference looks amphibious. A delegation is itself a corporate body. It implies the existence of two other corporate bodies—Delegated-from-Body and Delegated-to-Body. The kind of document whose authorship has to be determined may comprise memoranda submitted, resolutions tabled and utterences made, by the delegation at the conference, and report by the delegation to the delegated-from-body. Surely, the authorship belongs to the delegation. But the delegation is not an independent body. It is an organ. Its name has therefore to be only a sub-heading. The name of the body of which it is an organ should be the main heading. The question is, " Is it an organ of the Delegated-from-Body or of the Delegated-to-Body ? " Again, " Which body takes the ultimate responsibility for the thought-content of the document created by the delegation ? " " Is it the Delegated-from-Body or the Delegated-to-Body ? " There can be no difference of opinion about the answers to these questions. The ultimate responsibility rests with the Delegated-from-Body. The delegation is an organ of that body. Rule 79 of *Ala* is, therefore, faulty.

What should have been the intention of *Ala* in entering a delegation as an organ of the Delegated-to-Body ? Probably, it had the desire to bring in one place all the documents by and on the conference and even those related to it in some way or other. To achieve this end, *Ala* ignores the definition of author, while ostensibly choosing author heading for main entry. The main heading prescribed by *Ala* 79 is in reality a subject heading, if at all. It is not proper to make it the heading of main entry. The heading of main entry should be the name of the right author. The subject heading can only belong to a specific added entry.

Curiously *Ala* 79 adds insult to injury. It has not only denied the claim of the name of the author to form the heading of the main entry ; but it has denied it even the right to form the heading of a specific added entry.

Ala Rule 84. **Laws.**—Enter laws, decrees, and other acts having the force of law under the country, State, or other jurisdiction with the form-heading " Laws, statutes, etc.". Common forms of publications are :

General collection.	Political codes.
General codes.	Commercial codes.
Civil codes.	Official editions of a special act or acts on a particular subject (*e.g.*, banks, income tax, etc.)
Penal codes.	Non-official editions or compilations of acts.
Judicial codes.	Official drafts (or Legislative bills) for individual laws and codes.

Obviously, in all these cases except the last, the heading should be merely the name of the territory of the enacting sovereign power. This has been discussed in section 4301. No doubt, the various laws, for example of a country, will thereby be scattered among the various other entries under the name of the country. They will be scattered by the alphabetical arrangements of their titles, in author-entry. They can be brought together only by subject entry and not by author entry. Probably the intention of *Ala* is that such a publication need not be given author entry. Perhaps, the unexpressed reason for so intending is that both author and subject entries will have the same term as main heading. If so, it is desirable to state explicitly that the author entry is not necessary and leave it there. This rule for subject entry should not be inserted in the chapter on author entries. It is not the business of the rules for author entry to deal with subject entry. This is a violation of the Canon of Purity.

This confusion between author entry and subject entry can very well be used by *Pin* as an argument to show the danger of artificially putting up a governmental author, and perhaps even the absurdity of doing so.

Ccc preserves both author entry and subject entry. Of course, the subject entry is the main entry. There the subject is indicated by the call number in the leading section. The heading gives the correct name of the governmental author. In the alphabetical index part, the author entry occurs with the correct author heading. Of course, the name of the subject will also occur in the index part, as the heading of a class index entry.

Ala Rule 85. **Constitution**. Enter constitutions, and official drafts of proposed constitutions, under the name of the country or State with the form sub-heading " Constitution."

This is also a case of a violation of the Canon of Purity. Surely, the author of the South Africa Act, 1909, is Great Britain and not South Africa. South Africa's constitution was only its subject matter. Therefore, the heading prescribed by *Ala* 85 is only subject heading. The author heading is " Great Britain."

One of the examples given under this rule throws a lurid light on the confusion between author and subject entry. The second example would imply the two following entries :—

Main Entry

South Africa—Constitution

South Africa Act, 1909.

Reference Entry

Great Britain—Laws, statutes, etc.

See also

South Africa—Constitution

This is a case of a cross reference index entry referring from one subject entry to another subject entry. The aberration is traceable to failure inevitable in building a code of rules without a preliminary chapter on terminology before beginning the rules themselves.

Ala Rule 84B. **Laws of territories, Dependencies etc.** Enter the laws of States and territories, including dependencies, with or without a degree of autonomy, under the name of the jurisdiction or territory to which they apply, rather than under the name of the country or countries to whose sovereignty or suzerainty they have been successively subject and whose law making or executive powers have promulgated the laws.

This rule is doubly faulty both as Rule 84 and Rule 85.

Ala Rule 87. . **Charters**. Enter charters for colonial, provincial or local governments and for other corporate bodies under the name of the government or the body to whom the charter is granted.

The revelation of the fault of prescribing subject entry in the place of author entry reaches its height in this rule. The corporate author is the corporate body responsible for and conferring the charter. In the case of a charter of a city, it is the government of the country or the state within whose territory the city lies. Surely, the city is not responsible for the charter ; nor does it confer it. The second example given under this rule brings out the fault very clearly.

Main Entry

CINCINNATI, HAMILTON AND DAYTON RAILROAD COMPANY.
Charter and by-laws of the Cincinnati etc.

Reference Entry

OHIO—LAWS, STATUES, etc.
See also
CINCINNATI, HAMILTON AND DAYTON RAILROAD COMPANY.

The true author is denied the right to be the heading of the main entry of its work. The subject is made its heading. The true author's name can only occur as the main heading of a pseudo-subject entry. For, " Ohio—Laws, Statutes etc. " is neither the name of the author nor the name of the subject of the document.

Ala Rules 88A and 88B are on treaties. They continue a similar violation of the Canon of Purity by adding the sub-heading " Treaty " to the heading which is the name of the government.

Ala Rule 89E. Enter a collection of decisions on a single subject under the editor or compiler. If limited to a single court, make added entry under the court.

Surely, the thought-content of a collection of decisions of a single court has that single court as the author. This rule demotes the author to the heading of an added entry and promotes the collaborator to the privilege of being the heading of main entry.

Ala Rule No.	Document	Author heading: Name of
90B	Report of civil action	Plaintiff
90C	Report of contest of election	Plaintiff
90D	Report of criminal trial	Defendent
90E	Report of impeachment	Defendent
90F	Report of court martial	Defendent
90G	Admiralty proceedings	Vessel

105

7

The question in these cases is : Is the plaintiff (or defendent) the author or the subject of the document. No doubt a full report of the case contains an account of the plaint or the defence state-ment of all parties concerned. It also contains perhaps a verbatim report of the chief examination and the cross examination of the parties and the witnesses. It may also contain the argument of the advocates of all the parties. It must necessarily contain the verdict of the jury if any, and the judgment of the court. Surely, the plaintiff or the accused is not the sole author of the report. Nor is the contribution of each separable, from that of others, into distinct parts. And yet, the report cannot be regarded to be of joint authorship. Indeed such a report is a composite work in one sense. And yet, it does not have clear-cut parts for each of the different contributors. In this, it resembles a document embodying correspondence between several persons. There, however, the thought-content of the document gets developed jointly by all the correspondents. We cannot apply the same description to a report of a trial in a Court. Perhaps in the circumstances, a more appropriate course will be to treat such a report as a composite book. *Ala* rule 5 prescribes for the heading, the name of the editor. But the document may be without an editor. Then the names of the court which co-ordinates, and guides the course of the trial and finally summarises the entire course and gives the judgment, the real focus or the culmination of the report, has a better claim to be the author heading than the plaintiff or the defendant. The reason for the prescription of the *Ala* rules is probably the urge to put up as the heading that name which is likely to be looked up—especially in famous trials. But is it not really the subject heading rather than the author heading ? The name of the plaintiff or the defendant will more appropriately come as an answer to the ques-tion, " What is the subject of the document ? ," rather than to the question, " Who is the author of the document ? " Moreover, in the well-known famous trials series, the dominant term in the title of the book is the name of the defendant. This is significant in the same way as the word " Algebra " is in the title " Text book of Algebra ." It is of subject-significance.

4324 *Vat*

Similar remarks apply to the following corresponding rules of *Vat.*

Rules 115 to 118 (Constitutions, laws, statutes, tariffs, treaties, charters, privileges.)

Rule 122 (Criminal trials).
Rule 123 (Celebrated trials).
Rule 124 (Civil trials).
Rule 125 (Acts of martyrs).

44 Joint Corporate Author Heading

Ccc Rule 124. If the title-page indicates two or more Joint Corporate Authors, the Heading is to be constructed on the analogy of rule 122 (for Joint Personal Author Heading).

The other codes do not have an explicit rule on joint corporate authors.

45 Pseudonym Heading

Rdc Rule 7. Enter pseudonymous works generally under the Author's real name, when it is known, with a reference from the pseudonym ; but make the entry under the pseudonym with a reference from the real name, when the writer habitually uses his pseudonym or is generally known by it.

Pin Rule 73. There serve as author's names and become entry words

1 Those appellatives by which definite persons have been permanently named ; and

2 Pseudonyms, even when they are to be recognised as such at the first glance.

Rule 169. If different names come under consideration for the same author, the one being the real name, the other a pseudonym, then the real name becomes the entry word, with a reference from the pseudonym.

Rule 170. If, however, the pseudonym has established itself in usage in such a way for better known authors and they are preferably cited under it, then it becomes the entry word, with a reference from the real name.

Ala Rule 30A. Enter works published under pseudonym under the author's real name when known, except as qualified below in (1) to (3) and B.

1 Exception is made in favour of entry under pseudonym....When real name is unknown, or the author wishes it withheld.

2 When the pseudonym has become fixed in literary history (including current criticism) and biography, and is therefore, the name looked for by the informed reader.

This rule may be followed in cases where current popular authors are better known by pseudonym than by real name, if they have never published under the real name.

3 In cases where the real name and the pseudonym are used with about equal frequency and are therefore equally well known, the real name is likely to gain in ascendency and is therefore to be favoured.

B Other combinations of circumstances arise in which an individual case may require a special attention. For example, it is ordinarily better to enter under the real name authors who have written under several pseudonyms, especially if they have ever published under the real name ; but exception might be made for a well-known pseudonym.

Vat Rules 51, 52 and 55 are in substance the same as those of *Ala* rules. In addition it gives

Rule 57 a nickname, which has been taken from the place of birth, or has been formed in some other manner, may become the entry word if it is regularly used in the place of the real name.

Ccc Rule 125. If the title-page gives only a Pseudonym in the place of the author's name, the Pseudonym is to be used as the Heading.

Rule 1251. If the title page gives the real name of the author also in a subordinate manner, it is to be added in circular brackets.

Rule 12511. If the title-page gives the real name of the author and adds the pseudonym in a subordinated manner, the former is to be chosen for the heading. The latter is to be added in circular brackets.

Rule 1252. If the real name of the author can be found out from outside the work, it is to be added in square brackets after the pseudonym.

Rdc has started deviation from the Canon of Ascertainability.

Pin did not so deviate.

Ala and *Vat* have perpetuated the deviation started by *Rdc*.

Ccc is insistent on loyalty to the Canon of Ascertainability. It treats pseudonym on a par with alternative name. This is discussed in section 491 and its sub-divisions. *Ccc* has faults in drafting. It has mixed up ideas about choice and rendering in the same rule. These should be separated and put into separate rules. *Ccc* has also been influenced by *Rdc* tradition in its rule 1252. This fault also should be removed. Some of the remarks in the commentary to *Rdc* 7 have been incorporated as rules in *Ala* and *Vat*. They show the difficulty of the problem of pseudonym when unaided by a set of normative principles fixed for cataloguing. No doubt, these normative principles have to be distilled out of unaided tentative practices. But once the cycle of scientific method, described in section 18, is established, it is an advantage to frame catalogue codes with the aid of normative principles. At the time of *Rdc*, the cycle had not quite established itself. However, the struggle in grappling with the problem described in the commentary on *Rdc* 7 is revealing. The first paragraph in the commentary shows :—

1 The struggle in distributing weightage between 1 Canon of Ascertainability, 2 Canon of Permanence, and the convenience of readers, *i.e.*, Laws of Library Science ;

2 The tendency to draw the line too far away from the convenience of the reader to meet the convenience of the cataloguer ; and

3 The invocation of a standing committee to watch and give directives. Paragraphs, that follow in that commentary, show the veering round towards the convenience of the reader and incidentally towards the Canon of Ascertainability also. The last paragraph shows the play of the Principle of Local Variation.

46 Collaborator Heading

Rdc Rule 21. Reporters are usually treated as authors of reports of trials, etc. Translators and editors are not to be considered as authors.

Rule 98. Collector, Collecting editor (is a substitute for author).

A stenographic reporter is hardly more an author than the printer is ; but it is not well to make fine distinctions.

A collection of works should be entered under the translator if he is also the collector.

Pin The rules of chapter 1 " extension and restriction of the author concept " prescribe collaborator heading as shown below :—

Rule 36 (Chrestomathies etc. under editor).

Rule 39 (Collections of sagas under editor).

Rule 40 (Collections of laws under editor).

Rule 41 (Editions of inscriptions of unknown authors under editor).

Rule 42 (Editions of texts with work of editor as principal matter under the editor).

Rule 43 (Translations with independent significance, say as linguistic land marks under editor).

Rule 49 (Representation of artistic and cultural subjects when originator not named in the title under editor).

Pin does not permit use of collaborator heading for main entry of any single work.

Ala The following rules prescribe collaborator heading :—

Rule 7B (4). Results of expedition when prominence is given on the title-page to the editor of the results, under editor.

Rule 8B. Collection of inscriptions without a distinctive name and not being the property of a private individual or of a corporate body, under editor.

Rule 9A (4). Reproduction of miniatures or other ornamentations without text and with artist unknown, under editor or compiler.

Ccc Rule 126. If the title-page does not give the name of a Personal Author or the names of Joint Personal Authors or indicate Corporate Authorship or give a Pseudonym or Pseudonyms in the place of the name of the author but contains the name of a collaborator that name is to be used as the Heading and a descriptive word is to be added thereafter indicating the role of the person.

Ccc aims to minimise title headings for anonymous works. The other codes put an anonymous book under a collaborator only in one or two specified cases. *Ccc* is able to respect the Canon of Ascertainability without exception and choose collaborator heading for any anonymous book with a collaborator mentioned in the title-page. The reason for this is simple. Its rules are for a Classified Catalogue. In it, the main entry is call number entry. The call number section is prepotent. The heading is totally impotent. Moreover, the call number heading presents all the main entries of all the editions of an anonymous work together, in a consecutive sequence, irrespective of the variations of its title or of its editor from edition to edition. The prescription of collaborator heading in other codes even for the few specified cases is faulty ; for the different editions of the anonymous work will thereby get scattered. This offends the Laws of Library Science.

461 Competing Collaborators

Rule 1262. If the title-page gives the name of each of two or more of kinds of collaborators,—the name belonging to one and only one kind is to be chosen as Heading ; for this purpose, the order, in which the kinds are enumerated in the definition (of collaborators) is the order of preference.

This rule is faulty. It violates the Canon of Ascertainability. It would be more in keeping with this Canon to choose for the heading the name of the collaborator occurring first or in the most dominant type on the title-page.

462 Joint Collaborators

Ccc Rule 127 prescribes for joint collaborators the analogy of rule 122 for joint authors.

Rdc, *Pin*, and *Ala* do not prescribe rules to cover this case.

47 Title Heading

Rdc Rule 120. Make a first word entry (Entry made from the first word of the title not an article) for all anonymous works. (If the author's name can be ascertained, make the main entry under the author).

Rule 121. For anonymous biography, if the title mentions the subject of the life omit the title entry, leaving only the subject entry.

Pin Rule 69. If the author is neither named in the title nor to be ascertained from any other source the entry word is taken from the real title.

Rule 70. If the author is not named in the title, but is ascertained from another source, his name becomes the entry word.

Ala Rule 32. Enter works published anonymously under author when known.

Rule 32G. If the author is not known, enter under title. Enter a translation of an anonymous work under the translated title.

Vat Rule 179. Anonymous works are entered under their title. Only those works are considered to be anonymous whose authors remain unknown after a full and careful search.

It is customary to catalog an anonymous biography under the name of the person written about. But even in this case it is better to follow the general rule, especially as the work will appear in the dictionary catalog under the name of the person as subject.

Rule 189. Translations of anonymous works are entered under their own title in the various languages.

Ccc Rule 128. If the Heading cannot be chosen in accordance with any of the other rules of this chapter the first word of the title of the book, excluding an initial article or an initial honorific word, if any, is to be used as the heading.

There is fundamental difference between *Ccc* and all the other codes. The rule of the former speaks of the book. It bases its rule on its title-page. It abides by the Canon of Ascertainability without question. But the other codes call for search outside the book. They are thinking of the work and not of the book while cataloguing the latter.

471 ANONYMOUS BIOGRAPHY

Rdc definitely prescribes subject heading for main entry of an anonymous biography. *Vat* refers to this and records its dissent.

472 ENCYCLOPAEDIA

Rdc Rule 191. Make a form entry of encyclopaedias and indexes.

Ala Rule 5B. Enter encyclopaedias and dictionaries under title unless decidedly better known by the name of their editors.

Vat Rule 223. Works which result from the collaboration of a number of authors under the direction of an editor (Encyclopaedies, dictionaries, handbooks, etc.) are entered under their title, unless they are definitely better known under the name of their editor.

Ccc Rule 128. If a book is a general biographical dictionary or an encyclopaedia belonging to the class generalia, Science General, Useful Arts or Social Sciences......, the First Word of the title of the book, excluding the initial article or an initial honorific word, if any, is to be used as Heading.

Rdc does not explicitly mention anything about the main entry of an encyclopaedia. Can the above rule on form entry be taken to mean that that should be the main entry? *Ala* and *Vat* do not give a definite rule. They leave the heading to be decided by whatever "is better known." *Ccc* is categorical. Its rule is on the assumption that a general encyclopaedia will be remembered by title, and that on a specific subject by the name of the editor.

473 GENERIC AUTHOR STATEMENT

Ala Rule 32.   If the author is not known (but authorship is indicated by a descriptive or generic word or phrase preceded by an article, *e.g.*, " by a lover of justice," " by a physician," " by a bishop of the Church of Englnad,") enter under title.

Vat Rule 184 is similar.

Ccc has no rule on the subject.

A more elegant way of dealing with this case is to mention this idea in the definition of anonymous book in the chapter on terminology.

474 PERIODICAL PUBLICATION

Rdc Rule 133.   Periodicals are to be treated as anonymous and entered under the first word, not an article or a serial number.

Pin Rule 61.   Pocket books, special calendars, directories, annual reports of institutions and associations, and other quasi-periodical series are arranged according to their real title, even if every volume is the work of one (permanent or changing) author.

Rule 62.   Periodicals are arranged under their real title.

Ala Rule 5C (1).   Enter a periodical under its latest title....... In the case of a periodical which has ceased publication make exception in favour of entry under an earlier title used for a much longer period than the later title.

A periodical issued by a society, institution, or government body is ordinarily to be entered under its title.

Rule 5C (2).   Enter a newspaper under its latest title.

Vat Rule 230.   Periodicals are entered under their latest title, and no account is taken in the entry of any earlier title or titles.

Ccc Rule 712.   The Heading (of a periodical publication) is to be

1   the name of appropriate corporate body,....... if

either

(*a*) the Periodical Publication is of corporate authorship

or

(*b*) it is published or sponsored by or is the organ of a learned Society, though it may be only of a composite nature, not amounting to a case of corporate authorship ; and

2   the first word of the title...... if it is

neither

(*a*) a publication of corporate authorship

nor

(*b*) published by nor an organ of a learned Society.

The choice of heading for a periodical publication has not yet extricated itself fully from a severe aftermath of the controversy of the seventies of the last century about the recognition of the very concept of corporate authorship.   The powerful plea of *Rdc* on the need for recognising a learned society as author of its *Abhandlungen* down the entire range of alphabet right upto its *Zeitschrift* has been quoted in section 2382. This plea overreached itself. The urge for producing effect led to equating a mere " Sponsor " to an " Author." This has been discussed in detail in section 25. *Rdc* itself had felt the awkward result of such an overreaching. In the preamble to the commentary on its Rule 133 *Rdc* tries to extricate itself from this awkwardness by restricting the meaning of the term " Periodical." This restriction was not made by a precise definition capable of definite application unmarred by ambiguity.

This created a nebulous and more or less conflicting tradition in the choice of heading for periodicals. This is the aftermath of the successful fight of *Rdc* in another sphere. *Ala* perpetuated this tradition. *Vat* accepted it.

Oh ! the inexorability of tradition ! Particularly of tradition packed with fault !! In edition 1 (1934) *Ccc* Rule 712 saw that " Society was not author but only publisher of a " society periodical." And yet, it prescribed the choice of the name of society as heading, as if it were author. Edition 3 (1951) walked up almost to the door mat. It introduced the word sponsor in the amended form of Rule 712. And yet, it prescribed that the name of the sponsor or publishing society should be chosen as heading. In actual application difficulties mounted up. This was due to the intensification of the incidence of the 18 idiosyncrasies of periodicals with the increase in the number of periodicals in the world. These 18 idiosyncrasies are listed, discussed and dealt with in chapter 8 of *Ccc*. The difficulties were brought home more and more unmistakably in the working of the " the three card system " of administering periodicals, published first in a crude form in *Library administration* (1935) of Ranganathan, and refined later, guided by horse sense, as it were. " The three card system " prescribed title entry for the file of registration cards. And yet, inhibition caused by the *Rdc* tradition prevented the transfer of this change-over, to main entry in catalogue. The persistence of the aftermath of *Rdc*'s fight for recognition of the concept of institutional authorship led to a crisis during the preparation of *Union Catalogue of learned periodical publications in South Asia* (1953).

The crisis was in the conflict between the implementation of the *Rdc* tradition and the Canon of Consistency. It is crises that lift one from the rut of irrational ways imposed by blind tradition. In this case also, the crisis led to some rationalisation. Rationalisation was possible because the leading section of main entry was the prepotent class number ; it could rope in under one leading section of main entry all the volumes of a periodical, whatever be its idiosyncrasies devloped in course of time. Rationalisation also led to a clear distinction between the function of main entry and that of alphabetical added entry. This enabled the assignment of satisfying sponsor-approach to a periodical by an added entry with sponsor heading. This finding was implemented in the *Union catalogue*. Its helpfulness was demonstrated. The following will be the consequential amended form of Rule 712 of *Ccc* :—

Ccc Rule 712. The Heading (of the main entry of a Periodical Publication) is to be

    1   its title followed by the name of its sponsoring body, if any ; and

    2   the name of the appropriate corporate body, if it is of corporate author-ship and not merely of corporate sponsorship.

4741 Redundant Rules

The following rules are redundant :—

Ala Rule 5D (almanacs, year books, etc.).

        5E (directories).

475 Borrowed Heading

Ala Rule 5C (4). Enter a collection of extracts by various authors from a single periodical or newspaper under the name of the periodical or newspaper. Make added entries under the title of the collection and the name of the collector if given.

For entry of a collection of extracts by various authors from different periodi-cals, see 5A.

The work of a single author republished from a periodical entered under the name of the author, if known, or under title if anonymous has no added entry for the *periodical*. But an added entry is usually made under the *Newspaper* for the work of a single author republished from it, especially if the author is an editor or an official correspondent or if the article is anonymous.

Vat Rule 232. When the title of a periodical has been connected over a period of years with a diversified publishing enterprise, and therefore may be considered a real firm, its name is used as the author heading for its publications.

The above two rules demonstrate the danger of framing a code of rules without either a chapter on terminology and a chapter on normative principles or of forgetting the feeble definition given in the glossary of terms. The danger is laid bare by the version of *Vat*. It amounts to pricking the bubble of " borrowed heading " prescribed by *Ala*. For *Vat* calls the bearer of the name used as " borrowed heading," " real firm " and " publishing enterprise." Surely, the name of publisher occupying the heading of the main entry of one of its publications amounts to usurpation. This is wrong.

But what should have been the motive behind the backing of such usurpation by *Ala* and *Vat* ? Obviously, they regard the name of the source of the " collection of extracts " as a sought-heading. This is right. But it is not right to make it the name of the main entry. The source can figure in the main entry only in a note—Related Book Note. Then the source will get an added entry. This added entry will satisfy the needs of source-approach.

The divided mind of *Ala* in this matter is demonstrated by the very wording of its rule 5C (4). In the second sentence of the first paragraph, it concedes to the title of the collection and the name of the collector the right to claim the status of the heading of an added entry. In the second paragraph, it deals with extracts from different periodicals. Consistency with the prescription of the first sentence of the first paragraph of the rule would demand the use of the names of the different periodicals, as in the case of joint authorship. The third paragraph of the rule carries some light with it. If the collection of extracts form the work of a single author, the author's name is given the right of becoming the heading of the main entry. The source is demoted to the status of added entry. Even here, *Ala* is far too unsteady. It would concede the right to become the heading at least of an added entry only to a newspaper. It denies this right to a periodical. Evidently, *Vat* finds this exception within exception to be too maddening. It has replaced *Ala*'s complex of rules and confused hits, by a single straight hit. In doing so, it has laid bare the inappropriateness of the rule.

The correct rule should prescribe the treatment of the " collection of extracts " on its own right as a book. The heading of its main entry should be the name of its author, or collector or the title, as it may be. The name of the periodical publication forming its source should be made the heading of an added entry as for source material.

48 Composite Book

481 ORDINARY COMPOSITE BOOK

Rdc Rule 99. Several works published together *without a collective title* are to be put under the author's name which appears first on the title-page, even though the collector's name is also there.

Rule 100. For the convenience of the public it is better that the catalog's recognition of the collector should in certain cases take the form of reference or added entry rather than of main entry. Therefore entry is made under title and not under collector for ;

Rule 101. *Anonymous Collections*, unless the collector's name is wellknown and the collector is usually called by it.

Pin Rule 66. A collection of individual works with a comprehensive collective title is put under that.

Ala Rule 4A (1). Enter a work produced by collaboration of two or more authors...... under the author chiefly responsible for it.

Rule 4A (2). If origin, chief interest or responsibility is not closely identified with or attributable to any one of the contributors enter under the first-named author if there are not more than three and the title of the whole work is applicable to each of the contributions...... otherwise enter under the title.

Vat Rule 3. Individual works, which are printed together in a single volume with a common title-page that lists each of them are entered under the name of the first author mentioned.

Rule 4. If the works are issued under a common title, this title becomes the main entry-word...... However, if there is an editor or compiler, the entry is made under his name.

Rule 5. If a composite work or collection represents considerable editorial work on the part of a person or institution, the main entry is made under the editor, unless the work is better known under its title.

Ccc Rule 61. An ordinary composite book is to be dealt with as a simple book ignoring the names of the contributors except for index entries.

The rules of *Rdc*, *Ala*, and *Vat* are vitiated by lack of definiteness of prescription. There is the usual capitulation to the cult of " unless better known otherwise ". Of course, this violates the Canons of Ascertainability and Consistency. *Pin* overlooks the collaborator altogether and prefers title entry in all cases. *Ccc* strictly follows the Canon of Ascertainability. However, it fails to provide for the composite book with a common title-page that lists each item. *Rdc* Rule 99 choosing the name of first-mentioned author in preference to compiler's name is of doubtful helpfulness.

482 FESTSCHRIFTEN

Rdc Rule 108. Festschriften in honour of a man, may be entered under his name, with the addition of *subject*, or *testimonial*, or a similar word.

Pin Rule 57. Personal publications without author statement are put under the name of the person to whom they relate. If they concern several persons, they are put under the name of the first. If, however, the author is named, they are put under him. Also collections which relate to one person are treated like anonymous publications.

Ala Rule 5A (*c*). Enter Festschriften and similar collections published by a society or an institution in honour of a person, or to celebrate an anniversary under the society or institution. When not published by a society or an institution, enter under editor, if the editor's name appears prominently in the publication ; otherwsie enter under title.

Vat Rule 226 practically follows *Ala* except that the name of editor is not to be given the privilege of becoming the heading of main entry.

Rdc prescribes subject entry itself to be treated as main entry. *Pin* follows this *Rdc* tradition with one exception that if there is an author mentioned in the title-page, the author entry should become the main entry. The last sentence in its rule is difficult to understand. *Ala* and *Vat* prefer sponsor heading for the main entry if a corporate body is the sponsor. This is as bad as making the name of sponsoring body the heading of a main entry of a periodical. This has already been discussed in section 474. *Ccc* does not have to provide a special rule. For Festschrift is covered by its definition of ordinary composite book. However, in its first edition (1934), *Ccc* had fallen a victim to the *Rdc* tradition. Its then Rule was 611. On rationalisation, it later found its mistake. Rule 611 was omitted in later editions.

483 ARTIFICIAL COMPOSITE BOOK

Rdc Rule 106. Enter separate works forming the collections under their respective authors.

Pin Rule 66. A collection without a collective title is put under title of the first work.

Ala Rule 5A (2). Enter two or more writings by different authors published together but having no collective title,.......under the heading appropriate to the first work in the collection.

Vat and *Ccc* also prescribe in their Rules 224 (last para) and 621 respectively, the heading of the first constituent work as the heading of the main entry for an artificial composite book.

484 MULTI-VOLUMED COMPOSITE BOOK

Ccc Rule 522 category 5 introduces the prescription for a multi-volumed composite book into that for a multi-volumed simple book. This is a fault in drafting. The proper course is to leave multi-volumed composite book to the care of the rules for composite books. If at all, by way of caution an introductory note

117

may be inserted in chapter 6 " Composite books," in the words
" the rules of this chapter are applicable equally to single volumed
and multiple volumed composite books."

49 Change of Name

Change of name is not uncommon in the universe of :—

  1 persons ;

  2 geographical entities ;

  3 corporate bodies and their organs ;

  4 series ;

  5 books ; and

  6 periodicals.

Even simultaneous currency of alternative names for the same
entity is not unusual. The Laws of Library Science make it a
duty of the catalogue to disclose to readers.

  1 All books by the same author or with the same collaborator, whatever be the alternative names of them, which
the different books may have on their respective title-
pages ; and

  2 All copies of the same document whatever be the alternative titles which the different copies may have on
their title-pages.

There are three ways of making the catalogue fulfil this duty :—

  1 To respect the Canon of Ascertainability in each case,—
i.e., to follow the title-page. This will violate the Canon
of Currency. But it will satisfy the Canon of Permanence ;

  2 To respect the Canon of Currency and choose the latest
name. This would mean changing all the concerned
entries every time there is change of name. This will
violate the Law of Parsimony, the Canon of Permanence,
and the Canon of Ascertainability.

  3 To respect the Law of Parsimony and choose as heading
the earliest of the names. This will satisfy the Canon of
Permanence. But it will violate the Canons of Ascertainability and Currency.

Whatever be the way followed, in each of the cases there should
be a cross-reference index entry with the chosen name as referred-
to heading and each alternative name as the referred-from heading.

These alternative names should be given on the back of the main entry card.

Before leaving this section it may be helpful to enumerate briefly the causes for change of name.

Change of personal name may be made for various causes, such as,

1 Adoption of pseudonym for reasons of secrecy ;
2 Wilfulness ;
3 Change of nationality ;
4 Change of secular status ; such as peerage and coronation ;
5 Change of ecclesiastical status ;
6 Marriage ;
7 Law, as it happened in Thailand a few decades ago and in Japan about a century ago and so on ;

Change of geographical name may be made for political, administrative or even sentimental reasons.

Change of name of corporate body may be made for political, administrative, or even sentimental reasons. It may be made by law, or by executive action, or by public usage.

Change of name of series—rather simultaneous use of alternative names for a series—is not altogether uncommon. Examples have been given in *Ccc*.

Change of name of a book may be made for commercial reasons or for evasion of international copy-right convention, or sometimes even by the author to focus the content of the book in a better manner.

Change of name of a periodical publication is a common occurrence. It is doubtful if one in a ten thousand periodicals has escaped change of title. Several examples of this are given in the commentary on rule 832 of *Ccc*.

Variant forms of the name of any entity, caused by change in language, spelling, morphological form, in transliteration or any other cause may also be deemed alternative names for the purpose under consideration.

491 Alternative Name of Person
4911 *Ccc*

Ccc is not bothered at all in the choice of one of many possible alternative names of a person. It steadfastly follows the Canon of Ascertainability. The title-page of a document mentions only one of the alternative names in the majority of cases. *Ccc* chooses that name for the heading of the main entry.

Occasionally the title-page of a document mentions two names but one of these is printed in a more dominant type. *Ccc* chooses that name in the application of the Canon of Ascertainability. But with regard to the alternative name *Ccc* is prepared to go outside the title-page in order to prescribe the cross-reference index entries to be given to satisfy the Canon of Sought-heading. Thus *Ccc* by-passes the need for special rules for the choice of one of many possible names of a person for use as heading of main entry or of book index entry.

Ccc ought to have treated a pseudonym also as simply an alternative name. It need not have given special rules on pseudonym. Because of the peculiarity of the case, it might, if at all, invite special attention to this problem in a commentary on the basic rule 121. But it has succumbed to faulty tradition originated by *Rdc*. It has framed special rules for pseudonym. In so doing, it has been led to a further error. It has prescribed in rule 1252 the mention, in the heading, of an alternative name not found in title-page. These special rules should be deleted.

Ccc Rule 1218. If an alternative or secondary name of a Personal Author is given in on title-page, it is to be added, in circular brackets, after the primary name in the heading. The name thus added is to be preceded by the symbol " *i.e.*"

4912 OTHER CODES

The other codes have not been guided by the Canon of Ascertainability in the choice of one of may names of a person for use in heading of main entry. The Canon of Sought-heading has played the will-o'-the-wisp with them. This has made them hunt for the " best known name ". They have provided an unusually large number of rules on the choice of one of many alternative names. The result is perplexing. The other codes have not provided rules to cover the case of more than one name of author being mentioned on title-page.

4913 *Rdc*

Rdc was the first to fall a prey to the will-o'-the-wisp. Here is the basic rule directing the cataloguer to keep on chasing the will-o'-the-wisp :

Rdc Rule 40. Put the work of authors who change their name under the best known form, provided the new name be permanently adopted.

Rdc itself has been sensitive to the unwisdom of the hunt for the " best known " name. For, it adds the following commentary :—

Do not worry about the proper form of changed and transliterated names, nor spend much time in hunting up facts and deciding. If the necessary references are made, it is of little importance which form is chosen for the main entry, provided, of course, that the library always chooses the same heading.

This commentary is evidence of *Rdc* having had a glimpse of the right way of reconciling the Canon of Ascertainability and the Canon of Sought-heading. But it has misconceived the true import of the Canon of Permanence.

Rdc Rule 32. Give the names, both family and christian, in the vernacular form, if any instance occurs of the use of that form in the printed publications of the author.

Except that the following go under the Latin form :—

(*a*) ancient Greek authors, (*b*) certain medieval names and several from the renaissance and reformation periods, (*c*) popes.

In the commentary on this rule *Rdc* shows the effect of a glimpse of the Canon of Ascertainability. The commentary reads :—

This is the British Museum rule. It will obviously be sometimes impossible and often difficult to determine this point in a library of less extent than the Museum ; the cataloguer must make up his mind to some inconsistency in his treatment of mediaeval names, and be consoled by the knowledge that if proper references are made no harm will be done. Against a too great preference for the vernacular Professor De Morgan writes in the preface to his " Arithmetical Books " " I have not attempted to translate the names of those who wrote in Latin at a time when that language was the universal medium of communication. I consider that the Latin name is that which the author has left to posterity, and that the practice of retaining it is convenient, as marking, to a certain extent, the epoch of his writings, and as being the appellation by which his contemporaries and successors cite him. It is well to know that Copernicus...... (was) Zepernik...... But as the butcher's bills of these eminent men are all lost, and their writings only remain, it is best to designate them by the name they bear on the latter rather than the former."

De Morgan's robust common sense, disciplined in mathematics, which trains the mind in picking out the relevant and masking away everything else, has hit upon the wisdom of making

121

the title-page and the Canon of Ascertainability the sheet anchor of cataloguing practice.

The following rules of *Rdc* are redundant :—

Rdc Rule 24C.   (Change due to marriage.)

25 and 26 (Change due to elevation in secular status, such as peerage.)

32 and 33 (Change due to difference in language.)

34 (masculine and feminine forms.)

35 and 36 (change due to variant spelling.)

37 and 39 (Change due to variant transliteration.)

These rules could have been avoided if alternative name had been defined properly, if it had been made to include creation not only by total change of name, but also by change caused in the name by its version in different languages, by change in spelling, by change in morphological form and by change due to transliteration.

4914 *Pin*

The following are the basic rules of *Pin* on change of name of person :—

Pin Rule 78.   The same author always arranged under the same name.

Rule 79.   The author is arranged under his original and complete name, if another appellation has not supplanted it in custom.

The latter rule perpetuates the chase of the will-o'-the-wisp set in vogue by *Rdc*. However, Rule 78 answers the Canon of Permanence.

The following rules are redundant :—

Rules 94 to 96, and 165 to 166 (Change due to change in ecclesiastical and secular dignity.)

Rules 167 to 168 (Change due to difference in language.)

These rules merely show the application of the basic rules to particular cases. They are therefore redundant. Their proper place is in the commentary on the basic rules.

4915 *Ala*

The following is the basic rule of *Ala* on change of name of person :—

Ala Rule 45A.   Enter under the adopted name of a person who in civil life has changed his name unless the original one is decidedly better known. This includes legal changes of name, assumed name, such as, pseudonyms and professional names that have been adopted for general use, and also cases in which merely the spelling of the name has been altered.

Ala rule also is in the grip of the *Rdc* tradition of chasing the will-o'-the-wisp of ' better known ' name, unmindful of the Canon of Ascertainability, the compromise arrived at between this Canon and the Canon of Sought-Heading and the Canon of Permanence. However, it is noteworthy that *Ala* has recognised here that pseudonym is change of name. But in spite of this recognition, it has found it necessary to give a special set of rules for it in its Rule 30 and its subdivisions.

The following rules of *Ala* are redundant :—

Rule 45B (Change due to difference in language.)

Rule 46 (Change due to marriage.)

Rule 47 to 53 (Change due to change in ecclesiastical dignity.)

Rule 55 to 56 (Change due to coronation.)

Rule 57 (Change due to change in secular dignity.)

The contents of these rules deserve only to be mentioned in a commentary on the basic rule 45A.

4916 *Vat*

The following are the rules of *Vat* on change of name of person :—

Vat Rule 58. When a person assumes a new name in civil life, this name becomes the entry word.

Rule 65A. Generally a religious is entered under his surname or under the name assumed in religion.

Rule 65B. If a religious completely drops his name to take a new name, as is the case with Capuchins......, the assumed name is used for the entry.

Rule 65C. If the name of a religious is found in various linguistic forms......the original name or the adopted name is the entry word.

Rule 65D. If a religious has under his secular name and is better known by it, the main entry is made under his secular name.

Rule 71B. Persons (noblemen) known by their family name are entered under it.

Rule 71C. German noblemen are regularly entered either under their family name followed by their forenames and rank, or else under the family name combined, with the title, followed by their forenames and rank.

The above rules of *Vat* give a measure of the perplexity unavoidably created by the avoidance of using the Canon of Ascertainability and the Canon of Permanence as the sheet anchor of cataloguing practice, and of failure to see that the Canon of Sought-Heading can well be taken care of by cross-reference index entries using the preferred name as the referred-to heading and each of the alternative names as the referred-from heading. The corresponding rules of *Ala* also demonstrate the same perplexity.

492 Alternative Name of Geographical Entity

Name of a geographical entity can occur in the title portion of an entry and in the heading. When it occurs in the title portion it is subject to the same rules as the title portion itself. In most cases it will have to be in the language of the title-page. If the script is different from the script of the library, transliteration is prescribed. A few special codes prescribe translation of the title into the language of the library. When this is done, a few prescribe also the repetition of the title in the original language and script of the title-page. The position is different in the construction of the heading. When a geographical name is part of a name of an institution, the Canon of Ascertainability should have its sway. As it forms part of a proper name, the catalogue code has no right to change it in any manner. But in a governmental or subject heading, geographical name is brought in only by cataloguing convention. It is cataloguer's own creation. It is open to the convention to prescribe the choice of the geographical name in the language of the library. Such a convention exists in the case of a continent, country, and a few big cities, of an ocean, sea, and bay, of a major mountain, river, and desert, and so on. But in other cases, it seldom exists. Therefore the name of such a geographical entity will have to be only in the language of the document.

4921 *Rdc*

Rdc Rule 42. Give names of places in the English form.

By implication this has to be done only when there is an English form. Further this rule violates the Principle of Local Variation. " English " should be replaced by " Language of the library ".

Rule 43. But if both the English and foreign forms are used by English writers, prefer the foreign form.

It is not clear if this rule is applicable only if all the writers do so. If not, there will be violation of the Canon of Consistency. This should not be allowed to happen in a heading improvised by cataloguing convention.

Rule 44. Use the modern name of a city.

4922 *Pin*

Pin has no rule on the subject of alternative names of a geographical entity.

4923 *Ala*

Ala Rule 150A. Give countries, self-governing dominions, colonies, and protectorates in the conventional English form.

Rule 150B. Give local geographic name usually in the vernacular form but where well-established English form differs, prefer the English term.

Ala also violates the Principle of Local Variation.

4924 *Vat*

Vat Rule 89. Geographical names are given in the vernacular except that names of countries and large geographical units are given in the traditional Italian form.

Rule 89*a*. Names of continents, countries, kingdoms, colonies, mandated countries, and similar definite political and geographical divisions are given in the Italian form.

Rule 89*b*. The Italian form of names is used for regions, provinces, states, large peninsulas, islands, and groups of islands which have their own physical and ethnic character and tradition, various groupings of countries and kingdoms, and the individual states and lander of Germany and Austria.

Rule 89*c*. The Italian form is also used for the names of all the great physico-geographical units which transcend political and administrative boundaries, *i.e.*, oceans, gulfs, straits, ocean currents, rivers, mountain ranges, plains, plateaus, forests, capes, and similar geographical units.

Rule 89*d*. If the Italian form of a foreign geographical name has not been definitely established, but is variable or arbitrary, the vernacular form is preferred.

Rule 90. Other geographical names, which do not have a corresponding Italian form are given in the vernacular.

Rule 100. Cities and towns, villages, hamlets, and manors are given in the vernacular form.

The rules of *Vat* are clearer than those of the other codes. But these too fail to satisfy the Principle of Local Variation.

4925 *Ccc*

Ccc fails to give rules on names of geographical entities. Rule 1231 mentions " favoured language " as the language to be used for the name of a geographical entity. This is not sufficient. *Ccc* should give a special set of rules on the subject.

493 Alternative Name of Corporate Body

Change of name of a government appears in cataloguing practice, only as a change of name of geographical entity. But it is not so in the case of an institution. Special rules become necessary, if the Canon of Ascertainability is not followed.

Rdc has no rule on the subject.

Pin does not have to deal with this problem.

Ala rule 91A (1). When a society has changed its name, enter under the latest form.

Ala violates as usual the Canon of Ascertainability and the Canon of Permanence.

Vat Rule 140. A Society is entered under the first word, not an article of its present or latest title.

Vat also violates as usual the Canon of Ascertainability and the Canon of Permanence.

Ccc does not have a special rule on the subject. Because it strictly follows the Canon of Ascertainability.

494 Alternative Name of Series

Ccc Rule 1423. If a series has alternative names, the names are to be written one after the other, with an intervening " or ".

This rule is on the writing of the note section of the main entry. This should be followed up by mention of " Alternative names of series " in Rule 321, which enumerates the items to be chosen as heading of series index entry. But this rule fails to do so. This should be rectified in the next edition of *Ccc*.

495 Alternative Name of Book

We shall consider here only the titles of anonymous pedestrian books. Classics will be considered in chapter 5.

4951 *Rdc*

Rdc Rule 132. *Translations* of anonymous works should be entered in the same heading as the original, whether the library possesses the original or not.

This is a violation of the Canons of Ascertainability and of Sought-Heading. Evidently, this is done to bring the entries of the original and the translations in juxtaposition. The use of cross reference index entries will be sufficient to tie up the alternative titles. There is no need to violate the Canons mentioned above.

Rule 147. Anonymous works that change their title in *successive volumes* are to be entered under the first title...... unless the greater part of the work has the later title, or the whole is much better known by the later title, in which case entry should be made under that.

This rule also is a violation of the Canon of Ascertainability.

4952 *Pin*

Pin Rule 220. If the different titles of the same work are written in different languages, the original title is taken as the main title. If it cannot be ascertained with certainty which is the original title, the first is decisive...... Moreover, it is a matter of indifference whether the titles occur on the same leaf or on different leaves and whether or not a parallel to text corresponds the parallel title.

In Different Books

Rule 221. Here, too, the original title serves the main title.

Rule 222. So far as possible the title of the original also remains decisive for the arrangement even when the original itself is not actually in the library.

Rule 223. If, however, the title is known mostly in a language other than the original, then the entry word is taken from that.

Rule 224. For the arrangement of the books of the Bible, the titles which they bear in the Vulgate are decisive.

Rule 225. The entry is likewise taken from the translation when the original has been lost ; of several translations that one is chosen which has acquired the authority of an original.

Rule 226. If the works corresponding to the different titles are not merely translations but revisions, each title is treated by itself.

These rules are more detailed than those of *Rdc*. This is helpful. But the very details expose the deviation from the Canon of Ascertainability. It demonstrates the helplessness rising out of the ' cult of known most '.

4953 *Ala*

Ala Rule 32A is in substance the same as *Rdc* Rule 147.

Rule 32E. If the first word of a title entry may be spelt in more than one way, follow the spelling of the title-page.

This rule would have become redundant if the Canon of Ascertainability had been strictly and consciously made the basis of the code.

Rule 32G is in substance the same as *Rdc* 132.

4954 *Vat*

Vat rules 184, 187, and 189 are in substance same as *Ala* 32E, *Rdc* 147 and *Rdc* 132 respectively.

4955 *Ccc*

Ccc is not in need of a rule on this subject. It never deviates from the Canon of Ascertainability. It also satisfies the Canon of Sought-Heading through cross reference index entries.

496 Change of Name of Periodical

The uncanny frequency of change of name of periodical baffles almost every catalogue code.

4961 *Rdc*

Rdc Rule 145. A periodical which changes its name is to be entered under each title.

Each entry will have the imprint that belongs to that title and a note " preceded by " or " continued as " or both as required.

Or the periodical may be catalogued in full under the first title with a note of the changes.

The later form is the best when the volume numbers are continued through two or more sets.

For the class-mark the most practical rule (though it is one that makes some trouble to classifiers and cataloguers) is :

Rule 146.　Take the class-mark of a periodical that changes its title from the best known title, which is usually the last after it has been running a year or two.

The alternative suggestions contained in the commentary on Rule 145 show the baffling nature of the cataloguing of periodicals caused by change of title.　Rule 146 shows that *Rdc* has had a glimpse of the advantage of classified catalogue in facing this problem.

4962 *Pin*

Pin Rule 227.　If different titles occur in periodicals, the original title remains decisive.

Rule 228.　If, however, the original title was changed shortly after the publication of the first part the later title becomes decisive.

The alternative suggestions made in the above two rules indicate the impracticability of smoothly solving the problem created by change of title of periodical, in alphabetical cataloguing practice.

4963 *Ala*

Ala Rule 5C (1).　Enter a periodical under its latest title....... In the case of a periodical which has ceased publication, make exception in favour of the entry under an earlier title used for a much longer period than the later title.

Rule 5C (2).　Enter a newspaper under its latest title.

These rules of *Ala* throw even a more lurid light than the rules of *Rdc* and *Pin* on the perplexity caused by change of title of periodical, in alphabetical catalogue.

4964 *Vat*

Vat Rule 235d.　When the title of a periodical has changed the entry is made under the latest form and earlier titles are recorded in a note.

It is not necessary to specify all the minor variations in the title ; a note " title varies " or " title varies slightly " will suffice.

This is settling down to the cult of " latest name " unaffected by the worries created by *Rdc*, *Pin*, and *Ala*.

4965 *Ccc*

Ccc has given a comprehensive and elegant prescription to meet all the possible idiosyncrasies of periodical publications.　Its twin *Dictionary catalogue code* has tried to emulate it without success. A comparison of the performance of these twins shows the versatility of Classified Catalogue as compared to Dictionary Catalogue. This study is given in detail in part 4 of *Theory*.　A brief summary is also given in section 8213 of *Library catalogue* ; *Fundamentals and procedure* (1950).

Ccc Rule 8 analyses the idiosyncrasies of periodical publications into 18 categories.   Of these, the categories numbered 31 and 32 concern change of title.   The following are the rules relevant to the subject.

Ccc Rule 831.   (When title of a periodical changes), a separate Main Card is to be made for each different title and heading.

Rule 8311.   The Class Number in each such card being the same, the cards are to be treated as a set of " Continued cards " as per rule 0381.

The above rule satisfies the Canon of Ascertainability.   And yet it does not scatter the different titles.   It keeps them all together in a helpful way in chronological sequence.   The *Union catalogue* of *learned periodical publications in South Asia* (1953) demonstrates the efficiency of Classified Catalogue based on these and other rules dealing with all the 18 idiosyncrasies of periodical publications.

CHAPTER 5
RENDERING

In this chapter we shall consider the rendering of the heading, generally, of main entry. The conclusions are also applicable to heading of added entry. Choice of heading is half the battle in cataloguing. Rendering of heading nearly exhausts the other half. Style of writing forms only a trivial fraction. Rendering involves many details for consideration and prescription. We shall begin with some general directives. We shall then examine in detail the prescription for each kind of heading, enumerated in chapter 4 " Choice ".

501 Kind of Heading

From the point of view of rendering, it is convenient to consider separately each of the following kinds of headings. Against each kind of heading, its genesis is briefly indicated.

1 Personal Author Heading. In many cases, the title-page or its equivalent of a document mentions the name of a personal author.

2 Geographical Heading. In cataloguing convention, the name of a geographical entity is used to denote the government having that entity as its territory.

3 Government Author Heading. In many cases, the title-page of a document indicates a government or an organ of it as its author.

4 Institution Author Heading. In some cases, the title-page of a document indicates an institution or an organ of it as its author.

5 Conference Author Heading. In some cases, the title-page of a document indicates a conference or an organ of it as its author.

6 Collaborator Heading. In a few cases, the title-page of a document does not give or indicate the name of personal or corporate author. It gives only the name of a collaborator, such as, editor.

7 Title Heading. In a few cases, the title-page of a document does not give or indicate the name of personal or corporate author or of collaborator. But it gives only the title.

8 Joint Heading. In a few cases, the title-page of a document gives or indicates the names of two or more authors or collaborators.

502 Puff Element. Reduced Name

Some words in a name may be honorific. They are not essential elements in the name. They may form a term of courtesy, reverence, endearment, academic distinction, office, or any other attribute of that kind. This class of words in a name is called " Puff Element ". It usually lies at the beginning or end of name. But occasionally it is found to occur even somewhere in the middle. In Buddhistic personal name, for example, the puff element " Bhikku " may occur somewhere in the middle. On the title-page, puff element is often printed. But it need not be included in the heading of a catalogue entry. It is removable while rendering the name for use as heading. For convenience of reference, a name with puff element may be called " Gross Name ". A name with the puff element removed may be called "Reduced Name".

503 Inversion. Entry Word

The reduced name used as heading is often made of two or more words. These words are mentioned in a certain sequence, on title-page and in public usage. We shall call this the " Natural Sequence ". The first word in the natural sequence may be drawn from a class of words, not very numerous. Some other word in that sequence may be drawn from a class of words, relatively more numerous. This is the case in the names of most persons and of most departments of government. A word drawn from a more numerous class has greater potency in arrangement than one drawn from a less numerous class. The Canon of Prepotence would recommend the use of the most potent word in the natural name as the entry word in heading. This would involve " inversion of the natural sequence of the words in the name ". Obviously the question of inversion cannot arise at all in a single-worded reduced name. Many ancient names are single-worded. Even modern Burmese names are often single-worded. Equally obviously, the question of inversion does not arise even in a multi-worded name, with its most potent word occurring as first word in the natural sequence. It is said that Chinese names have this quality. For convenience of reference, a reduced name with its words inverted so as to satisfy the Canon of Prepotence, may be called " Inverted Name ". The problem of inversion should be considered for each kind of heading. And the necessary rules should be provided in a catalogue code.

504 Impotent Attachment. Entry Element

It may happen that reduced name contains some word(s) after the prepotent word. Such word(s) occur in South Indian personal names. "Ayyar", "Mudaliar" and "Sastri" are oft-recurring examples. There are about three hundred such words. They are normally patronymic words. They denote ancestral denomination of religion, civil or military rank or vocation. Unlike puff element, they are irremovable. Unlike the other words in the reduced name, they are more or less impotent. They are liable to be omitted without much loss in the individualising capacity of the name. For convenience of reference, such a word may be called " Irremovable Impotent Attachment-Word ". If the title-page mentions an irremovable attachment-word, the cataloguer should not remove it in rendering the name in heading. It must be attached to the entry word. Entry word along with its irre-movable attachment-word is Entry Element.

505 Potent Attachment. Entry Element

In some names, entry word may be followed by another potent word. Because it is potent, obviously it cannot be removed. Because it is potent, we cannot call it a mere attachment. Unlike an irremovable attachment, its omission results in considerable loss in the potency of the entry word. Such a potent word may be linked to the entry word by a hyphen or by an auxiliary word. Or, the entry word and the succeeding potent word may occur quite unconnected by word or symbol. A combination of the entry word and the succeeding potent word, taken along with the connecting symbol or word, if any, should be treated as inseparable while rendering the name in heading. This inseparable combina-tion is Entry Element.

506 Secondary Element

The irremovable word(s) occurring in the reduced name before the entry word, form(s) the Secondary Element in the name. In the heading, the secondary element is added after the entry element. The entry element and the secondary element are dis-tinguished from each other in the heading, by difference of type-face. The entry element is entered in a more dominant type-face or script than the secondary element—say the former in caps or in black face cap and lower case or cap and small caps ; and the latter in cap and lower case or in white face.

The secondary element may also be marked off by a comma or by enclosure in circular brackets. This happens in author heading and in collaborator heading. This does not arise in title heading. Even in a personal name heading, if the first word in the reduced name is the entry word, the succeeding words need not be so separated or marked off.

507 Homonym. Individualising Element

A heading is a noun. It is the name of an entity. The name may be capable of denoting more than one entity. It is then a homonym. Obviously, a homonymous heading does not individualise. To make it individualise, the homonym should be resolved. To resolve a homonym, another element should be added. The additional element added for this purpose may be called Individualising Element.

5071 INDIVIDUALISING TERM

The Individualising Element may have to be attached after the homonym. Then, it may be called " Individualising Term ". Individualising term may denote year of birth in the case of a person. It may denote the species of geographical category in the case of a geographical entity. It may denote the place and/or year of foundation in the case of a Corporate Body. It may be, some other word such as " Poem ", " Drama ", " Classic ", " Book ", " Engineer ", " Lawyer ", and so on. An individualising term is usually entered in the same type face or script as the secondary element. It is separated from the secondary element by a comma or in some other consistent way.

5072 ANTERIOR HEADING

The individualising element may have to be attached before the homonym. Then, it may be called Anterior Heading. This happens in individualising a homonymous name used to denote an organ of a corporate body. Many anterior headings may have to be attached in succession to resolve the homonym completely. The final result may be called Multiple Heading. The first heading in the multiple heading may be called Main Heading. The second or a later heading may be called Sub-Heading. Sub-head-ings may be distinguished among themselves as first, second, etc. sub-heading respectively.

5073 Posterior Heading

The individualising element may have to be attached after the homonym. Then, it may be called Posterior Heading. This happens in individualising the name of a subject. Many posterior headings may have to be attached in succession to resolve the homonym completely. The final result is a Multiple Heading. The terms Main Heading, Sub-Heading, etc., are applicable here also.

51 Personal Name Heading

511 European Culture

Rdc Rule 24*a*. Put under the surname in general all persons not included under rule 23 (*i.e.*, not being sovereigns, saints, friars, oriental authors, and a few others known only by their first name).

Pin Rule 107. For authors of modern times the family name becomes the entry word.

Ala Rule 37. Enter persons of modern times under the family name follow-ed by the forenames.

Vat Rule 39. Modern authors and other persons are entered under their surname, followed, after a comma, by the forename or forenames written in full.

Ccc Rule 1211. In the case of Christian and Jewish names of modern times, the surname is to be written first and the forename or forenames are to be added thereafter.

5110 Parts of Name

A personal name in a modern European cultural group is in many words. These words fall into two parts :—

1 **Family Name.** This denotes the family of the person. Generally, this name would have been taken in the distant past. It may be occasionally changed. Normally, it is a name inherited by the person at birth. It is already there. It gets attached to him. It is also called " **Surname** ".

2 **Given Name.** This denotes the individual within the family. It is given to him by the parents sometime after birth. That is why it is called Given Name. The ritual of giving the name is called christening. It is therefore called **Christian Name**. In public usage and on title-page, the given name comes before the family name. It is therefore called " **Forename** ". To match this term, the Family Name is sometimes called " **Last**

Name ".   There may be more than one Given Name.   Sometimes, they are all given equal weight by the person concerned.   Some others omit some of the forenames in giving the name on title-page.   For example, " Charles John Huffam Dickens " appears on title-page as " Charles Dickens ".   Here the Canon of Ascertainability should be obeyed.

51101 FAMILY *vs.* GIVEN NAME

In a European cultural group, Given Name is drawn largely from Biblical names.   In the course of centuries, a few other names also have been brought into use.   In spite of this addition, the class of Given Names is small.   Perhaps it does not exceed 2,000.   On the other hand, Family Name had been drawn from the names of a variety of entities, such as,

> Place, *e.g.*, London, Kent and Dewsbury ;
> Physical feature, *e.g.*, Hill, Lake, and Forest ;
> Material, *e.g.*, Stone, Slum, and Cage ;
> Vocation, *e.g.*, Butcher, Carter, and Miller ;
> Animal kingdom, *e.g.*, Lamb, Parrot, and Hare ;
> Plant kingdom, *e.g.*, Rice, Plant and Tree ;
> Colour, *e.g.*, White, Brown and Black ;
> Biblical name, *e.g.*, Cain, Paul, and Mathews ;
> Size, *e.g.*, Long and Short ;
> Heavenly body, *e.g.*, Morgansterne ; and etc.

Indeed, there is hardly any class of names from which a family name cannot be drawn.   Thus the class of family names is far more numerous in an European cultural group than the class of Given Names.   Therefore, the Canon of Prepotence would make the Family Name the entry word in the heading of a catalogue entry, be it main entry or added entry.

51102 THE PAST

But, it had taken centuries for sheer folk-sense to grasp this at least unconsciously.   Before the invention of printing, the number of books written was small.   The number of authors was even smaller.   Therefore, the potency of the Given Name was great enough to individualise authors to a high degree of helpfulness.   It was therefore used as the entry word.   The words in a name were not, therefore, inverted in the distant past.   The Given Name continued to have sufficient potency for about two centuries after the invention of printing. Conrad Gesner of Zurich, reputed to be the first universal bibliographer, arranged the entries in his *Bibliotheca universalis* by the Given Names of authors. But he felt the unhelpfulness of such an arrangement. He therefore added a summary list of authors with the words in each name inverted. This was in 1516. *La liburia* (1550), an Italian bibliography, also arranged the entries by the Given Names of authors. So did the French bibliography *Premier volume de la bibliotheque* (1584). Arrangement by Given Names continued till the eighteenth century in some libraries.

51103 CHANGE-OVER

The first change-over from Given Name to Family Name in the heading of a catalogue entry was in 1595. It was in the *Catalogue of English printed books*. Its author was Andrew Maunsell, a draper turned book-seller. He wrote, " They make their alphabet by the Christian name. I, by the Sir name." This bookseller had unconsciously seen the greater potency of the Family Name as compared to Given Name. This marks the triumph of the Canon of Prepotence. Andrew Maunsell had all the courage of an iconoclast and tradition-breaker.

51104 THE PRESENT

All the catalogue codes of the present follow the lead of that pioneer. But, they seem to have adopted the pioneer's practice, blindly as a new tradition. No rationalisation appears to have led to its adoption. No statistical sense seems to be guiding the choice of entry word even today. For, the cataloguers brought up or indoctrinated in European culture have largely fallen a pray to an illusion. The Family Name happened to be the last word in a name in public usage and on title-page. This was in a name of a European cultural group. Then, they began to regard the last word in any name of any cultural group as the family name. They also treated it, by sheer habit, as the word of the greatest potency in the name. Thus, they made the last word the entry word for any author heading or any personal name heading. This landed them in the ridiculous practice of making an impotent attachment—such as, Ayyar, Mudaliar, and Sastri—the entry word. This irrational extension of European practice to non-European names needs correction. This correction should be based on statistical analysis.

51105 THE FUTURE

Nearly half of humanity, measured in terms of cultural groups, had been in a state of cultural exhaustion since the invention of printing. In these exhausted cultural groups, authorial activity had been nil or negligibly small. Books have been written in the last few centuries mostly by persons of a few European cultural groups. This intensified the illusion mentioned in the preceding section. But to day, the other cultural groups of the world are waking up. They are entering the ascending phase of their present cultural cycle. Documents have begun to originate from all such cultural groups. Such documents are sure to increase in number. Documents originating from European cultural groups will soon cease to be the only documents or even the most numerous group of documents. Cataloguing practice should therefore get out of the groove cut for the rendering of names of European cultural groups. Multiworded names in other cultural groups should be statistically studied. The entry word in such a name should be chosen in accordance with the Canon of Prepotence.

51106 A CONFUSION

Such an investigation of the problem is diffracted today by certain happenings in the cultural groups entering into renascence. These happenings are the result of cultural contact between one cultural group in an active state and another cultural group in a passive state. The first few authors among the newly awakening cultural groups have been over-powered by the urge to imitate European cultural groups in manipulating their names. Any such author contracts all but the last word in his name, into initial letters. He leaves on the title-page only the last word in his name uncontracted. It even happens that this last word is but an impotent attachment to his name. This phase of blind imitation will not last long. The cataloguing profession in the world should be on the alert. It should not base its rules for the choice of the entry word in the name of a person, on the indications of such abnormal ways of the manipulation of name by authors in the transition period. It should follow the rational path of statistics. It should make a statistical study of the class of words from which the various words in a name of each cultural group are drawn. With this statistical knowledge, it should spot out the word of the greatest potency within a name. It should thus propitiate the Canon of Prepotence. No doubt, the imitative habit of the newly awakening cultural groups will cause great confusion for some time. But the cataloguing profession should keep their head clear through this disturbing period of transition.

512 NON-EUROPEAN CULTURAL GROUPS

Rdc does not prescribe rules for the different cultural groups outside European culture. Its only rule on such names is the following :—

Rdc Rule 23*e*. Put under the Christian or forename oriental authors.

The impracticability of this simple rule has made *Rdc* add the following commentary on this rule :—

This rule has many exceptions. Some Oriental writers are known and should be entered under other parts of their name than the first...... In *Arabic* names words of relationship Abu (father), Umm (mother) Ibin, Bin, (Son), Ahu, (brother), though not to be treated as names by themselves, are yet not to be disregarded. They form a name in conjunction with the word following and determine the alphabetical place of the entry. But the article (changed by assonance to ad, ar, as, at, and az,) is neglected...... In all Oriental names the cataloguer must be careful not to take titles, as Emir, Bey, Pasha, Sri, Babu, Pundit, for names. A useful list fills up *pp.* 76-79 of Linderfelt's *Eclectic card catalogue rules* (1890)...... In regard to East Indian names...... if there are two names, enter under the first, which is the individual name, with a reference from the second ; if there are three or more, enter under the third, which is the family name, with a reference under the first or individual name ; the second name is neglected.

The above is an over-simplification. This gives wrong results in most cases. But it demonstrates the awareness and the cautious approach of the pioneer *Rdc* to the rendering of a name belonging to a non-European cultural group. Some of the later codes have seen the need to have different rules for names of different cultural groups.

5123 China

Ala Rule 67. Enter a Chinese writer under the family name...... The given names are hyphenated and the first only is capitalised...... The courtesy name is not used officially and does not appear in the heading except occasionally in the case of distinguished personages who have come to be generally known by that name rather than by their real name, in which case it takes the place of the given names.

Ala's commentary is as follows :—

Chinese surnames date from approximately 3,000 B.C. As among other peoples with whom surnames were a later development, they were derived from place of origin or domicile, occupation, hereditary title, etc.

. Every Chinese rightfully has three names, a family name and two given names. Of these given names, the first, as a rule, indicates the generation and is common to all members of a family belonging to the same generation. The second is the personal name. Each individual may have also one or more courtesy names...... He may, in addition, have one or more pseudonyms and in some cases a posthumus appellative.

Obviously, the first name, the Family Name, is the entry word. All the other irremovable words in the name form the Secondary Element.

A pseudonym or courtesy name should be treated as an alternative name.

The other codes do not provide any explicit rule for Chinese name.

5122 Japan

Ala Rule 66. Enter Japanese writers under the family name followed by the given name.

By an Imperial edict of 1870, a Family Name and a Given Name were made obligatory in the name of every Japanese. Thus, the choice of entry word in the name of an author or person of the modern period is quite simple. This was probably the effect of the pressure of European Culture. Before 1870, only a nobleman, or a member of the military class or a specially privileged member of the lower classes had a Family Name. Others had only Given Names.

The other codes do not provide any explicit rule for Japanese name.

5123 Burma

Ala Rule 69A. Enter Burmese writers under their names in full without inversion, in the normal Burmese order, followed by the term of address.

There is no Family Name in Burmese culture. A name may consist of one, two or three words. A statistical study of the relative potency of the different classes of words from which the various words in a Burmese name are drawn, has yet to be made. What is the function of each word in a name ? Do the different functions get represented in the same sequence in all names ? These are some of the questions to be investigated. Then only a satisfactory rule can be framed.

Again, the honorific words—the term of address, as it is called —are no doubt impotent. For, there are only a few such words. They are "Maung," "Ko," and "U" for men and "Ma," and "Daw" for woman. Moreover they are not permanent. As one grows older, "Ko" is changed to "U." In these circumstances, they deserve to be treated as removable words. But tradition in Burma calls for their retention. How did this tradition arise ? Is it not possible for cataloguing convention to ignore it ? These questions also require investigation.

The other codes do not provide an explicit rule for Burmese name.

5124 Viet-Nam

Ala Rule 68. Enter Annamese writers under their names, in full, without inversion in the normal Annamese order. Connect the three names by hyphen and lower case the middle word or name.

A full Annamese or Viet-Namese name usually consists of three words. These are respectively Family Name, a middle word which is not substantial, and Given Name. Family Name is mostly of Chinese origin. There are only about two hundred Family Names. Thus a Family Name has little potency. It is not eligible for use as entry word. The middle word usually indicates sex, in the same way as Mr., Mrs., and Miss. The Given Name is usually drawn from an indefinitely large reservoir. This reservoir consists of many of the common words. The Given Name, therefore, satisfies the Canon of Prepotence. It is therefore eminently fit for use as entry word. The rendering of Viet-Namese names in catalogue entries has not yet been studied on rational grounds. In the past, three practices had prevailed :—

1 In the first practice, the words in the name are written in the sequence found in public usage and on title-page. Even the middle word is retained. All the words are hyphenated.

2 In the second practice, the words in the name are inverted. The Given Name is made the entry word. The other words are made Secondary Element. Both the hyphens are retained in the Secondary Element.

3 The third practice is similar to the second. But the second hyphen is omitted in the Secondary Element. The current tendency is to follow the third practice and to omit all hyphens

except to connect a two-worded Given Name or a two worded Family Name.   The present tendency is also to omit the middle word.   It is for the cataloguing profession of the cultural group concerned to study this problem from the angle of the Canon of Prepotence.   Based on such a study, a firm rule should be esta-blished.   Such a firm rule will accustom people to its acceptance. There is nothing gained by evading such a responsibility on the part of the cataloguing profession.   The escapist attitude of drifting along in this matter is not desirable.   Viet-Namese name lends itself to standardisation in the rendering of personal names in the heading of a catalogue entry, much more easily than the names of certain other cultural groups.

5125 Thailand

Prior to 1916 a Thai-name consisted only of a Given Name. If it contained more words, the Given Name occurred as the last word in public usage and on title-page.   King Rama VI spent some years in Europe.   He was impressed by the prevalence of surname in Europe.   On returning home in 1916, he promulgated a law making adoption of surname compulsory.   Surnames were given officially to families.   The king himself gave them to high officials.   High officials gave them to lower officials.   An official hierarchy was established for bestowal of surnames.   Since then, normally, a Thai-name consists of a Given Name and a Family Name.   To reinforce Family Name, there is a move to encourage the abbreviation of the Given Name to its initial letter.

Honorific words also get prefixed to name.   The following is a list of such honorific words :—

Chaophya	Koon	Khun	Nangsao	Phra
Dekying	Koonnai	Luang	Nang	
Dekohai	Koonnying	Nai	Phya	

These honorific words are all removable in catalogue headings. Generally, a Buddhist can become a priest for a short period. He then gets a name as a priest.   Even after withdrawal from priesthood, he may retain that name as middle word in his name. It is for consideration of cataloguers of Buddhist group whether such a middle word may not be deemed removable in the heading of a catalogue entry.   This question has to be considered by cataloguers in Thailand as well as in Ceylon.

5126 Indonesia

In Indonesia, four cultural groups co-exist :—Hindu, Buddhist, Christian and Muslim. The Christians have adopted the European practice of having a Family Name and a Given Name. The other communities have been all along escaping this European influence. However, a small fraction of the people of the present generation imitate the West by adopting the name of the father as if it were family name. They give the Given Name as the first word and the father's name as the last word. In the case of these few names, the Family Name should be used as the entry word ; and the Given Name should be used as the secondary element. In any other case, the Given Name is the entry word. Honorific word occurs in Indonesian names. It generally varies with the island to which the person belongs. In Java, for example, the honorific words prefixed to a name are Mas, Raden, Raden Mas, and Raden Aryo. In Sumatra, the honorific words are Soetan, and Raden Pandji.

5127 Arabic Culture

Pin Rule 146. The personal name (*ism*) becomes the entry word, with a reference from the place epithet (*Nisba*) and, if necessary, also from the first name expressing relationship (*Kunja*).

Ala Rule 64. Enter Arabic, Persian, and Turkish writers, upto about the year 1900, living in Mohommedan countries and writing only, or predominantly in their native tongues, under the given name compounded with the patronymic (the latter preceded by the word "*Ibn*" ; in rare cases "Akhu," as well as with the surname and nickname, usually derived from place of birth or residence (*nisba*), occupation, physical peculiarities, etc.

Vat Rule 84 is very much on the lines of *Ala* Rule 64.

Ccc Rule 12132. If the personal name or *ism* occurs on the title-page, it is to be written first.

Rule 12133. If the personal name is followed by '*ibn*' or its variants, that word and the personal name immediately following it are also to be written first, but after the personal name mentioned in rule 12132.

Rule 12134. If there be a second and later '*ibn*' or its variants, all such '*ibns*' and their variants and names governed by them are to be ignored.

Rule 121361. Nick names or *Urfs* are to be ignored.

Ccc gives an elaborate analysis of the structure of Muslim names in section 1213. The terms "ibn" and "Abu" may not only be introducers of patronymics ; but they also occur as integral parts of certain Given Names. These two uses can be distinguished only by those who are born in Arabic Culture or are familiar with

it. In recent years, Egyptian Muslims have begun to adopt
Family Names. From 1921 Family Name is being also used in
Iran. In Turkey a law of 1934 prescribed the adoption of Family
Name by the head of each family and the registration of the same
before July 1936. Wherever such a Family Name is adopted, it
is the last word in the name in public usage and on title-page.
It should be made the entry word in the heading of a catalogue
entry. In Malaya, a Muslim name follows the Arabic tradition
in a simplified form. In India and Pakistan, the structure of
Muslim name is different. Some simulate the West. They contract all the words but the last in their name. Then, there is no
difficulty. Most have two-worded names. Both the words of
such names should be taken together as Entry Element. In some
names, a third word may occur as prefix or suffix. Then, the
Entry Element will be made of two words. These will have to be
spotted out on the analogy of two-worded names. There may
also be impotent, honorific or academic words at the beginning
or end of the name. These will have to be spotted out and removed.
It may be difficult for foreign cataloguers to spot out the Entry
Element in all such cases. Perhaps, the only course is to append
to the rule on Indian and Pakistani Muslim names, a schedule of
two-worded Entry Elements or, if possible, a schedule of starters of
such elements, as in the case of two-worded Family Names in
Maharashtra, Bengali and Sinhalese names described in section 5146.

513 India

Indian culture has, no doubt, an ineffable unity of its own.
From the cataloguing angle, however, it may be taken to be a
complex of cultures. The structure of the name of a person has
undergone different changes in different cultural groups during
the last two centuries. In spite of several exceptions, the name in
most of the cultural groups has arrived at a fairly stable structure.
But the function of each word in a name differs from one cultural
group to another. These cultural groups are virtually linguistic
groups. Generally speaking, the South Indian linguistic groups
have escaped the urge to imitate the West. The other linguistic
groups have been influenced by the British practice.

5130 STRUCTURE OF NAME

In India, Family Name is strictly *Gotra* Name. Generally

speaking, it had its origin in prehistoric days. Except in some
sections of South India, a family traces its ancestry to one or other
of a few hundred Vedic Rishies. Each family name is usually
after the name of a Rishi, such as Bharadwaja, Kaundinya, Kausika,
Srivatsa, and Viswamitra. The prescription for rituals and many
social usages were taken by each family from the tradition associated with its Rishi. The Gotra Name was used only in private,
intimate occasions, such as prayer, ceremony and marriage. It
was not brought into public use. On the other hand, till the
cultural impact with the West during the last two centuries, the
Given Name has been the only name brought into public use.
It was usually drawn from the names of God. But everything in
the world is believed to be a manifestation of God. Therefore,
the name of any entity can be used as Given Name. Here are
some Examples :—

Place, *e.g.*, Chidambaram, Kasi and Thirumalai ;
Physical feature, *e.g.*, Giri, Ganga and Sukhavanam ;
Material, *e.g.*, Thangam, Muthu and Swarnam ;
Plant kingdom, *e.g.*, Tulsi, Champakam and Aswatha ;
Colour, *e.g.*, Karuppan, Shyam and Neelamegam ;
Heavenly body, *e.g.*, Ravi, Indu and Revathi.

Indeed, there is hardly any class of names from which Given
Name cannot be drawn. However, there is one class of names which
has contributed most to Given Names. These are the names of the
different human manifestations of God mentioned in ancient lore.
Even out of this group, about a dozen names are oft-recurring :—
Rama, Krishna, Govinda, Subrahmanya, Ganapathi and Visvanath
among males ; Sita, Lakshmi, Rukmini, Uma, Sarojini and Sarada
among ladies ; and various modifications and combinations of these
names. To resolve homonyms, it has become the practice to add
father's name and if necessary, the name of the place of birth. In West
India, the father's name was added after the Given Name. In
South India, the father's name and/or the name of place of birth
are/is added before the Given Name. Moreover, in all parts of
India, other than South India, a surname was also added at the
end. Thus, the structure of a modern Indian name has become
one of many words. The functions of the different words in a
name vary from one cultural group to another.

51301 Maharashtra

In Maharashtra, a patronymic surname had been in use for several centuries. Mahamahopadhyaya Poddar, the Maharashtra historian, told me that lists of such surnames are now in the possession of the priests in important pilgrim centres, such as Banaras and Nasik. These are different from Gotra Names. These are based upon the names of ancestral village, profession, or trade. These names too were not used as part of an author's name in earlier years. But after the advent of the British, they were brought into public use by being added at the end of the name even as Western Family Names. This became a common practice about the middle of the nineteenth century. The surname is never contracted on title-page. The Given Names of oneself and of the father are liable to be contracted. The number of Maharashtra Family Names is quite large. Taken along with the two preceding Given Names a Maharashtra Family Name is reasonably non-homonymous. For names of persons belonging to the later half of the nineteenth century, it is safe to prescribe the last word in the name as the entry word. But in the case of an earlier name it is wrong to use the last word as the entry word. For, it is the Given Name of the father. The first word should be the entry word. For, that alone is the Given Name of the person. Here are some examples :—

> **Gokhale** (Gopala Krishna) is the rendering of Gopal Krishna Gokhale ;
>
> **Tilak** (Bala Gangadhara) is the rendering of Bala Gangadhara Tilak.

51302 Gujarat

In Gujarat, the structure of a name is similar to that in Maharashtra. The function of each word in a name, taken in succession, is also similar to that in Maharashtra. The evolution in structure has also been similar. The choice of entry word also should therefore be similar. However, in some names, the father's Given Name may not occur. Therefore, for a cataloguer not born and brought up in the culture of Gujarat, a two-worded name will give trouble. In a modern name the second word should be made the entry word. In a pre-mid-nineteenth century name, the first word itself should be the entry word. There seems to be no way of helping a foreign cataloguer out of this difficulty, except to give a list of two-worded names of the earlier period—particularly of the first half of the nineteenth century. A rule should be inserted that a name in that l⸱st should not be inverted while rendering it for heading. Here are some examples :—

> **Gandhi** (Mohandas Karamchand) is the rendering of Mohandas Karamchand Gandhi.
>
> **Gandhi** (Devadas) is the rendering of Devadas Gandhi.

51303 Bengal and Orissa

In Bengal, the adoption of surname came into vogue after the British advent. Honorific, academic and vocational patronymic words were given the status of Family Name. This is different from *Gotra* name. This was made the last word in the name. Moreover, the Given Name was split into two words. While contracting the Given Name, the initial letters of each of its parts are given on title-page. Thus, a Bengali or Orissa name has normally three words. The first two words are the two parts of the Given Name ; and the last word is the Family Name. The number of words available for use as Family Name is not more than a few hundreds. They do not therefore satisfy the Canon of Prepotence. I saw an instinctive and unconscious resistance to the use of Family Name as the entry word, among most of the Bengalis whom I met in a conference to discuss this problem. However, cataloguing practice is definitely choosing the Family Name as the entry word in a Bengali or an Oriya name. Moreover, there is also a tendency to increase the number of words eligible to be used as Family Name. It is for the people and the cataloguers of Bengal and Orissa to decide whether the Family Name will continue to satisfy the Canon of Prepotence even when the authors increase in number with the intensification of the present renascence. According to the following practice, the following examples may be given :—

> **Chatterjee** (Bankim Chander) is the rendering of Bankim Chander Chatterjii.
>
> **Tagore** (Rabindra Nath) is the rendering of Rabindra Nath Tagore.
>
> **Panigrahi** (Siva Ram) is the rendering of Siva Ram Panigrahi.

51304 Uttar Pradesh

In Uttar Pradesh and other Hindi areas, Family names were improvised in the nineteenth century. These are quite different from *Gotra* names. They are patronymics of one kind or another. As in Bengal, this Family Name is made the last word in the name. Again as in Bengal, the Given Name is broken into two parts. If this practice in naming had been stabilised, there would not be much difficulty in rendering a Hindi name in the heading of a cataloguing entry. But after the political awakening of India, a tendency has started to drop the Family Name. At the same time, the Given Name left behind continues to be written in its split form, as two distinct words. But people remember that in reality they should be read together as a Single Word. Therefore, in such a two worded-name, it is wrong to use the second word as the Entry Word. The two words should be together taken to form the Entry Element. There is no Secondary Element. Except for a person born and bred up in the Hindi cultural group, it will be difficult to recognise such a two-worded name to consti- tute a single word and to render it for heading without inversion. For Example, but for the recent tendency to drop the Family Name, the name of the present President of India should be rendered as **Srivastava** (Rajendra Prasad). But, in actuality, his name occurs in the title-page only as Rajendra Prasad. It should not be rendered as **Prasad** (Rajendra). But, it should be rendered as **Rajendra Prasad.** Before the introduction of Family Name under the British influence, it would have occurred only as a single word in the form **Rajendraprasad.**

51305 North Kanara

Linguistically, North Kanara falls within the South Indian cultural group. However, in the structure of name, the people of North Kanara follow the practice of their Northern neighbours, the Maharashtras. Therefore, the rule for rendering a North Kanara name in catalogue entries is similar to that for a Maha- rashtra name. This is quite different from that of the majority of Kannada speaking people living in Mysore, Coorg and South Kanara. This difference in practice among the Kannada speaking people cannot be got over easily by a cataloguer not born and brought up in the Kannada cultural group.

51306 South India

In South India, we find quite a different practice from that in the other parts of India. South India has resisted the influence of European culture in the structure of name. Family Name has not been adopted. Normally, the last word in the name is the Given Name of the person. In Telugu, Kannada and Malayalam cultural groups, the name preceding the Given Name of a person is the Name of a Place—usually the ancestral one. In the Tamil cultural group, usually the name preceding the Given Name of a person, is the Given Name of the father. Not infrequently the latter is preceded by the Name of a Place. If this structure of a name and function of the words in it hold good universally, the choice of the Entry Word would be very simple. The last word can be prescribed as the Entry Word. The preceding word(s) can be prescribed as the Secondary Element. But there are complications. An impotent, irremovable attachment-word often follows the Given Name on title-page. There are a few hundreds of such irremovable, impotent attachment-words. It is difficult for a cataloguer not born and bred in the South Indian cultural groups to distinguish these irremovable, impotent attachment-words from the Given Name. As an aid to cataloguers, *Ccc* gave for the first time a list of such irremovable, impotent attachment-words. The rule prescribes that the Given Name of the person followed by the irremovable, impotent attachment-word should be taken as a whole as Entry Element.

51307 Ceylon

Ceylon is bilingual. A Tamil name of Ceylon has to be rendered in the same way as a Tamil name of India. But a Sinhalese name presents a different structure. Dutch influence has introduced the adoption of Family Name. The Given Names are often made of European words. As in a Siamese name, a name added during temporary or permanent priesthood may be inserted anywhere amidst the words in a name. The Family Name is usually the last word. Therefore, the choice of Entry Word is simple. The only difficulty is to spot out the priesthood name and remove it. A cataloguer not born and bred within the culture should be helped to spot it out, by adding a list of such priesthood names under the rules in the catalogue code.

51308 Pakistan

Muslim name in Pakistan and India presents features similar to those of any other names in Uttar Pradesh. Muslim name in South India is generally similar. But some names show the features of any other name in that region. A slightly fuller account has been given in section 5127.

5132 *Pin*

Pin Rule 154. The personal name (in Northern India usually the first of the series, in Southern India usually the second) becomes the entry word ; reference is made from the additional names according to need.

Kasinatha-Panduranga Paraba with a reference from **Paraba.**

Nelluri **Ramachandrayya** Pantulu Garu with references from **Nelluri** and **Pantulu**.

Rule 155. Reference is not made from caste and similar designations, such as,

Das(a), Sen(a), Gupta, Josi ; Garu, Naidu etc.

Rule 157. Names used in modern times according to Western usuage are as a rule treated like modern family names.

The first two rules are totally wrong. Giving a reference from the place name " Nellore " is as extravagant as giving a reference from a Given Name like " William." Giving a reference from " Pantulu," an irremovable impotent attachment-word is equally extravagant. Again, the first four words, given as examples under rule 155, have now become entry words. To deny them even a reference is certainly wrong. Lastly, how is a cataloguer to apply Rule 157 ? What is a name 'used in modern times according to Western usage' ? How is he to distinguish such a name from one not following Western usage ?

5133 *Ala*

Ala Rule 70A. Enter Indic writers prior to the middle of the nineteenth century under the personal name (usually the first) and refer from the family name or surname (usually the third). When there are only two names, refer from the second.

Rule 70B. Where family names have been adopted according to Western usage, enter it under the family name, ... Refer from parts of name not chosen as entry word.

These rules are naively over-simplified. To give reference from every word not chosen as entry word is a counsel of despair. Its adoption will flood the catalogue with cross reference entries. These will hide the substantial entries. The sections 5130 to

51308 have shown the unhelpfulness of rendering Indian names according to the *Ala* Rules.

5135 *Ccc*

Ccc Rule 1212. In the case of modern Hindu names, the last substantive word in the name is to be written first and all the earlier words and initials are to be added thereafter ; except that, in the case of South Indian names, if the last substantive word merely indicates caste or community and the penultimate word is given in full on the title-page, the two last substantive words are both to be written first in their natural order.

The rule gives a list of the more common South India words indicating caste or community, referred to in the body of the rule. This is about the best prescription given so far for the rendering of an Indian name. But, even this rule gives wrong results in the case of a Hindi name in which the surname is omitted and the Given Name stands split up into two distinct words. Another difficulty will be experienced by foreign cataloguers in applying this rule. This will be caused by the honorific words at the beginning or the end of a name. The complication gets more complicated when the same word can be used both as a removable honorific word in some names, as an irremovable impotent attachment-word in some other names and as the only unabbreviated words in still other names. "Sri" and "Sastri" are words belonging to this category. No help can be given in this matter to a cataloguer not born and bred in the cultural sub-group of India concerned. But a list of other honorific words can be given along with the cataloguing rule. This list will help anyone to remove any of these honorific words in rendering the name in the heading of a cataloguing entry.

514 Double or Treble Entry Word

The above are the complications commonly arising in the rendering of the name of a person in the heading of a catalogue entry. But these do not exhaust the complications. A name belonging to a European cultural group may have a Double Family Name. This complication arises also in Viet-Namese Given Names, prescribed for use as entry word. Double Family Name occurs also in the name of a person in the cultural groups of Maharashtra, Gujarat, Bengal, North Kanara and Ceylon. When a Double Family Name is hyphenated, there need not be any difficulty ; otherwise, there is difficulty. Moreover, a Given Name of South

India is occasionally split up into two or three words. Then all these splits taken together should be regarded as the Entry Element. If in addition there is also an irremovable impotent attachment-word, it too should be taken along into the Entry Element. Here are some examples :—

> **Ganapathi Subramaniya Pillai**
> **Siva Sankara Narayana Pillai**
> **Venkata Narasimham Pantulu**

It is hardly possible for any cataloguer not born and bred within the respective cultural group to handle successfully, and with ease and accuracy, all such idiosyncrasies.

5141 *Rdc*

Rdc Rule 28. Treat compound names according to the usage of the authors' fatherland, though if it is known that his practice differs from this usage his preference should be followed. Compound names then go :

> *a* If *English*, under the last part of the name, when the first has not been used alone by the author.
> *b* If *foreign*, under the first part.
> *c* In foreign compound names of women also although the first part is usually the maiden name and the second the husband's name, the entry should generally be under the first.

The number of provisos in the above rule is too great to give consistent results. The terms ' usage,' ' though,' ' if ' and ' generally ' nullify the value of the rule. The commentary of *Rdc* itself adds further to the nullification. Here they are :—

> This rule secures uniformity ; but like all rules, it sometimes leads to entries under headings where nobody would look for them. It is advisable therefore to make some exception...... Moreover, it is not always easy to determine which is compound surname in French. A convenient rule would be to follow the authority of Hoefer, Larousse, Querard, and Lorenz, in such cases, if they always agree ; unfortunately, they often differ. References are necessary whichever way one decides each case, especially when the second part of a foreign compound name has been used alone.

In French a forename is sometimes joined to a surname by a hyphen. In such cases even a general rule like " use a hyphenated double family name, as if it were a single word, as the entry element " gets nullified.

5142 *Pin*

Pin Rule 115. In compound names of all kinds—whether the individual parts stand next to one another disconnectedly or are connected with one another by a hyphen, a preposition, or a conjunction—the first part becomes the entry word. Whether a compound name exists is in cases of doubt to be determined by a reliable biographical or bibliographical work.

This looks like a simple, easily workable rule leading to consistent results in cataloguing. But *Pin* itself is not sure whether such a uniform rule would be truly helpful to the reader. Therefore it prescribes a plethora of cross-references in its next rule.

Rule 116. A reference is made as a rule from the second part of a compound name.

Pin has also to make several exceptions to the general rule 115. This is done in its rules quoted below :—

Rule 118. If in compound names the second or one of the following names is customarily preferable, this becomes the entry word, with references from the others.

Putility (Gans Edler Herr zu), with a reference from **Gans.**

Fouque (De La Mottee), with a reference from **La Motte.**

Fenelon (Salignac De la Mothe), with references from **Salignac** and **La Mothe.**

Surely, it is not easy for a foreign cataloguer to make himself familiar with all such involved idiosyncrasies. A foreign reader too may not be expected to wade through so many words or to get the right word stick to his mind. Surely, the cataloguing profession should, at the international level, do something to save the time of the cataloguer and the tempo of the reader alike in such cases.

Rule 119. In Hungarian compound names, that are not connected by a hyphen, the second name regularly becomes the entry word.

Csoma (Koeroesi Sandor), with a reference from **Koeroesi** ; but **Pariz** (Papai), with a reference from **Papai.**

Rule 120. If authors bear in front of their surname the family name of their mother, their god-parent, etc—this is customary especially in Holland, England and Scandinavia,—such family names have only the value of forenames ; but reference is made from them, if necessary. In this connection it is to be noted that in Dutch names the addition introduced by *Van* frequently denotes only extraction.

Allen (Heron—), with a reference from **Heron.**

Dirichlet (Lejeune), with a reference from **Lejeune** ; but

Mill (Stuart), without reference from **Stuart** ; and

Hulshoff (van Oosterwijk), without reference from Van Oosterwijk; but **Lambrechtsen van Ritthem** (Nikolaus Kornelis).

Even this is not definite. For the next rule of *Pin* mentions an exception.

Rule 121. Such combinations are treated like real compound names, however, if they have been assimilated in foreign languages and the first name has found its way into use here (in Germany) ; reference is always made from the second name.

Prince-Smith with a reference from **Smith**.

Rule 122. Forenames that are united to the family name by a hyphen retain the value of forenames.

Cohn (Lassar-) is the rendering of **Lassar-Cohn**.

Rule 124. Apparent compound names, when they originate through the combination of the names of different authors who have participated in a work, are analysed into the individual names.

Fischer (Franz) and **Ellinger** (Josef) is the rendering of Fischer-Ellinger.

It is hardly possible for a foreign cataloguer to deal with such idiosyncrasies.

5143 *Ala*

Ala Rule 46. Enter a married woman under her latest name unless......
she has consistently written under another name.

The heading is to consist of (1) husband's surname, (2) her own forenames, and (3) her maiden name, when known, in parentheses.

Viterbi, Bona (Benvenisti).

Rule 46F. Compound names consisting of a combination of the surnames of husband and wife are frequently found on the title-pages of books by married women. As a rule these are not treated as compound names, but are entered according to general rule for married woman, (46). However, exceptions are sometimes made, especially in the case of foreign names if custom favours entry under the compound form.

(1) In Spanish names the customary usage is for a woman to add to her own surname the surname of her husband, connecting the two by the preposition *de*. Ordinarily the part of each surname which represents the mother's surname is dropped, but is sometimes retained if the mother's name is a particularly distinguished one, or, as a means of identification if the father's name is a very common one.

Enter according to the general rule for compound names, the entry word in this case being the woman's maiden name.

Molinay Vedia de Bastianini (Delina).

The data for this name are as follows :

Father's name	: Octavio T Molina.
Mother's name	: Manuela Vedia de Molina.
Maiden name	: Delfina Molina y Vedia.
Husband's name	: Rene Bastianini.

(2) The usage in Portuguese and Brazilian names is less consistent than in Spanish, but in general, names are formed in the same way. At present however, the tendency is toward the use of the last surname, the husband's, rather than the full compound form. Enter under the last surname, with reference from any other surnames which forms part of the name.

(3) The Dutch custom is to use a hyphenated compound in which the

husband's name is followed by the wife's maiden name. Treat as any compound name.

(4) In Italian names the compound form is frequently found, the wife's name sometimes preceding and sometimes following the husband's name. In general enter under the maiden name or the married name according to the rules for married women, using the compound form only when it is the author's consistent usage, or when it is impossible to distinguish between maiden name and married name.

(5) German, Swiss, Scandinavian and Russian married women who use a compound form of name on the title pages of their books are entered according to the general rules for married women unless the compound form is known to be the preferred usage.

5144 *Vat*

Vat Rule 40 is in substance the same as *Ala* Rule 38. So also *Vat* Rule 59 is in substance the same as *Ala* Rule 46 and 46F.

These rules will break the back of any foreign cataloguer.

5145 *Ccc*

Ccc Rule 12111. Compound surnames and forenames are to be written in their entirety.

This is an over-simplified rule. It has overlooked all the complications actually occurring in compound Family Names found in European cultural groups. The problem is not so perplexing in regard to compound Family Names found in the Asian cultural groups. In the first place, in South Indian cultural groups, there are no Family Names. Therefore, compound Family Names do not arise. Moreover, marriage does not result in change of name either for man or for woman. But in the cultural groups that have adopted family name, on marriage a woman merely gives up her maiden family name and takes over the family name of her husband. Complications like those in the European cultural groups do not arise.

5146 ASIA

Double Family Names do exist. In Viet Nam, compound family name is usually hyphened. So is the compound Given Name prescribed to be Entry Element. They do not therefore give any trouble. In other cases, a compound Family Name is not hyphened. In my investigation for Unesco's Project on the Rendering of Asian Names, I found that the number of compound Family Names are only a few. There are about fifty compound Family Names in the cultural groups of Maharashtra, Gujarat and Kannada. In Bengali and Sinhalese cultural groups, it has been tentatively found that there are only about six " starters " of two-worded Family Names. If the penultimate word in a reduced name is any one of them, that word and the end word together form a two-worded Family Name. Three Bengali words and three Sinhalese words are also " starters " of three-worded compound Family Names. If any such " starter " occurs as the third last word from the end in a name, that word and the two succeeding words together form a three-worded Family Name. I have given a list of double Family Names and of the " starters " of double and treble Family Names in table 3 of my *Report* to Unesco on the Rendering of Asian Names in Headings of Catalogue Entries. As stated in section 5127, a similar schedule will be necessary for Indian and Pakistani Muslim names also.

515 NAME WITH PREFIX

Some names in European cultural groups have prefixes added to Family Names. In some names, the prefixes are merged in the Family Names. Then no problem arises in the rendering of such Family Names as entry words. But in some cases, the prefixes are written as if they are separate words. These prefixes may be articles, or prepositions, or combinations of them. The rules for rendering Family Names with unmerged prefixes are complicated. Cataloguers of foreign cultures are obliged to apply these rules in darkness, as it were.

5151 *Rdc*

Rdc Rule 29. Put surname preceded by **Prefixes** :

   a   in *French* and *Belgian*, under the prefix when it is or contains an article Le, La, L', Du, Des ; under the word following when the prefix is a preposition de, d'.

   b   in *English*, under the prefix, no matter from what language the name is derived.

   c   In all *other languages*, under the name following the prefix.

   d   *Naturalised names* with prefixes are to be treated by the rules of the nation adopting them.

   Thus German names preceded by "von" when belonging to Russian are to be entered under Von. Eg. **Von Vizin** and not **Vizin** (von). Prefixes are d', de, de La, Des, Du, L', La, Le, Les, St, Ste, da, dal, dalla, dalle, dai, dagli, del, della, delle, dei, degli, da, dos, das, ten, ter, thor, Van, vander, van't, ver, am, auf, auf aus, aus'm, in, im, von, vom, zu, zum, zur, A', Ap, O', Fitz, Mac, M', Mc.

   For non-European cataloguers, it is no wonder that names with unmerged prefixes are a source of bewilderment.

5152 *Pin*

Pin Rule 108. The simple unconnected article in front of the name is disregarded, in Germanic languages ; in Romance languages, however, it is attached to the name.

Rule 109. The simple unconnected preposition in front of the name as well as in front of the article and the name is never taken into account.

Rule 110. If preposition and article are blended or firmly connected (*a, auf'm, aus'm, im, vom, zum, zur* ; *ten, ter, thor, vander, vander, van't, var* ; *du, des, del, della* ; *dei, d' de, degli, delle, dal, dalla, dai, dagli, dalle, do, da, dos, das, etc.*) they are attached to the name.

Rule 111. If the preposition blended with the article is similar to a simple preposition as, for example, Portuguese *da* (from *de ÷ a*) and *do* (from *de ÷ o*,) Italian *de'* or *de* (for *dei*), reference is made from the basic form of the name.

Rule 113. Attributes and prefixes permanently preceding the name are attached to the name. So in particular *Saint* (*Sankt, sainte, san, santo* etc., always in the full form of that language to which the name belongs), the Norman *Fitz* (*i.e.,* " son of "), the Irish-Scottish *Mac, Mc,* or *M,* (*i.e.,* " son of "), the Irish *o'* (*i.e.,* " Grand child of," " descendant of "), the Welsh *Ap, Ab,* (*i.e.,* " son of "), etc.

Rule 114. Prefixes that are not permanent are disregarded.

How is a foreign cataloguer to know when a prefix is permanent or not. Barring this, *Pin* has given the rules on merged prefixes in the clearest form known.

5153 *Ala*

Ala Rule 39 is in substance similar to the rules of *Pin* given in section 5152.

5154 *Vat*

Vat Rules 42 to 44 are in substance similar to rules of *Pin* given in section 5152.

5155 *Ccc*

Ccc rules 12112 and 121121 are in substance similar to the rules of *Pin* given in section 5152.

5156 Indian Name

There are a few prefixes occasionally attached to the entry word in an Indian name. In most cases, they are honorific ; therefore, they may be removed in the heading of a catalogue entry. But a prefix is sometimes merged with the entry word ; then there is no difficulty ; it forms part of the entry word. Occasionally, an honorific word is treated as irremovable though not merged with the entry word. " Sri ", including its variant " Shri," is an honorific word of this kind.

Shri Sankara is rendered as **Sankara.**
Shriprakasa is rendered as **Shriprakasa.**
Sri Aurobindo is rendered as **Sri Aurobindo.**

These conflicting usages cannot but baffle a foreign cataloguer. The last mentioned may baffle even an Indian cataloguer. Moreover, the merging and the non-merging of Sri are practised indifferently in printing the same name on title-page. This makes confusion worse confounded. Other such tantalising honorific words are yet to be investigated.

516 Any Remedy ?

The rules mentioned in the sub-sections of section 51 are bewildering. One code differing from another is the least part of it. The exceptions within exception in the same code are the worst features. One may not be far wrong in saying that the rules are as shapeless as liquid. This, of course, is no wonder. Each catalogue code virtually attempts the impossible. It seeks to cover diverse cultural groups. The culture of each group is, moreover, a living culture. Change is a characteristic of anything living. Further, the structure of one's name is one's own prerogative. It is open to any one to defy the practice of one's community. Neither a catalogue code nor a cataloguer has the right to interfere with that prerogative. It is futile, in these circumstances, to codify cataloguing rules for names of all cultural groups. Futility cannot but characterise a national catalogue code. It is even more so in an international catalogue code. But cataloguing cannot be done with any consistency whatever, without the aid of a catalogue code. This is a dilemma. Is there a way out of it ? Is there any remedy ? Yes, there is. I can think of two remedies. In either of them, a cataloguer or a catalogue code will have to depend on outsiders.

5161 Help from Publishing Trade

The first remedy seeks the help of the publishing trade. The publisher is in touch with the author. The author knows what he takes to be the prepotent word(s) in his name. Even if he is too preoccupied with his own work to think about it, the publisher who is an extrovert business-man, can find opportunity to think with the author and make him show his preference. Of course, the publisher himself needs some guidance in the matter. It is the duty of the library profession to provide him this guidance. To do so, the profession should do some field work. It should consult cultural sociologists. It should contact the author-world. It should plough into this field its own experience of the psychology of reader's approach. Since the World War II, a National Standards Organisation is being established in country after country. The National Standards Organisation provides a helpful forum for all the interests to meet. It provides the anvil on which an agreed standard can be beaten out. Standards Work does not attempt to tie down any practice with a thong. Man has now learnt to reconcile standardisation and the change necessary for progress. The literary language has been a monumental example of such an elastic standardisation being applied unconsciously by the common folk. A similar thing cannot be impossible for the very restricted interests concerned with the determination of the relative potency in the words in a name, and in the determination of the most potent word in it. If this is granted in principle, the exploitation of it at the practical level is not difficult. The agreed findings of all the interests concerned can be indicated, by suitable typographical device, in printing the name of a personal author on the back of the title-page of a book or its equivalent in any other form of document. Chapter 7 of this book gives a draft standard for the author-statement in the back of title-page or its equivalent. One should not hastily brush aside the practicability of promoting such a standard. " Publishers won't agree ", is the summary disposal of some ! This is unfair to the publishers. We have not till now approached them with such a request. " The aesthetic design of the back of the title-page will not allow this ", is the second line of opposition ! But aesthetic design is a work of art. It is creative art. There can be no limit to what can be achieved by creative art. Our duty is merely to tell the artist what our requirement is. It will simmer in his mind ; and imagination or intuition will sooner or later throw forth the proper design. The International Standards Organisation should cooperate with the International Publishers' Association in this matter. The corresponding national bodies too should co-operate with each other in each country. Then, an international standard can be established. Then, the present wastage in cataloguing man-power in determining the correct way of rendering a personal name in the heading of a catalogue entry can be eliminated. Readers too will soon get accustomed, by the suggestion of the typographical dominance in the back of the title-page, to look up the catalogue for the correct entry word.

5162 International Co-operation

International co-operation in the cataloguing field is another means of getting out of the present chaos in the rendering of a personal name in the heading of a catalogue entry. A detailed scheme for international co-operation is given in chapter 9 of this book. This scheme entrusts the cataloguing of each book to the National Central Library of the country of origin of the book. It should be competent to determine all the issues in the rendering of a personal name belonging to its cultural group. In cases of doubt, it has expert guidance within its easy reach. In the case of a living author, it can even take his own advice. The scheme suggests every other country copying the catalogue entry established by the home-country of the book.

5163 Instability

The international situation may upset the international co-operation suggested in section 5162. In times of war, correct cataloguing work will be jeopardised. There is no way of escape from this.

5164 Past Books

Neither of the above remedies is available in regard to the collection of books printed before the remedies are adopted. But they have been already catalogued in some library—particularly in big national libraries—in one way or other. Most of them are likely to be more or less dead materials. Of course, a classic of permanent value will be an exception. But by its very being a classic, it is sure to be brought out in new editions. Generally speaking then, the older books will be largely of antiquarian interest. Its seekers will be specialists. They will be few in number. Their antiquarian zest will carry them through hurdles. On this assumption, the existing catalogue of the older collection of a library may be provisionally sealed. Stray books coming out of it into active use may be transferred from time to time from the old collection to the new. Its catalogue entry can also be brought into line with that for the new collection. This is the Method of Osmosis. This has been described in section 3475 of chapter 3.

5165 Future Books

One of the two methods of escaping from the present chaos in the rendering of a personal name in the heading of a catalogue entry should always be available. During intervals of international peace, both the methods will be available. The library profession need not any longer drift in chaos. Future books should be catalogued consistently, economically and in comfort. This should be so irrespective of the country which catalogues and the country which produces the book. Cataloguing of future books need not be a heart-break. Future books need not be held over from public use or given a temporary treatment, in order to correspond with authors and publishers and experts living in far-off countries, or in order to go into the market place, as it were, to find out " usage " —past usage, current usage, and future usage !

5166 Canon of Ascertainability

Let it be repeated. The elixir of cataloguing work is the Canon of Ascertainability. The Five Laws of Library Science urge the cataloguing profession to extend the sphere of this Canon. Hitherto, the choice of heading alone has been left to the care of this Canon. The Fourth Law of Library Science now insists upon a further step being taken. To Save the Time of the Reader, the library profession should save the time of the staff. To save the time of the staff in cataloguing, the region of the sway of the Canon of Ascertainability should be extended. To extend its sway, it is necessary to push the attention of the library profession even to the pre-natal stage of a book or document. The particular moment before the nativity of a book needing attention, is the moment of the design of the back of the title-page of a book or its equivalent in a micro document forming but a tiny part of an independent macro document. This is the essence of the first method described in section 5161 " Help from the Publishing Trade ". This is the next forward step to be taken by the library profession. Let us not doubt our capacity to take this step. Let us not hesitate to take this step. Let us march on.

517 Pseudonym

5171 DESCRIPTIVE WORD

Rdc Rule 204. Add *pseud* to the heading for all sorts of false names of whatever origin.

Ala Rule 30A (para 2). Exception is made in favour of entry under pseudonym followed by the abbreviation " Pseud."

Vat Rule 52. When the real name of an author remains unknown, the work is entered under the fictitious name, followed by the term *pseud*.

Ccc Rule 125. The pseudonym......is to be followed by the descriptive word ' *Pseud* ' written as a separate sentence.

Obviously, *Ala*, *Vat* and *Ccc* have blindly followed the tradition set by *Rdc*. Is it necessary for the catalogue to mark a name used by an author as an alternative name of himself, to be a pseudonym ? Does this not belong to the profession of historical bibliographers rather than cataloguers ? Which Law of Library Science throws this obligation on the cataloguer ? Whatever be the treatment given to an alternative name of a person, it will look after a pseudonym too. *Rdc* itself appears to have come very near this view in the commentary on its Rule 204. It says :—

So much is necessary to prevent mistake on the part of the public ; but it is a waste of time for the cataloguer to rack his brains to discover which of the ingenious names invented by Pierquin de Gembloux (cryptonym, geonym, phrenonym, etc.) is applicable in each case: for the only result is that readers are puzzled.

The latter half of the above quotation shows the sensitiveness of *Rdc* to the undesirability of the heading of a catalogue entry giving more information than what is necessary for a reader bringing up to the catalogue a particular name or information to find his book. But *Rdc* has failed to see that even the information " *pseud* " would not be brought up by a reader. The addition of the descriptive word " *pseud* " will also puzzle a reader. This is not relevant infor-mation. *Ala*, *Vat* and *Ccc* also have failed to see that it is not relevant. Such is the inexorability of tradition. But *Pin* has escaped the clutches of this tradition.

5172 OVER-INFORMATION

Rdc Rule 205. When an author uses a single pseudonym add it to his name.

Ccc Rule 1251. If the title-page gives the real name of the author also in a subordinated manner, it is to be added in circular brackets after the descriptive word " *Pseud* ". The real name of the author is to be preceded by the symbol ' *i.e.* '.

Rule 12511. If the title-page gives the real name of the author and adds the pseudonym in a subordinated manner, the former is to be chosen for the heading. The latter is to be added as a separate sentence and enclosed in circular brackets after it. The descriptive word ' *Pseud* ' is to be added as a second sentence within the bracket.

Rule 1252. If the real name of the author can be found out from outside the work, it is to be added in square brackets after the descriptive word ' *Pseud* '. The real name of the author is to be preceded by the symbol ' *i.e.* '.

The rules 1251 and 12511 of *Ccc* are in accordance with the Canon of Ascertainability. But the rule 1252 of *Ccc* is not in conformity with it. Nor does it satisfy the Canon of Relevance. It is obviously a blind following of the tradition started by *Rdc* Rule 205. The other codes have escaped the clutches of this tradition. The rule on cross reference index entry for alternative name is quite sufficient to take care of the problem created by the discovery of the real name hidden by the pseudonym.

5173 MULTI-WORDED PSEUDONYM

Vat Rule 53. In choosing the form of entry, fictitious names are treated according to the same rules as real names.

Rule 54*a*. The whole expression without inversion is used as the entry in the case of compound pseudonym made up of two words, of which the second often has the value of an adjective (as in the names of the Arcadia and other literary bodies), or pseudonyms made up of two or more words which represent a single idea, a synthetic expression, or a whimsicality.

Rule 54*b*. When a pseudonym is composed of a name preceded by a title, degree, or appellation, often with a burlesque or satirical meaning, this addition is placed after the name, except in Italian names.

These details in pseudonymous headings are not provided for in the other codes. In this respect, *Vat* is more penetrating than the other codes.

5174 INITIONYM

Rdc Rule 96. Part of the author's name when only a part is known, (is a substitute for the author's name).

Ex for a book " by J. B. Far ... " ... the entry is to be made under **Far** ... (J.B.). For a book " by L.M.P. ", the entry is to be made under **P.** (L.M.).

If the last initials are plainly, from the style of printing or from other evidence furnished by the book, those of a title, the entry will be under the initial preceding them ; thus for book " by *B.F., D.D.* " the entry is to be made under **F.** (B.).

Even mere printer's marks as *** or ... or !!!, unaccompanied by any letters, though they cannot be considered as names, may be used as headings for a reference for the sake of bringing together all the works of an author using them.

Rdc's rule implies that the last initial should be made the Entry Element and that the earlier initials should be taken to constitute the Secondary Element.

Pin Rule 72. The work is also treated as anonymous when the author designates himself :

1 with mere letters or sign ;
2 only as author of another work ;
3 with a mere appellative, such as, " by a citizen ".

Pin is prone to swell the category of anonymous works. The first category mentioned above is an example of this proneness.

Ala Rule 320 is in substance the same as *Pin* rule 72. But it provides for initionym or symbol being used as heading of a cross reference entry.

Vat Rule 56 is in substance the same as *Pin* rule 72.

Ccc Rule 1217. If the title-page contains only the initials of the name, the initials alone are to be used in the place of the name.

Rule 12171. If the full name of the author can be found out, it is to be added in square brackets after the initials-name. The full name thus added is to be preceded by the symbol " *i.e.* ".

Ccc respects the Canon of Ascertainability in its first rule. But it partially violates it in its second rule. Will it not be sufficient to give a cross reference index entry from the real name of the author, found only from outside the title-page ? *Ccc* differs from *Rdc*, in prescribing the initials to be rendered in the heading in the same sequence as in the title-page ; whereas, inversion is prescribed by *Rdc*. We have really to appeal to psychology to choose between these two alternative prescriptions. Perhaps, in the view of *Ccc*, the natural sequence of the initials is more likely to stick to the mind of the reader. Statistical consideration leading to inversion is not applicable to initionyms.

518 Homonym

5181 FORENAME

Rdc Rule 211. Distinguish authors whose family name is the same by giving the forename in full or by initials.

Pin Rule 132. For the further arrangement of identical family names, the forenames ... are decisive, no matter whether they have been taken from the title or supplied from some other place.

Ala Rule 40A. Give forename in the form most common in the author's native or adopted language.

Vat Rule 47. The forename is written in full.

Ccc Rule 12115. If the title-page contains only the initials of the forename or the forenames, but the surname is given in full and not as an initial, their full forms are to be found out and used. In case they cannot be found out, the initials alone may be used in their place.

As indicated explicitly in *Rdc*, the purpose of having Given Name(s) is to resolve homonym in the heading. The probability

for the resolution is greater with Given Names written in full than
in initials alone. This is the reason for the prescription of the
expansion even of a Given Name, represented on title-page by
initial only. This prescription violates the Canon of Ascertainability. We should think twice before violating this Canon. But
the commentary in *Ccc* raises a doubt in this matter. It says,

> In view of the difficulty and in some cases even of impossibility of getting
> the initials expanded, it is for consideration whether consistency may not be
> secured by using initials in all cases. No doubt this will increase the number of
> apparent homonyms. But this can be averted by the use of the usual other
> devices like date of birth, subject interest, and so on, to resolve homonym.

This suggestion also violates the Canon of Ascertainability. For, it
would imply replacing even a Given Name appearing in full on a
title-page by its initial. The arrangement will become chaotic
unless a person uses the Given Names in exactly the same way in
the title-pages of all his books. The problem of bringing together
all the entries of his name—having the same family name but
with the forenames in different forms—would become insoluble
unless the Canon of Ascertainability is violated. It is a dilemma.
Moreover, *Rdc* points out in its commentary that it will go against
common usage to contract the Given Name into initials in certain
cases. The commentary reads :—

> An exception may well be made in the case of man always known by a
> double-name : as Sydney Smith, or Bayard Taylor. Nobody talks of Smith or
> Taylor. Taylor, B., conveys no idea whatever to most readers. Taylor, Bayard,
> they know.

5182 PLAY OF PROBABILITY

To get out of the dilemma, we should first examine the probability for the creation of homonym. An ever-increasing pre-dis-
posing cause for homonym, is the number of persons to be named
exceeding the number of words available to name them. Creation
of homonym is intensified, by the social habit of naming a person
after the grand-parent or the great grand-parent. One of the
means permanently adopted to resolve homonym in many communities is to use two or more words to form a name. In small intimate circles one of the words proves sufficient. But in the wider
public context, all the words are brought into use. Then, assuming
the number of words available to name a person to be n, the number
of persons who can be named without homonym increases from
n to $n(n-1)$, if two words are used in each name. It increases to

n $(n-1)$ $(n-2)$, if three words are used in each name. Let us assume that, with the use of this device, we can name about a thousand million persons non-homonymously using all the languages of the world—nearly all the adults living in the world at any one time. But disturbances are caused by certain words being used unduly often—such as, Smith in the English-speaking community ; Hoffmann in the German-speaking community ; Jensen in the Danish community ; Ram in any Hindu community ; Subramanya in Tamil community ; and Mohamed in the Muslim community. Consequently, homonym occurs even among contemporary authors, though in a smaller proportion than in the community as a whole, in the measure of the proportion of authors to the people as a whole. The term " junior " is often used to resolve this homonym. This may prove efficient among contemporaries. But it cannot be of use in distinguishing persons born several generations apart.

5183 OBLIGATION TO EXPAND

In the world of authors, there is another factor intensifying the probability for homonym. An author is virtually immortal. Once a person writes a book, he is immortalised in a bibliography, and in the catalogue of his National Central Library, and perhaps even in the catalogues of some service librarires. Thus as authors cumulate through the ages, the probability for homonym goes on increasing. In these circumstances, the resolving power of Given Name is inconveniently lost, if it is reduced to an initial. The proper course is obviously to prescribe by rule that all Given Names should be given in full in the heading of a catalogue entry. But it costs considerable money, man-power, and time to hunt outside the title-page for the expansion of initials in names. It is truly the business of the profession of historical bibliography to do it. There should therefore be a division of labour here. It is uneconomical to cross the boundary of this division of labour between historical bibliographer and library cataloguer. This is in regard to books of the past.

5184 OTHER COMPLICATIONS

The books of the past give some additional trouble. There is for example the problem of omitted Given Names. Complication sets in, if an author is not consistent in omission. All the codes, except *Ccc*, prescribe the restoration, in some measure, of omitted Given Names. This also makes the cataloguer either depend on historical bibliographer, or himself become one. The apologetic direction, "neglect them in arrangement" occurring at the end of *Rdc* Rule 212, is significant. The commentary of *Rdc* on this rule is almost pathetic :

> He (the consulter of the catalogue) does not quickly recognise Charles Dickens in **Dickens**, Charles John Huffam or Leigh Hunt in **Hunt,** James Henry Leigh or Max Muller in **Muller**, Friedrich Max. Besides, the eye finds the well-known name more quickly if the others are, as it were, pushed aside.

Why search for the omitted words and then "push them aside"? The *Ala* had the courage to disown this shadow of the historical bibliographer. *Ccc* followed this example.

5185 PERSISTENCE OF HOMONYM. YEAR OF BIRTH

In a retrospective bibliography and in the catalogue of a National Central Library, homonym may persist even beyond the capacity of fully written Given Names. An additional device for resolving homonym becomes necessary. The Chinese wisely reserve the middle word in a name to denote the generation to which the person belongs. In the name of other cultural groups, the year of birth is a powerful resolvent. It can be further re-inforced by the addition of the year of death, in due course. Many codes have recourse to the use of this.

Rdc Rule 213. Distinguish authors whose family and forenames are the same by the dates of their birth and death, or if these are not known, by some other label.

Pin Rule 175. Different authors with the same family name, whose forenames are lacking or are completely alike, are arranged chronologically, according to the date of publication of the oldest of their works existing in the library.

Ala Rule 42. For medieval and modern names add dates of birth and death in the heading when they can be discovered with a reasonable amount of search.

Vat Rule 38. In all cases, the name is followed, if possible, by the date of birth, and eventually, of death ; this serves the purpose of placing the author or the person in his period.

Ccc Rule 1219. If two or more personal authors have the same name, they are to be individualised by the addition of the respective dates of birth or death or both or, if this method is not practicable, by the addition of the individualising word indicating their profession or any other such distinguishing features.

Now the use of two or more words in the name of a person has already become common to guard against the occurrence of a homonym and the wastage of labour that will be needed to resolve it, as time advances and the number of authors increases, and thereby the probability of homnoym increases. It is desirable to make it equally common to add the years also to the names of authors, as the probability for homonymous multi-worded name also will increase with time. Year is a sharp resolvent of homonym. But to do this, it takes considerable correspondence and time-lag. This is so tiresome that the cataloguer is tempted to use the same year for later books bearing the same name in the author-statements found in the title-pages of different books. This exposes him to the mistake of overlooking a possible homonym. An instance actually occurred to my knowledge about twenty years ago. A friend of mine was an economist. He was already the author of a book on economics. I found an entry of an astrology book under his name, in a foreign catalogue. This was unbelievable to me. I asked my friend about it. He said he knew a name-sake of his who had written on astrology. I asked if he too was born in 1894. He said that he was much older than himself. "But 1894, your year of birth, has been added to his name." I replied. He was surprised. After a while he said, "When my first book was published, the Library of Congress asked for the year of my birth and I gave it. Evidently I am now credited with the astrology book of my older name-sake."

5186 Future Books

Most of the difficulties mentioned in section 51 and its subjections regarding homonyms may not arise in service libraries of "adult growth", which weed out books freely as and when they get worn out by use or outmoded in thought. But this cannot be so in a National Central Library. Books are now produced every year in thousands. Copies of these are, by law, preserved in several libraries of the world. Exhaustive national bibliographies are now promoted in annual, quinquennial, and decennial cumulations. The problem of homonym cannot be met in future without the aid of expanded Given Names and years of birth and, eventually, of death. Even in service libraries, occasions may arise when such persistent homonyms occur. It is therefore desirable that cataloguing time should be saved by a suitable device. This device may consist of an agreed international standard. This standard should stipulate that

    1 the author-statement in the title-page should give the

Given Names of the author(s) and the collaborator(s) in full, and not in initials ; and

    2 the supplementary author-statement on the back of the title-page should give the year(s) of birth of author(s) and of collaborator(s) ; and in the case of deceased persons, the years of death as well.

This can be done for future books. This will lead to international economy. The time of historical bibliographers can also be saved from the pursuit of trivial problems on the " equation of authors ". The library profession, the publisher's trade and the author-world should be brought together by Standards Organisations, to evolve an International Standard on this matter.

5191 Title

Rdc Rule 25. Put under the highest title British and foreign noblemen.

Rule 26. But in a few cases in which the *family name* or a lower title is decidedly *better known*, enter under that.

Rule 214 gives elaborate instructions about the title to be added to the name of a woman marrying a nobleman.

Rule 213 (para 4 of commentary). As late as 1760 unmarried women were usually styled *Mrs.* ... There is no objection to following this practice in cataloguing, as the object of the cataloguer is not to furnish biographical information but to identify the people whose works are catalogued.

Pin Rule 165. If different names come under consideration for the same author, the one being the original, the other just adopted in legal form, chiefly on entering on a new dignity or condition of life, then the latter becomes the entry word.

Ala Rule 57. Enter a nobleman under his latest title, unless he is decidedly better known by his earlier title or by his family name. (Then follows a long string of rules and illustrations about the rendering).

Vat Rule 71 is in substance the same as the *Ala* Rule 57.

Rule 71*c.* German noblemen are regularly entered either under their family name, followed by their forenames and ranks, or else under the family name combined with title, followed by their forenames and rank.

Ccc Rule 1215. Hereditary titles, if any, be mentioned in the title-page are to be added as descriptive words after the forename or forenames, as the case may be, or in the place of forename, if there is no forename. Place names if any, associated with titles of persons, who retain their surname after being raised to peerage, are to be ignored.

Rule 12151. In the case of a woman author not having a hereditary title, the descriptive word ' *Mrs.*' or ' *Miss* ' or the respective equivalent in the language of the title-page may be added after the forename or the forenames as the case may be, if it is found necessary.

    Ccc follows the Canon of Ascertainability strictly in the form in which the name of an author (or a collaborator) should be rendered in the heading of a catalogue entry. It also separates the rule for choice from the rule for rendering. But the other codes fail in this respect. Confining ourselves to rendering alone, it may be asked if the word designating even a hereditary title should be added at all in the heading, unless it is required to resolve a homonym. *Ccc* has given the name of the title the status of 'descriptive word'. It also makes it compulsory. Unless a word describes the role played by a person in the creation of the thought-content or the words of exposition of a work, or in the preparation of it for publication in the capacity of a collaborator, it is not proper to give it the status of 'descriptive word', still less to make it compulsory. The wording in the *Ccc* rule should be changed to "individualising word". Then it need be used only if it is necessary for resolving a homonym. In rule 1215 also, the same correction should be made regarding '*Mrs.*' and '*Miss*'. This suggestion is anti-traditional, but it is time that all such traditional rules are examined rationally and ruthlessly modified or even deleted if necessary.

5192 Monarch, Prince, Pope, Saint

Ala Rule 47A. Enter saints of the early and medieval church like other writers of the same period under the forename, using the Latin form, followed by the designation, 'saint' in English... The designation saint follows epithets or appellatives qualifying the name of the saint and titles of nobility, but precedes titles of office.

Rule 48. Enter a Pope under his Latin Pontifical name, followed by the title 'Pope'.

An anti-Pope is entered under his Latin Pontifical name ... followed by the title 'anti-Pope'.

Rule 55. Enter sovereigns and ruling princes under their forenames in vernacular, followed by title in English.

Enter the consort of sovereigns under forename in the form used in the country of the sovereign, with the title in English and the name of the sovereign in English form.

Rule 58E. Enter presidents or other high executives officially known by their surnames under the surname, and add the designation of their office.

Rule 56. In general, enter members of the immediate families of sovereigns under forename ... (the examples given under this rule add the titles after the forename though it is not specified in the rule).

Vat Rules 60 to 70 are in substance the same as the rules of *Ala* mentioned above.

Ccc Rule 1216. In the case of monarchs and members of a royal family, saints and popes, the forename with the individualising Roman numeral, if any, is to be written first and thereafter, as a separate sentence, a descriptive word or phrase specifying the position held by the person.

Obviously, *Ccc* unnecessarily makes the name of the position a descriptive word instead of an individualising word. All the remarks made in the commentary in section 5191 apply here also. In the case of official publications issued by a monarch etc., his name will not be the entry word. His designation preceded by the name of the country will be the heading. In the case of books written in personal capacity, the name of the office need not be prescribed, unless it is required for resolving homonym. *Rdc* appears to respect this principle.

Further, if the Canon of Ascertainability is strictly followed, a special rule for monarchs, popes, saints, etc., will not be necessary. For the way in which the name is printed on the title-page will determine the heading.

5193 Categories for Omission

Ala Rule 41B. Omit from the heading titles of address (Miss, Mr., Mrs., Frau, Mme, etc.) ; minor ecclesiastical titles (abbey, archdeacon, dean, rabbi, reverend, etc.) ; governmental titles, below the highest rank (vice-president, senator, governor etc.) ; military and naval titles ; academic and professional titles.

Ccc Rule 12152. All other (non-hereditary) titles are to be ignored. Honorific words at the end or the beginning, if any, are to be ignored. All other words describing the position, status, etc., of the author are to be ignored.

Ala and *Ccc* do well in explicitly providing for the categories of words occurring in the author-statement on title-page, but to be definitely omitted in rendering the name of a person in the heading of a catalogue entry. Otherwise, the Canon of Ascertainability would imply their retention, or at least the fact of their omission being indicated by dots or " etc. " or some other means. It is desirable to add to the categories mentioned in the rule " academic distinctions, relation to other persons, books, and institutions ". It goes without saying that any of the categories to be omitted may be used as individualising term to resolve homonym, if it cannot be resolved by the year of birth or other chronological device.

5194 Schedule of Terms for Omission

No doubt, *Ala* and *Ccc* have filled up by these rules a lacuna in *Rdc*, *Pin*, and *Vat*. But these rules satisfy only a formal requirement to propitiate, and to escape from the blind incidence of, the Canon of Ascertainability. They cannot be applied by a cataloguer to names belonging to the diverse cultural groups of the world. For, he cannot distinguish between honorific words and the words belonging to the Reduced Name, in the name of a person, as it occurs on the title-page. To help him in spotting out honorific and other words for omission, the rule should be amplified by annexures giving exhaustive schedules of all honorific words in all natural languages. Even then another complication will make unaided decision difficult for a foreign cataloguer. For, some honorific words in some languages can also occur either as Family Name or as Given Name or as an irremovable impotent attachment. Thus the problem of removable impotent words is insoluble by rules alone.

5195 SOLUTION

For the solution of the problem of removable impotent honorific, academic and other terms, we have to fall back once again on such terms being indicated in the author-statement on the back of the title-page. Terms indicating academic titles are also mentioned, because in some languages, in Indian languages for example, academic titles are full-fledged words taken from among those which can be used as Family Names, Given Names or irremovable impotent attachments. The author is the person who knows best which words in his name, as it occurs in the title-page, are removable on account of their being honorific or academic or for other reasons. It is the publisher who can extract this information from the author during one of his contacts with him. To miss this opportunity may amount later to digging the whole of the Himalayas to find *the* rat, as the saying goes. In fact the most reliable source, *viz.*, the author, may not at all be available, if the present is not availed of. Indeed, a stitch in time would certainly save nine in this matter. The library profession should have this problem included in the International Standard for back of title-page to be promoted jointly by itself, the publishing trade, the author-world, the National Standards Organisations, the International Standards Organisation and the International Publishers' Association. It should not despair in anticipation of the printer's or of the designer's resistance to the proposal. The capacity of the creative artist is endless.

He can find quite an aesthetic solution to combine a variety of type-faces with varying degrees of dominance, to indicate unequivocally the Entry Element, the Secondary Element, and the Removable Element in the Supplementary Author-Statement on the back of the title page and its over-flow.

52 Geographical Name Heading

A geographical name often becomes the Entry Element in corporate author heading. It may also occur as Secondary Element. It often occurs as individualising term. It is sure to occur as main heading or as a subheading in class index entry in classified catalogue and in subject entry in dictionary catalogue. It is therefore convenient to have a set of rules on the rendering of a geographical name in the heading of a catalogue entry.

Rdc and *Pin* do not give such special rules. *Ala* and *Vat* have separate chapters on them. *Ccc* mixes up the specification about geographical names, in the various rules for the rendering of the name of a government. This is a fault. This fault should be removed in the next edition.

521 Language

Ala Rule 150A. Give countries, self-governing dominions, colonies and protectorates in the conventional English form.

Rule 150B. Give local geographical names usually in the vernacular form but where a well-established English form differs, prefer the English form.

In deciding between different forms of place-names consult U. S. Geographic Board's *Sixth report* (1933) and the *Decisions* of its successor, the U S Board on Geographical Names ; Canada Geographic Board ; Permanent Committee on Geographical Names for British Official Use ; *Times Gazetteer of the World* ; *Bartholomew's survey gazetteer* ; *Lippincott's new gazetteer* ; *Longman's gazetteer* ; *Century cyclopedia of names* ; *Ritter's geographisch-statistisches lexikon* ; Vivien de Saint-Martin, *Nouveau dictionnaire de geographie universelle*, etc., giving preference in all instances to official sources.

Vat Rule 89. Geographical names are given in the vernacular except that the names of countries and large geographical units are given in the traditional Italian form. The vernacular form of geographical names is based on standard gazetteers and atlases, in particular the *Atlante internazionale* of the Touring Club Italiano.

Rule 89*a*. Names of continents, countries, kingdoms, colonies, mandated countries, and similar definite political and geographical divisions are given in the Italian form.

Rule 89*b*. The Italian form of name is used for regions, provinces, states, large peninsulas, islands and groups of islands which have their own physical and ethnic character and traditions, various groupings of countries and kingdoms, and the individual states and *Lander* of Germany and Austria.

Rule 89*c*. The Italian form is also used for the names of all the great physico-geographical units which transcend political and administrative boundaries ; *i.e.*, oceans, gulfs, straits, ocean-currents, rivers, mountain ranges, plains, plateaus, forests, capes, and similar geographical units.

Rule 89*d*. If the Italian form of a foreign geographical name has not been definitely established, but is variable or arbitrary, the vernacular form is preferred.

Rule 90. Other geographical names, which do not have a corresponding Italian form, are given in the vernacular.

Ccc Rule 1231 ... the name (in the favoured language of the library) of the geographical area.

As already stated in the introduction to this section, *Ccc* fails to have separate rules for geographical names. The above extract occurring in the rule for rendering the name of a government—which is the name of its territory—has the force of a rule for the rendering of geographical names in headings for catalogue entries.

Ccc provides explicitly for the following of the Principle of Local Variation, by stating its rule in terms of " favoured language of the library ". By this simple verbal device, it qualifies itself to be an international catalogue code. The other two codes become strictly national catalogue codes, in their wording of the rules for the rendering of the heading in a geographical name entry.

Vat is unnecessarily verbose. This is a fault in drafting. Its Rules 89 and 90 would become sufficient with a slight re-wording. *Ala* has nearly achieved such a result.

Ccc is very condensed. Its prescription of rendering in the " favoured language of the library " implies that the vernacular should be used for a geographical entity without a name in the favoured language of the library.

522 MULTI-WORDED NAME

Vat Rule 91*a*. In geographical names that consist of a generic physical qualification and a distinctive name, the latter precedes the former. The inverted part follows a comma, and is left in the language of the name itself. Such physico-geographical qualifications are ; lake, promontory, cape, mountain, pass, sea, river, gulf, strait, and forest as well as their equivalents. Names of important public works are treated similarly ; *e.g.*, castle, gate, street, road, rail road, bridge, canal, and light house.

The qualifiers follow the name in German, Dutch, and the Scandinavian and Slavic languages ; in English they sometimes precede and sometimes follow.

Rule 91*b*. When a generic word forms an integral part of a name, it is retained as the first part, without inversion.

173

Likewise, when the distinctive part is a common adjective, no inversion is made.

Rule 91c.   In the entry an adjectival noun is preferable to a compound name if it does not cause confusion.

Rule 91d.   The appellative is not inverted if it has lost its original meaning in a given expression.

Rule 91e.   The generic term is not inverted in the name of cities.

No other code makes a similar prescription for the inversion of the words in a multi-worded geographical name.   Even *Vat* is unable to make an easily workable prescription.   It is difficult to satisfy the Canon of Consistency in applying the above rules. How is a foreign cataloguer to distinguish a generic word forming a mere physical qualification and the same forming an integral part of the name ?   How is he to know that " Rio de " is a mere qualification in " Rio de Araguaya ", but an integral part of the name in " Rio de Janeiro " ?

Again, how is a foreign cataloguer to know when a distinctive part is a common adjective and when not ?   How is he to know that on this ground " Monte Cavo " should be rendered without inversion, but that " Monte Shasta " should be inverted in rendering ?

Or again, how is a foreign cataloguer to know that " Mount Pleasant " or " Lake Placid " should be rendered without inversion because the first word in each has lost its original meaning ?

Regarding a city, how is a cataloguer to apply Rules 91c and 91e consistently?   How is he to know that "Citta Sant' Angelo" should be rendered in full and without inversion, while " Citta del Vaticano " should be rendered as the mere adjectival noun " Vaticano " ?

The fact is that there are multi-worded geographical names. We may preferably use them as proper names without inversion. Their first words will not recur as often as the first words in a personal name—the first Given Name in the personal name. Therefore, the Canon of Prepotence will not require inversion in geographical names.   It will be particularly considerate to the Canon of Consistency likely to be violated by complicated rules, with exceptions, for inversions.

Moreover, in the case of the name of a place as governmental author heading, the Canon of Ascertainability should be the guide.

The presumption is that the title-page of the document mentions the name of the government in terms of the official name of its territory, be it sovereign government or local government.

In the case of the name of a place as a subject heading, this help cannot be had. Perhaps, a helpful rule may be that if the proper name in current use exists in the language of the library, it should be used. If it does not exist, the proper name in the vernacular should be used. In either case, an authoritative atlas or directory or list of names should form the basis. This rule would be not only easy to apply ; but, it would give the name of the geographical entity in the form in which a reader would look for it.

5221 Name with Adjective

Vat Rule 93g. Adjectives are inverted which designate points of the compass and other features, such as : high, low, lower, upper, etc., and their equivalents in other languages.

Rule 83c. Such adjectives are retained in the original position in the names of administrative districts and cities which are given in the vernacular.

The adjective is not inverted when it is followed by a generic noun.

The adjective " New ", as well as its equivalents in other languages is retained at the beginning of the names of cities.

The distinction made in *b* and in *c* is not, perhaps, necessary. People are using a term like " Far East " or " Extremo Orinte ", as if it were a proper name. If the words are inverted, the quality of being " proper " is lost both by the noun and the adjective. Such initial adjectives do not occur in many geographical names. Moreover, there are not many names of other species of entities beginning with such adjectival terms. Therefore the Canon of Prepotence would not want inversion.

Ala high-lights the tantalising situation caused by inversion, incidentally in the following paragraph occurring in its Rule 153 :—

Ala Rule 153. The name of the country is used in direct form even though inverted for its own entry.

Elisabethville, *Belgian Kongo* ; and not

Elisabethville, *Kongo Belgian* ;

Incidentally, it should be seen that the rendering of " Belgian Congo " (which is a country) in a language different from English, contradicts *Ala*'s basic rule 150A for the rendering of names of countries.

5231 Name Beginning with " Bad "

Ala Rule 156*b*. Enter German health resorts beginning with the word " Bad " under the name of the place, omitting " Bad ". Refer from name beginning with " Bad ".

Name of such a place is usually hyphenated, *e.g.*, Bad-Eilsen. Is it not better to use the inverted form in the Heading of Cross Reference Index Entry ?

523 Initial Article

Ala Rule 156A. Place names beginning with an article have the article as entry word. ...exeeption may be made in the case of place names familiarly referred to in English under the part of the name following the article.

Vat Rule 92. Articles which form an integral part of a local name are retained in the heading, but are disregarded in filing.

Vat differs from *Ala* by prescribing that the initial article should be ignored, though written.

Ccc has a general prescription that initial article should be ignored in any heading. Thus it would carry out the intention of *Vat*, without writing the article. As initial article in place name does perplex people, *Ccc* repeats its prescription about initial article explicitly in the commentary on its basic rule for geographical name.

524 Redundant Rules

The following rules are redundant :—

Ala 153D (name of a suburb) ;
Vat 94*a* and *c* (name of country) ;
     96 (countries no longer in existence) ;
     97 (annexed and merged states) ;
     98 (federated states) ;
     101 (colonies) ; and
     102*b* (successor cities).

If at all, the substance of these rules may be given in a commentary on the basic rules. Because, these merely re-iterate the basic rule as applied to particular cases.

525 Homonym

5251 AREA WITHIN AREA

Ala Rule 154A. When different political or administrative units have the same name, distinguish them by adding the particular designation in parentheses, preferably in English, though a term without a precise English equivalent is given in the vernacular form.

Vat Rule 103. Geographical homonyms are distinguished by means of appropriate qualifications which are given in parentheses and in Italian. The name alone without qualification, signifies the modern city or state.

Ccc Rule 123101. If more than one geographical area has the same name, and all such Geographical Areas can be arranged in an articulated sequence, each area being part of the preceding one, in the case of the Geographical area of the greatest extension, the heading is to be arrived at in accordance with Rule 1231. In the case of the others, the Heading arrived at in accordance with Rule 1231 is to be augmented by an individualising word or phrase indicating the nature of the Area, *e.g.*, Province, State, District, Thaluk, County, Commune, Borough, City, Town, etc. The descriptive word so added is to be deemed to be a separate sentence.

Ala, *Vat*, and *Ccc* agree in substance. But there is one difference. *Ccc* makes the additional term an individualising term. Further, *Ala* and *Vat* do not distinguish the homonym of area within area dealt with in this section, from the homonym of areas exterior to one another dealt with in section 5252. This is not as helpful as it can be, particularly when both kinds of homonym have to be resolved in the same case.

Moreover, *Ccc* satisfies the Law of Parsimony by prescribing that the individualising element denoting status may be omitted for the largest area denoted by the homonym. *Vat* makes some similar provision. It provides for the name of a city to be left without an individualising term. But it does not clinch it or deal with it exhaustively as *Ccc* does. *Ala* overlooks the Law of Parsimony.

5252 AREAS EXTERIOR TO ONE ANOTHER

Ala Rule 155. Distinguish two or more places of the same name, the same type of unit, and the same country by the addition, in parentheses, of the name of the province, " department ", county, etc.

Vat Rule 103 (para 2). City of the same name in different countries are distinguished by adding the name of the country in Italian. If Italian cities of the same name are not otherwise distinguished, the name of the province is added.

Ccc Rule 123102. If more than one Geographical Area has the same name and Rule 123101 is either not applicable or even if applicable it is not sufficient for individualisation, a word or group of words is to be added in square brackets in each case, consisting of the name of the largest Geographical Area, forming the territory of a Government containing it and sufficient for individualising it. The additional individualising term is to be omitted if the Geographical Area whose name is the Heading is either (*a*) a part of the mother country of the library or (*b*) a part of the favoured country of the library, the mother country not having an area of that name. The matter in square brackets is to be inserted immediately after the name of the place and before the individualising word, if any, required by Rule 12310.

It may be remarked at the outset that the term " Government " in the *Ccc* Rule cited, denotes both sovereign government and local government. *Ccc* gives a sufficient number of examples to bring out the need for the detailed and elaborate prescription it has given to resolve homonym among areas exterior to one another. *Ccc* further prescribes different styles of rendering for the individualising term denoting (1) designation of status, and (2) name of a larger containing area.

Ala and *Vat* recognise these two modes of the formation of homonym. But they fail to prescribe means for distinguishing the individualising terms necessary for the two kinds of homonyms.

Further, *Ccc* respects the Principle of Local Variation, by prescribing the omission of the individualising element if it is the name of the country of the library and in a certain circumstance if it is the name of the favoured country of the library. *Ala* and *Vat* do not make a similar provision in the matter.

5253 DIFFERENT GEOGRAPHICAL SPECIES

Vat Rule 93a. If it is necessary to distinguish the various applications of a name, a qualification or appellative is added, in parentheses and in Italian.

This is a distinctive contribution of *Vat*. No other code has visualised the need for this. The next edition of *Ccc* should add the following rule in the section to be opened for geographical name.

If entities of more than one geographical species have the same name, an individualising term is to be added consisting of the name of the species. The additional individualising term is to be omitted in the geographical area—country or county or city or town or village, etc.—capable of forming the territory of a government, sovereign or local.

The second sentence in the above draft rule is added in order to satisfy the Law of Parsimony.

5254 GEOGRAPHICAL *versus* PERSONAL OR WORK NAME

Homonym may also arise between geographical name and personal name or work name. But the homonym between geographical and personal name is already resolved by the fact that a personal name will have a secondary element following it. But to resolve the homonym between geographical and work names, the individualising term " Work " or its equivalent such as " Poem " " Drama " or " Fiction " should be added after the latter.

5255 CHANGE OF NAME

Vat Rule 102a. Cities and other localities which at different times have had various names are entered under their latest official name.

178

Rule 102*b*. If the various names represent different cities which have succeeded one another, or grown up in the same place in different areas, each of the names is used.

Rule 102*d*. Names of celebrated cities are given in Italian when the form of name has been greatly changed with the passage of time.

The first of the above rules violates the Canons of Ascertainability and of Permanence. It is also liable to violate the Law of Parsimony. For, if change of name occurs in the future, all the old entries will have to be re-done. The real significance or purpose of rule 102*d* is not clear. Moreover, change of name may occur even for a country or for a state forming part of a country. It has occurred in our own days.

Ccc does not have necessity for rules of the above kind. It depends upon the Canon of Ascertainability to do its work. Of course, the various alternative names of the same geographical entity will be tied up by cross reference index entries.

Rdc, *Pin* and *Ala* do not deal with change of geographical name.

526 Irrelevant Information

5261 GEOGRAPHICAL INFORMATION

Ala Rule 152. Counties in the United States and Canada when used as entry word are followed by the name of the state or province, elsewhere by the name of the country, in accepted abbreviated form.

Rule 153A. When used as entry word, cities and towns in the United States and Canada are followed by the name of the state or province, in accepted abbreviated form.

Rule 153B. Cities and towns other than those in United States and Canada are followed by the name of the country not by the name of the province or smaller division or region. The name of the region is used for cities and towns in areas whose political jurisdiction has been unstable, as, for example, Sardinia.

Designation follows the local usage if distinctive.

The name of the country is used in direct form even though inverted in its own entry.

Rule 153C. Enter largest or best-known city by its name, in America or elsewhere, without further designation.

Vat Rule 99. The name of the country and the Italian term of the local unit are added to the name of the district, after a comma and in italics. The name of the country is not added to Italian districts.

Rule 100. Cities and towns, villages, hamlets, and manors are given in the vernacular, followed by the name of the country. For larger and better known cities, the name of the country is not necessary.

Ccc does not give corresponding prescriptions. In its view, they are not necessary. The information prescribed by the rules of

Ala and *Vat* violate the Canon of Relevance. Unless the name of the country or state is necessary to resolve a homonym, the purpose of giving it in the heading of a catalogue entry is not seen. No doubt, it is correct geographical information. But it is not the business of the heading in a catalogue entry to give it. It will be in its place if it is given in a postal directory for writing addresses.

5262 HISTORICAL INFORMATION

Ala Rule 154C. For countries or other political units in which a different government needs to be specified in the heading for official publications, add to the usual name of the unit a word or phrase designating the period covered.

Publications of the colonial and territorial periods of states of the United States are distinguished by the designation " Colony " or " Ter ".

Vat Rule 95. Countries and peoples which have had periods both of independence and foreign domination are entered under their present name with the various governmental changes designated in parentheses. This form is used for government publications during the various periods, but in subject headings the simple name is used for works about a country, and the necessary period subdivisions are added.

Ala and *Vat*, in effect, appear to treat the name of one and the same geographical area in conditions of different political status, as if they are homonyms. To resolve such a homonym, they prescribe either the period in inclusive years of the political status, or its equivalent in descriptive terms, as the individualising element. This is no doubt correct political information. But, is it the business of the heading of a catalogue entry to carry the load of such political information ? In the view of *Ccc*, change of political status is no more different, from the angle of the rendering of heading in a catalogue entry, then change of personal status of a person. It is not the business of the heading to give information about status. Giving of such information violates the Canon of Relevance.

There is, however, a misleading element in this situation. A country or any other geographical territory is immortal. The number of entries with the name of any given geographical area in the heading will be great. It will keep on growing to inconveniently great dimensions. The effect of the prescription of *Ala* and *Vat* is to sort out such entries into smaller sub-groups. But really speaking, such a sorting out is the business of classification and not of cataloguing. The further details of this problem are better discussed under corporate name heading and subject heading. This will be done in sections 53, 593 and their sub-divisions.

53 Governmental Heading

5301 *Rdc*

Rdc Rule 46. Enter under places (countries, or parts of countries, cities towns, ecclesiastical, military, or judicial districts) the works published officially by their " rulers " (kings, governors, mayors, prelates, generals commanding, courts, etc.).

The inclusion of " judicial districts ", among the place names to be used as heading, is not correct. Because, a court is only an organ of a government. *Rdc* itself is conscious of this fault. For, it adds in a foot-note, " the relation of courts to judicial districts is a little different from the others, but it is convenient to treat them alike ". Indeed, the example given under the rule makes the name of the place merely the main heading ; and the name of the court, which is but an organ, is rightly given as sub-heading. It can be true only of a court with national jurisdiction. But, for a local court, it is not proper to use the local name as heading. In fact, all these remarks apply equally to " the works published officially by rulers ". For a ruler too is but an organ of the government. In modern times he is not the whole government. This small fault in *Rdc* should not be made much of. For to *Rdc* goes the credit of having boldly established the tradition of naming a government by the name of its territory.

5302 *Pin*

As it has been already stated in section 2232, sub-paragraph 2, *Pin* does not recognize corporate authorship in general, and governmental authorship in particular.

5303 *Ala*

Ala Rule 72. Enter under countries or nations, states, cities, towns, and other government districts, official publications issued by them or by their authority.

Ala's Rule avoids the fault in the rule of *Rdc*. But there are two terms in it which require attention. " Nations " does not fit in with the other terms in the Rule. It is a sociological term. It is not a geographical term. It should be removed from the list. " Government districts " is a homonymous term. At any rate its meaning is not definite. This term is not always used to denote the territory of a local government. In India, for example, it is

181

used to denote an administrative district of the government of the territory within which it falls—*e.g.*, revenue district, judicial district, postal district and so on. Surely, the revenue authority, the court, and the post office have no governmental function over their respective districts. They are only organs of the government of the whole territory, discharging the function of the government over a specified strip of the territory. It is again a creature of administration. In other words, it is an organ of the territory.

The phrase " by their authority " may mislead cataloguers. This is discussed in section 224 and its sub-sections.

Vat Rule 104. Official publications of government (national, provincial, municipal, etc.) and of special districts, (ecclesiastical, judicial, military, etc.) are entered under the name of the country, city, province, local district, etc. from which they emanate.

Vat's rule has combined the faults in the rules of *Rdc* and of *Ala*. Due to historical reasons, Roman Catholic ecclesiastical polity often runs independently of secular polity. Therefore, there is justification for the inclusion of the term " ecclesiastical " among " the authorities of special districts ". But the other authorities are merely organs of the government of the larger territory within which their respective territories fall. The clause " from which they emanate " is not happy. It is not clear what " which " stands for. Surely, the intention is " Governments ".

5305 *Ccc*

Ccc Rule 1231. If the Corporate Author is a government as a whole, the Heading is to consist of the name (in the language of the library) of the Geographical Area whose affairs are governed or administered by it.

This is a fool-proof prescription. The conscious or unconscious confusion between " government as a whole " and an " organ of it " is completely removed. It may be added further that the confusion is further eliminated by *Ccc* having given a precise definition of the term " government " in rule 1230. As a matter of fact, the confusion and the looseness of drafting in the other codes arise out of neglect to fix the terminology precisely, as a preliminary step. This has been already dwelt upon in chapter 2 of this book.

5308 Organ

When the author is not the whole government but only an organ of it, the main heading is the name of the government itself— *i.e.*, the name of its territory. The sub-headings are to be added according to prescribed rules. This is explicitly prescribed by *Ccc* in the following rule :—

Ccc Rule 123108. If the Corporate Author is not the Government as a whole but a dependent body of it, sub-headings are to be added according to the following and analogous rules.

The rules following the above one prescribe the rendering of the names of different organs of government as sub-heading. The term, "dependent Body" has been giving trouble in interpreting the rules. Even when the third edition of *Ccc* was published in 1951, no way could be found out of this difficulty. It is only, while writing this book, that this difficulty could be traced to failure to define precisely the meaning of the term "Dependent Body". We have now introduced the term "Organ" as a generic term to denote all the parts of government covered by the rules referred to in Rule 123108. Organ of a corporate body has now been differentiated from Institution dependent on Government, for its existence or finance. For this see 2285. And the various kinds of organs of a corporate body have also been defined and distinguished in sections 2221 to 2228.

The other codes have not given any such enabling rule, in general terms, to provide the name of an organ of a Government as a sub-heading.

531 Head

5311 *Rdc*

Rdc has no special rule for adding a sub-heading when the author is the head of government and not the whole government.

5313 *Ala*

Ala Rule 73A. Enter collections of messages to legislative bodies, proclamations, executive orders, and similar documents of sovereigns, presidents, governors, etc., covering more than one administration, under the name of the country or other jurisdiction, followed by the name of the office.

The clumsy need for repeating the phrase "under the name of the country" in each of the rules dealing with organs of government is due to the absence of a generic rule for all such government publications, such as the one given in *Ccc* Rule 123108.

Rule 73B. For single messages to legislative bodies, proclamations, executive orders, etc., include in the heading the inclusive years of the administration or reign and in parentheses, the name of the incumbent.

This Rule prescribes an individualising element as if the name of the office of the " Head of Government " is a homonym. Is it truly a homonym ?

It is not so in fact. Then, why does *Ala* prescribe an element resembling an individualising element? Probably the reason is as follows :—The office of the " Head of Government ", is virtually eternal. The number of documents with the Head of Government as author is never-ending. It grows from year to year. The titles under it as the heading are many—inconveniently many. These titles do not have sharp names. They are far too flabby and fussy. The potency of the first few words in such a title is negligibly small, in the arrangement of the title. Nor do these first few words stick to one's mind. In these circumstances, how is a reader to locate the one title he wants ? When there is an enormous number of items to search through, the human mind strives to sort out the items, on the basis of some convenient characteristic, into smaller subheads. This is an inherent and involuntary tendency of the human mind. In this case, the items to be sorted out or classified are titles. Obviously, one of the characteristics, that suggest themselves as a basis for classifying the titles in question, is the choronological characteristic. This accounts for *Ala*'s prescription "include in the heading the inclusive years of the administration or reign." The second individualising element— *viz.*, " the name of the incumbent "—is redundant. One of these two elements is sufficient. To give both is to violate the Law of Parsimony. But the *Ala* is in a dilemma. It is the name of the incumbent that is usually remembered by the reader. But its use as individualising element will scatter the documents according to the alphabetical idiosyncrasies of the names. In an alphabetical catalogue this alphabetical scattering is helpful. And a Dictionary Catalogue is an essentially alphabetical catalogue. But the classificatory urge of the human mind is inexorable. A chronological arrangement satisfies this urge better than an alphabetical one. The *Ala* has succumbed to it. The result is the usual formation of a classified pocket in a Dictionary Catalogue !

The proper course is to divide the catalogue into two parts :— The classified part to take full and exhaustive care of classificatory urge, and the alphabetical part to satisfy alphabetical approach and to serve as an alphabetical key to the classified part. Division of function is always conducive to clarity and economy. It marks a higher stage of evolution. Nature demonstrates it in living bodies and in social economy. It is so even in cataloguing too. We are thus forced to recognise the higher stage of Classified Catalogue as compared to Dictionary Catalogue.

Let us see how the titles with the head of government as author will get handled in classified catalogue. Without any loss of generality, we may take the concrete example of the documents with the sovereign of Great Britain as author. These will fall in two classes—serial and independent books. If Colon Classification is used the former will get the number V56,1:8m. Each of the volumes of the serial will get a book number made up of its year of publication. Thus the classified part will automatically arrange the successive volumes of the serial in the desired chronological sequence. If there be a second serial, its number will be V56, 1:8m1. This set will stand next to the first set. And the successive volumes of the second set also will appear in the classified part in the desired chronological sequence. Each serial will have two index entries :—(1) under the heading " Great Britain, Sovereign ", followed by the title of the serial, and (2) under the title of the serial as heading. Thus, whatever be the approach of the reader, he can readily locate an entry about the document. Let us consider next an independent document, say, one issued by Queen Anne in 1714. Its class number will be V56,1:8·L14 Similarly, each of the documents having the British sovereign as the author will get its own distinctive call number. This will arrange the documents in question in the desired chronological sequence. Even if there is later edition of the above-mentioned document, say, in 1955, its number will be V56,1:8·L14 N54. Thus, this edition will get arranged along with the first edition. For a reader making an alphabetical approach, the documents will be all arranged alphabetically under the heading " Great Britain. Sovereign ". On the other hand, a reader making a classified approach will get the key to enter the appropriate region of the classified part, through the entry in the alphabetical card having the heading " Archives. Sovereign. Great Britain ". The entry with this heading will ask the reader to look up the class number V56,1:8. When he looks up that class number, he will

12

find, arranged chronologically, all the documents of which the author has been a British sovereign. Even if the reader is not able to think of " archives ", but at least think of " Sovereign " which is the substantive word related to " Royal "—and he is likely to think of the documents as royal proclamations or royal messages—, he will be directed by the related entry in the alphabetical index to look up V56,1 in the classified part. Thus, again, the reader will get his entry whatever be his approach.

5314 Vat

Vat has no rule in the subject.

5315 Ccc

Ccc Rule 12311. If the Corporate Author is the Crown the first subheading is to consist of the term ' Crown ' or other equivalent term or designation according to the government in question. The second subheading is to be the name of the person holding the office, the name being written in accordance with the Rule 121 and its subdivisions, except that the descriptive term, if any is to be omitted. If deemed necessary, the period of office expressed as inclusive years in Arabic numerals may be added.

All but the first sentence should be omitted. In this rule, *Ccc* has blindly capitulated to the *Ala* tradition. As already explained in the commentary on the corresponding *Ala* rule, the last two sentences of this Rule of *Ccc* will completely nullify the alphabetical purpose of the alphabetical index. It will merely reproduce imperfectly and clumsily the very sequence in which the classified part features the documents in question. This is a violation of the Law of Parsimony.

532 Executive

Ccc Rule 12312. If the corporate author is the executive, the subheading is to be the name of the executive.

    Ex.—**Great Britain. Cabinet.**

No other code has a rule on the rendering of the executive of a government in author heading.

533 Legislature

5331 *Rdc*

Rdc Rule 47. Enter under the place the journals, minutes, acts, laws, etc., of Congress, Parliament, and other " Legislative Bodies ".

    Ex.—**France,** *Corps Legislatif.*

Rdc has not made its rule complete. Its rule prescribes merely the main heading. It does not prescribe the subheading. This has to be inferred from the example.

5333 *Ala*

Ala Rule 74. Enter the proceedings of sessions, debates, reports etc., (but not " acts " or laws), of legislative bodies under the name of the government with the name of the body as subheading, subdivided as needed by date of session and/or branch ... In the case of the United States Congress, when dates are given, give also the number of the Congress and the session.

All the arguments against the introduction of the " date of session " given in the commentary in section 531 hold good in this case also.

5334 *Vat*

Vat Rule 112. Publication of parliament and legislative ... bodies are entered under the name of the country in Italian, followed by their special names. in vernacular. Local government bodies are treated in the same way except, that the name of the place is given in vernacular... The separate houses of a legislative body are entered under the name of the legislature.

Ex.—1 **Italia. Parlamento.**
2 **Italia. Parlamento. Senato.**
3 **Italia. Parlamento. Camera dei Deputati.**

The examples bring out the intention of the rule clearly. In the two later examples, the intermediate subheading " Parlamento " is made compulsory. What is the purpose served by this ? The author of the document is presumably the *Senato*. This subheading is therefore necessary. The name of the government is *Italia*. Therefore, it should form the main heading. An inter_mediate subheading between these two will be necessary only as an individualising element, if the name of the organ, which is the author, is a homonym. In this case, " Senato " is not a homonym. Therefore the intermediate subheading " Parlamento " violates the Canon of Relevance as well as the Law of Parsimony. Surely, it is not the business of a heading of a catalogue entry to inform the reader, by implication or suggestion, that the legislature has sub-organs or that it is bicameral.

Ccc Rule 12313. If the Corporate Author is the legislature, the subheading is to be the name of the Legislature.

Explicit or implicit indication of all the codes is that the name of the legislature should be in the language found on the title-page.

Ccc is able to make its rule simple because it has prescribed the main heading in a separate Rule *viz.*, Rule 123108. Therefore, the rule on legislature has to prescribe only the subheading.

534 Administrative Department
5341 *Rdc*

Rdc Rule 324. In arranging government publications make all necessary divisions but avoid sub-divisions.

This rule is too laconic. *Rdc* itself seems to have sensed this. It therefore gives a long commentary and a number of examples. Here are some extracts :—

It is much clearer—and it is the dictionary plan—to make the parts of a division themselves independent divisions.

> *Ex.*—**United States. Navigation, Bureau** of ; *and not*
> **United States. Department of the Navy. Bureau of Navigation.**

There are, however, certain divisions or sections which have no independent existence and should be subordinate as *Division of Statistics* under several departments or bureaus, and the various divisions of the Library of Congress (*Catalogue division, Order division*).

The subordination of bureaus and offices to departments is adopted simply for convenience, and is changed from time to time as the exigencies of the public service demand. There is no corresponding convenience in preserving such an order in a catalogue, but inconvenient, especially in the case of the above-mentioned changes. The alphabetical arrangement has here all its usual advantages without its usual disadvantage of wide separation.

Rdc has, as a pioneer, argued out the position on the basis of robust commonsense. Eighty years later, we see how unerring its intuition had been. In modern terminology, it amounts to saying "Make the name of the territory the main heading. Make the name of the particular organ concerned the essential sub-heading, whatever be its remove from the parent body. If this sub-heading is homonymous, insert between it and the main heading the name of an appropriate organ of lesser remove, as an additional sub-heading. In each sub-heading, follow the Canon of Prepotence. Generic words, such as bureau, department and ministry, are virtually impotent. Therefore, invert the words in the name of the organ, so that the potent element becomes the Entry Element in the sub-heading. It usually demotes the subject-jurisdiction of the organ. The remaining words in the name of the organ form the Secondary Element. As usual, subordinate the Secondary Element in dominance of style ". This will be made clear in the rules of *Ccc* given in section 5345.

5343 *Ala*

Ala Rule 75. Enter executive departments, ministries and secretariate as sub-headings under the country or other jurisdiction.

Rule 75A. Enter bureaus or offices subordinate to an executive department, ministry, or secretariate directly under the name of the jurisdiction, not as a sub-heading under the department, ministry or secretariate.

When, however, the bureau or office does not have distinctive name so that one of the same name might exist in another department, enter under the department.

Ala Rules virtually follow the *Rdc* rules. The second paragraph of rule 75A is not fully expressive of the intention. The intention is seen in the examples given. There, the name of the department is made the first sub-heading and the name of the bureau also is made the second sub-heading.

This lacuna in the rule should be removed. Moreover, *Ala* violates the Canon of Prepotence. It is not easy to see why the correct lead given by *Rdc* half century earlier has not been followed. However, *Ala* puts, in its examples, the inverted form of the name of the organ as the referred-from heading in a cross reference index entry.

Rule 75B. Divisions, regional offices and other units of departments, bureaus, commissions, etc., subordinate to these departments, bureaus, commissions, etc., are usually entered, if required, as sub-headings to the departments, bureaus, commissions, etc.

Drafting cannot be more verbose or indefinite than this. A correct definition of organ and of different removes of organs, as a preliminary step in the chapter on terminology would have made the rule clearer.

5344 *Vat*

Vat Rule 106*a* and *b* practically follow the *Ala* Rules 75 and its sub-division quoted in section 5343. There is, however, a paragraph of some value in *Vat*'s Rule. It reads :—

Two objectives in every case should be kept in mind in selecting the entry for government publications ; complicated and over-long headings should be avoided ; and the specific character of an office should be brought out when this is not already apparent from its name.

This directive is rather vague. It is based on allergy rather than on objective normative principles.

5345 *Ccc*

Ccc Rule 12314. If the Corporate Author is a Department of Administration or any of the sub-divisions of a Department, the sub-heading is to consist of the name of that specific body, provided the name of that specific body does not occur also as the name of a sub-division of some other department.

Rule 123141. If there is no special name for the specific body, the designation of its officer is to be used as its name.

Rule 123142. The word or group of words in the name of the specific body indicating the sphere of work is to be written first and the other words in the name are to be added thereafter (according to the general rules on the style of writing).

Rule 123143. If two or more sub-divisions of one and the same department have the same name, they are to be individualised by the addition of a word or a group of words which may be one of the following :—

1 The geographical area over which the sub-division has jurisdiction, if the sub-division is made on geographical basis.

2 The main function of the sub-division, if the sub-division is made on a functional basis ;

3 The name of the headquarters of the sub-division, if the sub-divisions are usually or more conveniently individualised that way ; and

4 Any other word or group of words that may be appropriate, necessary and sufficient.

Rule 12315. If the Corporate Author is a sub-division of a Department, whose name occurs also as the sub-division of some other Department, the first sub-heading is to consist of the name of that body in the hierarchy of Department, Division, Sub-division and so on, which is the least remove from the specific body which is the author and admits of being used as a sub-heading under Rule 12314. The second sub-heading is the name of the body in the hierarchy which comes next to what contributes the first sub-heading and so on with the third and further sub-headings until the name of the specific body which is the name of the author, is reached.

Rule 123151. The words in each sub-heading are to be rendered and written on the analogy of rules 123141 and 123142.

Ccc spells out in detail the implications of *Rdc* Rule 324.

Rule 12314 is new. It is a necessary rule. It has not been given in the other codes. The ways of resolving homonyms, given in this Rule arc on helpful lines.

But *Ccc* Rule 12315 over-reaches the objective. Its objective is to resolve homonym. For this purpose, it may not always be necessary to put in as sub-heading, the name of each one of the bodies in the hierarchy mentioned. In some cases, it will violate at once the Law of Parsimony and the Canon of Relevance. This fault can be removed by the addition of the following sentence at the end of that rule :—

Ccc Rule 12315 (last sentence). The number of intermediate sub-headings so added should be the minimum necessary to resolve the homonym.

With the use of the terms, " organ " and " remove ", Rule 12315 can be made less verbose. It can be re-stated as follows :—

Ccc Rule 12315. When the name of the organ which is the author is a homonym, the name(s) of the necessary and sufficient number of organ(s) of lesser remove are to be inserted as intermediate sub-headings.

In one of the Seminars of the Department of Library Science of the University of Delhi, it was argued on behalf of the Law of Parsimony that the Secondary Element in the name of an organ of a government—particularly of an administrative department—may be omitted. The argument used was on the following lines :—The rendering of the name of a government and any of its organs is made artificially by cataloguing convention. This convention retains in the main heading only the potent word *viz*., the name of the territory of jurisdiction. This convention ignores the Secondary Element, such as " Government of." Is it not desirable to slim the sub-heading also similarly ? Can we not have a convention that in rendering the name of an administrative department, it is sufficient to have only the Entry Element, *viz*., the subject of jurisdiction of the department ? Can we not ignore the Secondary Element, such as, " Ministry of." " Department of," and " Bureau of " ? The result will be as follows :—

India. Education *and not*
India. Education (Ministry of).

A serious difficulty arose. Such a proposal was found to create a homonym. The heading " India. Education " may mean either the author heading " Ministry of Education of the Government of India," or the subject heading " Education in India ."

Both the Corporate Author Heading and the Subject Heading are the creation of cataloguing convention. Each of them constitutes an artificial language. It is improper and unwise to let homonyms to come into an artificial language specially designed by the cataloguing profession. Thus the seminar decided against the simplification proposed for propitiating the Law of Parsimony.

535 Judiciary

Rdc Rule 46. Enter under judicial districts the works published officially by their courts.

Ala Rule 89A. Enter courts under their names (statutory titles) as sub-headings under the countries, states, etc., from which they derive their authority.

Vat Rule 121a. Supreme courts are entered under the name of the country, followed by their special title ; provincial courts under the name of the province ; and local courts under the name of the locality.

Ccc Rule 12316. If the Corporate Author is a Court of Law, the sub-heading is to be the name of Court.

All the codes agree in making the court a sub-heading. As

shown in its Rule 54, *Rdc* also means this. The example given under this Rule shows it. But what should be the main heading ? Here all the four codes do not agree. *Rdc* and *Vat* go together; *Ala* and *Ccc* go together. Further, *Ala* and *Ccc* do not agree totally.

Ala prescribes the name of the government, from which a court derives its authority, for use as main heading. The application of this will require a knowledge of the Constitution Act of each country. Even then, this may give unhelpful results. For example, the High Court of a Constituent State of India " derives its authority " from the Union Government of India. Its judges receive their Instrument of Instruction from the President of India. The court itself has been created by the Constitution Act of the Union Government. Then, according to the prescription of *Ala* all the High Courts in India should be entered with " India " as the main heading. Each should be individualised by adding the name of the Counstituent State as the individualising term. A more helpful view seems to be to view a high court as a constitutional organ of the government of the constituent state itself. Here is a parallel. The legislature of a constituent state is also created by the Constitution Act of the Union Government. And yet none of the codes prescribe that the main heading for a state legislature should be " India " and not the name of the state. This is because a state legislature is a constitutional organ of the government of the state. Again, a Borough Council is created by an Act of Parliament. But, the main heading for its entry is only the name of the borough. This is prescribed because it is an organ of the local government of the borough. The same argument holds good also in the case of High Court. Thus, the main heading for the High Court of a constituent state should be the name of the state itself, and not " India ."

In applying the Rules of *Ccc*, the above-mentioned result is got by reading Rule 12316 with Rule 123108. The latter Rule asks the question, " Of what government is the High Court, say of Bengal, the organ ? " The question is not, " Which government created it " ? Obviously the answer to the first question is " Bengal." With this answer given by Rule 123108, Rule 12316 can only be interpreted to mean that the heading for a document of the High Court of Bengal should be rendered as

Bengal. High Court *and not as*
India. High Court. Bengal.

But a local court within a constituent state does not form a constitutional organ of the " government of the locality," unless it happens to be a court established for the discharge of judicial functions vested in the Local Body. The courts in the different districts and towns are not established; they are established by the constituent state for such a purpose for the discharge of its own judicial functions. They, therefore, form an organ of the High Court, which itself is an organ of the constituent state.

Vat's prescription—it makes explicit the implied prescription of *Rdc* and therefore *Rdc*'s prescription also—that the heading of local court should be the name of the locality would be faulty if it is applied to cases where the court is not a constitutional organ of the local body.

5351 DIVISION OF A COURT

Ccc Rule 123161. If a Division or a Department of a Court is the Corporate Author, a second sub-heading is to be added consisting of the name of the specific body written on the analogy of the sub-divisions of Rules 12314 and 12315.

Rule 123162. If a sub-division of a Division or a Department of a Court is the Corporate Author, a third sub-heading is to be added on the analogy of Rule 123161 ; and so on in the case of further sub-division.

The other codes do not give a rule on this subject.

Ala, however, indicates concurrence with *Ccc*'s Rule, through an example given under its own Rule 89A.

The Law of Parsimony would, however, challenge, the prescription of *Ccc*. It would ask, " Should the name of the parent court be inserted as a sub-heading before the name of the branches of that court ? " It would argue that this is not necessary unless it is needed to resolve a homonym created by the name of a Branch Court. Let us take the King's Bench Division of Great Britain. This name is not borne by any other court of the country. Therefore, it should be sufficient to render the heading as,

Great Britain. King's Bench Division. *and not as*
Great Britain. High Court of Justice. King's Bench Division.

The Law of Parsimony would support this. The old blind tradition of having the latter heading should be given up. If the object is to bring together the documents by all the divisions of the High Court, it is the business of classification to secure it and not that of the catalogue.

5352 HOMONYM

Ccc Rule 1231601.   If two or more Courts of Law of the same Government have similar names, they are to be individualised by the addition of a word or group of words denoting their respective areas of jurisdiction; or, if such areas are not definite or are not conveniently named, denoting their respective headquarters or giving any other appropriate individualising features.

The other codes do not give a rule on this subject.

Ala, however, indicates concurrence with the *Ccc*'s Rule through the examples given under its own Rule 89A.

Vat by-passes homonyms of this kind, since it prescribes the name of the locality and not of the territory of the sovereign power, as the main heading. *Rdc* too should be taken to have done so.

Ccc resolves the homonym by the addition of an individualising element in the usual way.

5353 Joint-Court

Ala Rule 89B.   Enter joint courts of two or more governments under the name of the court followed by the name of the place if there is a permanent seat.

A note under the above Rule gives the following information :—

Exception has been made by the Library of Congress for the Permanent Court of Arbitration and the Permanent Court of International Justice, both located at the Hague and entered under the place.

No other code has given a Rule on this subject.

54 Institution
540 Basic Rule

5401 *Rdc*

Rdc Rule 61.   Enter corporations and quasi-corporations both English and foreign under their names as they read, neglecting an initial article or serial number when there is one.

Specification

This includes associations, societies, clubs, guilds (Rule 72), business firms (Rule 74), institutes, private schools (Rule 87), colleges and universities (Rules 65, 75, 76, 80), libraries (Rule 77), galleries (Rule 77), museums (Rule 77). Ecclesiastical organisations, churches (Rule 81), convents, monasteries (Rule 83), and all similar bodies, provided they have an individual name.

Rdc Rule 61 is reduced to very limited application by its Rules 71 to 84. *Rdc* Rules 71 to 73 prescribe the use of the dominant word(s) in the name as the entry word(s). Rules 75 to 81, 83 and 84 prescribe the name of the place of the institution as the entry word respectively in the case of academy, university, library, museum, gallery, observatory, exposition, church, monastery, convent and National Bank—unless they have a distinctive name.

5403 Ala

Ala defines "institution" to include only bodies coming under the rules of *Rdc* that prescribe name of place as entry word. The definition excludes the other bodies. These other bodies are called "Societies." *Ala* prescribes for a society more or less in the same way as *Rdc* Rule 61. Moreover, the Canons of Ascertainability and Permanence, and the Law of Parsimony are violated by the prescription of the latest name.

Ala Rule 91. Enter a society under the first word (not an article) of its latest corporate name.

Rule 92. Enter an institution (using the latest name) under the name of the place in which it is located.

Ala Rule 92A. Enter an institution of the United States or of the British Empire whose name begins with a proper noun or with a proper adjective under the first word of its name... For countries other than the United States and the British Empire follow the general rule of the entry under the place.

This exception has not been applied to tax-supported schools (Rule 107) nor to Carnegie, Passmore-Edwards and similar public libraries which because of their number as well as the nature of their grants and endowments tend to become better known, at least outside of their immediate neighbourhood, by the name of the city in which they are located than by their own name. Where only the building is a private donation, the library being otherwise endowed and supported by public taxation the presumption is particularly strong in favour of entry under the place.

To avoid doubt or complications in the order of filing, it has been found expedient to write the names of institutions beginning with the name of a place (city), in the form of entry under place, with sub-division.

Exception might be made, however, in names long established and well-known.

Colleges and other institutions named after Luther may be regarded as a group and entered under the conventional rather than the official form of name "Luther College," followed by name of place.

Rule 104. Enter state and provincial institutions of the United States and Canada under the name of the state or province. The name of the State or Province is to be followed by a period and the next word capitalised.

When the name of the institution begins with the name of the city in which it is located, transpose to the end of the entry.

There are certain institutions which, although not strictly official, *i.e.*, maintained and controlled by the state, are, on account of their names, most frequently looked for under the name of the state. These may best be entered according to the above rule.

195

Exception may be made in favour of entry under its own name for a state institution having a distinctive name which gives no indication of its relation to the state.

Rule 105. Enter American state historical and agricultural societies under the name of the state whether or not it is the first word of the name of the society. If the corporate name begins with the name of the state, the corporate form is to be followed ; if not, the name of the state is to be followed by a period.

Enter American state societies which are also state boards under the name of the societies.

Rule 106A. Enter agricultural experiment stations of the United States under the name of the states or territory in which they are organised. Include in the heading the name of the place where the station is located.

Rule 106B. Enter Canadian agricultural experiment stations under " Canada." Include the name of the place in the heading.

Rule 106C. Enter foreign agricultural experiment stations according to the general rule for institutions (Rule 92).

There are 14 rules forming exceptions to the basic Rule 92. Some rules are exceptions to exception ! One rule is an exception to an exception to an exception !! How is a reader to know the entry word of the main entry under which he should look up the catalogue for an institution ? How is the cataloguer himself to get guided through this maze ? Is it all merely a case of Local Variation ? No. It does not seem to be so. Surely, the rendering of the name of an institution in a main entry needs simplification. *Ala* itself seems to be doubtful of a cataloguer knowing when Rule 92 is operative. Therefore, it gives quite a number of redundant rules. Here is a list :—

Ala Rule 107 (Public Schools)
     Rule 108 (Private and Endowed Schools)
     Rule 109 [Indian Schools (U.S.A.)]
     Rule 110 (Radio Stations)
     Rule 111 (University and Union League Clubs)
     Rule 112 (Volunteer Fire Companies and Associations)
     Rule 113 (Mercantile Library Associations)
     Rule 114 (Gilds).

No advantage appears to be gained by such a complicated set of rules. This tradition need not be perpetuated. The distinction between 'society' and 'institution' may be dissolved.

5404 *Vat*

Vat virtually follows *Ala*. It has, however, an important new rule. There is no such provision in any other code. The following is the rule :—

Vat Rule 136c. Ancient institutions whose official or precise name is not known are entered under the name of the place followed by a fictitious name which indicates the nature and scope of the institution.

Ex. **Delphi. Oracolo.**

5405 *Ccc*

Ccc Rule 1232. If the Corporate Author is an institution as a whole, the Heading is to consist of the name of the institution. If the name occurs in many languages, that in the favoured language of the library and if it does not occur, that in the language, which occurs and is the earliest in the scale of languages of the library, is to be chosen.

Ccc makes no difference between society and institution. This has been already discussed in section 2282. For all corporate bodies other than a government (which includes local body in its definition) and conference, it prescribes the name of the body as the heading. Avoidance of using the name of a place as main heading and the name of the institution only as sub-heading has made its rule simple. It is easy to apply. It is equally easy for a reader to get familiar with the rendering.

Why do *Rdc*, *Ala*, and *Vat* disturb the hornet's nest by prescribing the name of place as main heading ? Various considerations might have led them to it. They are explained in the succeeding sections.

54051 HOMONYM

Probably, fear of homonym might have been a reason. Many institutions have the same name.—*e.g.*, Public library, Post office, Elementary school. These will occur as homonyms in large numbers. These homonyms can be best resolved by the addition of the name of the place as individualising term. So far, it is right. But the individualising term cannot be given greater dominance than the name of the body individualised. It should not be given the status of Entry Word. It should be added only at the end of the heading. *Rdc* seems to recognise it. *Rdc*'s Rules 85 and 86 deny entry under place to Y M C A, Mercantile Library Association and benevolent or moral or similar society. This is of significance in this connection. The commentaries under this rule emphasise the unhelpfulness of putting the name of the place as the Entry Word, instead of adding it at the end merely as an individualising term. Here are the commentaries :—

It has been usual to enter these under the name of the place, but this is objectionable because (*a*) it is an exception to the rule, (*b*) such societies are known in their own home by their own names (no one in Northampton, would ever think of looking for the Smith Charities or the Home Cultural Club under Northampton) ; the reasons (for Y M C A etc.) are the same.

It is curious that the foot-note of *Ala*, given as paragraph 2 under Rule 92A should argue just in the opposite way. It argues that Carnegie Library, for example, should be entered under the name of the place as main heading, because such libraries tend to become better known, at least outside of their immediate neighbourhood, by the name of the city ". Anyhow, the pioneer *Rdc* thinks just the opposite way.

54052 Change in Name

In spite of such a clear analysis, why does *Rdc* prescribe name of place as main heading for a university, school, church, bank, etc. ? Perhaps, it is for the reason that the name of such a body is not quite definitely remembered. The official or statutory name may be one. The name by which it is currently and popularly known may be another. The " University of Madras " is the statutory name. But people may generally call it " Madras University ". *Ccc* would argue as follows :—The heading of the main entry should be decided by the Canon of Ascertainability. Any alternative name likely to be brought up by readers should be used only as the heading of a cross reference index entry, exactly as has to be done in the case of an alternative name of a personal author.

54053 Resulting Creation of Homonym

Thus, fear of homonym and of alternative name cannot be sufficient reason for making the name of place the main heading and relegating the name-proper of an institution to the status of sub-heading. Apart from this, there is a third reason which makes it undesirable. That reason is adduced by the Canon of Prepotence. After all, the rendering of the name of a corporate author is based strictly on convention to be established by the cataloguing profession. It is not like the name of a personal author. This is given by others. This has got to be accepted by the cataloguing profession. The cataloguing profession has freedom to make its own convention for the rendering of the name of a corporate body in a helpful way. When building this convention of its own, the cataloguing profession should avoid the introduction of homonymous main headings. All the codes including *Rdc,* *Ala, Vat* and *Ccc* agree in making the name of place the main heading when the corporate author is a government including a local body. It is therefore desirable that, for no other corporate body, the main heading—artificially improvised by rules—should be prescribed to be the name of a place. *Rdc* appears to be conscious of this. For, in the commentary introducing the section " place preferred " just before its Rule 75, it says,

Note that the entries under place in rules 46-58 (on governmental authorship) are very different from those in rules 76-84 (for institutional authorship). The former are made because the place (country, city, or town) is the author of the work ; in the latter the place *is not the author* (italics are mine) but is taken for heading so that the entry may be more easily found.

54054 "More Easily Found"

The arguments like " more easily found " and " public's preference " are often the result of the boomerang action of a rule established in the days of inexperienced empiricism, without aid from normative principles because of their absence. When the cycle of scientific method is established and normative principles have been enunciated to guide the framing of catalogue code, it is necessary to draw the line in the right place between a conservative regard for custom and a wish to lead the public toward a desirable simplicity and consistency. In this case, it is desirable to accept the Canon of Ascertainability. If necessary, custom and the cult of " public's preference " may be propitiated by a cross reference index entry from the name of place, until a new generation of readers is raised, quite attuned to look for the name of an institution under its name itself. But custom should no longer be allowed to interfere with the heading of the main entry itself. They should not be given the right to cut off the sheet-anchor of cataloguing—*viz.*, the Canon of Ascertainability in the plane of principle and the title-page in the material plane.

541 Homonym

Ala Rule 91B (3). When necessary for identification in cases where headquarters of a society are not given, the name of the country, state, province, etc., is added.

Rule 91C. When two or more societies in the same place have the same name distinguish them by dates in the heading.

Rule 144C. If a firm is known only by the name of the owner or founder, add the designation " Firm " to the heading to distinguish it from the same name as personal entry.

Ccc Rule 123201.   If the name of the Institution does not individualise it the Heading is to be augumented by an individualising word or group of words, added as a separate sentence.   This is to consist of—

1 The name of its place if it is a localised institution ; or
2 The name of the country to which the institution belongs if it is a national body ; or
3 The name of the province, district, taluk, state, county, or any such division of a country, if it is provincial, etc., body ; or
4 The name of its headquarters, if it cannot be individualised conveniently by 1, 2, or 3, above.

Rule 123202.   If individualisation is not attained by Rule 123201, the year of foundation may be given as a further individualising term written as a separate sentence.

Both the codes agree in substance.   But the wording in *Ccc* is more precise and clear.   But *Ccc* should incorporate the substance of *Ala* Rule 144C.   *Rdc* and *Vat* do not go into this question.

542 Over-Information

Ala Rule 91B (1).   If the name of the place does not appear in the corporate name, add it in the established form when the activities of the society are local or when the location is an aid to identification for societies of non-distinctive or similar names.

Rule 91B (2).   The city is not added, ordinarily, to the names of societies whose headquarters have changed, or whose membership is nation-wide and whose branches may be located in different places.   In general, for national societies in United States prefer the omission of the city ; for foreign societies, the addition of the city may serve also to distinguish the country to which the society belongs.

Vat Rule 140.   If the name of the place in which it is located is not an integral part of the corporate name, it is added to the heading in the vernacular and in italics.

The addition of the name of a place to the name of a society in the heading of a catalogue entry violates the Canon of Relevance. It is necessary only for the removal of a homonym.   Of course, it is always necessary in a directory.   Indeed, the involved wording of the rules of *Ala* and the variety of exceptions, indicate that these rules attempt to impose, on the heading of a catalogue entry, the function of a directory.   Such over-information should be avoided.

543 Omission, Inversion, etc.

5431 OMISSION

Rdc Rule 61.   Enter corporations ... under their names as they read, neglecting an initial article or serial number when there is one.

Rule 72.   Enter guilds under the name of the trade.

*Eg.—***Sationers Company.**   *And not*

Master and Keepers of Wardens and Commonality of the Mystery and Art of Stationers of the City of London.

Ala Rule 94.   A society or institution whose corporate name is so little used as to be practically unknown may be entered by a shorter better known form.

Ccc Rule 1232.   If the Corporate Author is an Institution as a whole, the Heading is to consist of the name of the Institution in the shortest form found on the title-page, half-title-page, or any other part of the book and omitting honorific words and puffs if any, at the end or beginning.

All these codes have seized the problem of impotent initial words and puffs where they may occur.   *Ccc* tries to reconcile the Canons of Prepotence and Ascertainability, as it is usual with it. But *Rdc* and *Ala* are prepared to go beyond the title-page and render the heading according to " popular usage."

5432 RETENTION AND OMISSION!

Vat Rule 127*b*.   Initial adjectives that denote privilege (such as *Reale, Imperiale,* etc., and the corresponding words in other languages) are abbreviated but not inverted, and are disregarded in filing.

This is the survival of an old tradition.   The tradition itself originated at a time when it was not realised that the language in the heading of an entry of a catalogue is an artificial one and not a natural language.   In speech and in ordinary writing, courtesy, politeness and perhaps even elegance require the retention of initial adjectives denoting " privilege."   But in a catalogue-heading, such an obligation does not arise.   Such words are impotent from the point of view of arrangement, because they are so few in number ;   and they may be the initial words in many names. Why should we add to the puzzle of readers by writing them at the beginning of entries and at the same time " disregarding them in arrangement " ? '   If they happen to be a significant part of the name of an institution as in Royal Society of London, and Royal Observatory of Greenwich, they ought to be written ;   and they should be counted as potent while filing ;   they should not be disregarded.   This is rightly provided for in the next Rule of *Vat* and in a Rule of *Ala*.

Vat Rule 127*c*.   The adjectives, " municipal ", " free ", etc., and the corresponding words in foreign languages are written in full and become part of the filing medium.   The same applies to the words " Royal ", " imperial ", etc., when they contribute to the specific part of the meaning.

Ala Rule 93B. Omit from the name of a society or institution, the adjective or abbreviation of an adjective denoting royal privilege, except (1) when it forms the distinguishing part of the name and (2) in English names. In foreign names the adjectives denoting a national body is not to be abbreviated. Adjectives denoting pontifical privilege are not to be omitted.

Ccc treats all honorific words alike. It omits them all without making any exception for a particular language such as English.

5433 Retention

Ala Rule 93C. Titles of honour, distinction, or address occurring at the beginning of the name of a society or institution are to be retained.

Rule 93D. Enter a society whose corporate name begins with a numeral under that name, with the numeral spelled out in the vernacular.

Rule 93F. Enter a society whose corporate name contains initials under the form of name used by the society, with explanation of the initials in brackets when necessary for clearness.

Rule 143. Enter foundations and endowments, funds, etc., under their names. Retain, at the beginning of the name, forenames and titles of honour, distinction, or address which are given in full ; initials of forenames and abbreviations of titles may be omitted.

These rules for retention of certain kinds of first words are in addition to those mentioned at the end of section of 5432.

5434 Inversion

Rdc Rule 71. When a corporation is much less known by the first words of a name than by a later part enter by the later part.

Ex.—**Christian Endeavour** (Young People's Society of).

Rule 73. Enter bodies whose legal name begins with such words as Board, Corporation, Trustees, under that part of the name by which they are usually known.

Ex.—**Harvard College** (President and Fellows of).

Rule 74. Enter the name of firm under the family name rather than the forename and do not fill out the forenames.

Ex.—**Friedlander und Sohn** (Raphael). *And not*
      Raphael Friedlander und Sohn.

Ala Rule 144*b*. The names of many foreign terms begin with the words or abbreviations denoting joint stock company. It is preferable in these cases to use an inverted form making entry under the first distinctive word.

Ala Rules 142 and 144A are similar to *Rdc* Rules 73 and 74. But Rule 142 adds the following exception :—

    If however a board is organised to administer the combined funds of several bodies, enter under its own name.

Vat Rule 138*c*. Inversion is used for French monasteries and abbeys whose names begin with " Notre-Dame de ".

These rules are in strict accord with the Canon of Prepotence. The elements recommended to be converted into Secondary Ele-

ment, though appearing at the beginning of the name of an institution, are impotent because of the smallness of their number and
the large number of names which may begin with them. The
observations of *Rdc* in a commentary on its Rule 74 is of significance.
It indicates the interdependence of " public usage " and the usage
unconsciously promoted by cataloguing convention in the light of
the Canons of Cataloguing. The conundrum " egg first or hen
first " applies here. *Rdc* rightly points out the double mind of
the public. The commentary reads as follows :—

This rule might be expected to include corporations, colleges, libraries, etc.,
whose legal names include forenames. Entry under a forename, as Silas Bronson,
Library, and especially under initials as T.B. Scott Public Library, is very awkward. But the public habit is not yet sufficiently settled to justify an exception.
I have never heard the Johns Hopkins University called the Hopkins University,
though the John Crerar Library is usually called Crerar Library.

To meet this inconsistent way in which the name of a corporate
body fixes itself in the memory of the public, *Ala* provides an exception under Rule 144A though it fails to do so similarly under
Rule 142. The following is the exception :—

Ala Rule 144A (Exception). Entry under forename may be preferred in a
few cases, favouring customary use.

Perhaps, Canon of Consistency may be satisfied in this place
also, by providing cross reference index entries to meet all cases of
exception.

Ccc does not deal with the various complications possible in
the name of an institution, provided for by the Rules of *Rdc* and
Ala. Its intention is evidently not to have recourse to invertion
in the name of an institution, but to follow strictly the Canon of
Ascertainability even in the sequence of the words, as given on the
title-page. As for other possible alternative approaches by readers,
it would satisfy them by cross reference index entries, as if they
were alternative names.

5435 INCORPORATED SOCIETY

Ala Rule 95. Omit in the heading for an incorporated society the term
indicating incorporation, unless that term is the initial word of the name or
forms a distinguishing part of it.

Rule 144. Enter firms, business corporations (including those owned by
governments), hotels, railway companies, etc. under the corporate name. The
terms incorporated (Inc), limited (Ltd), etc., or their equivalents if included in
the corporate name are to be retained.

The substance of this rule has been missed by the other codes.

544 Change of Name

Ala Rule 91A (1). When a society has changed its name, enter under the latest form.

Vat Rule 136a. Institutions which have changed or modified their name are entered under the latest form.

Rule 136b is redundant.

Rule 140. A society is entered under ... its present or latest title.

Rule 142 (last sentence) is redundant.

As usual, *Ala* and *Vat* violate at once the Canons of Ascertain-ability and Permanence and the Law of Parsimony. *Ccc* does not need a special rule to deal with change of name. The Canon of Ascertainability prescribes that the name occurring on the title-page should form the heading of main entry and all specific entries. It depends upon cross reference index entries to tie together the different names. *Ala* and *Vat* too do use cross reference index entries to tie up all the old names to the latest name.

545 International Body

Rdc Rule 62. Societies extending through many lands or having authorised names in several languages go under the English form of the name ;

     a but if no publications have appeared in English enter under the name in the language in which most of the publications have appeared ;

     b if publications have appeared successively in various foreign languages, but not in English, use the best known name ;

     c if there is no difference in this regard take the name used in the first publication.

Ala Rule 97. Enter a society extending through many lands, or having authorised names in many languages, under the English form if it is used officially (*i.e.*, if it appears on any of the society's publications) ; otherwise under that official form of the name which occurs most frequently.

Vat Rule 147. International societies that have official names in various languages are entered under the Italian form, provided that Italian has been accepted as an official language ; otherwise in the language which is used most frequently in the publications.

Ccc Rule 1232 (second sentence). If the name occurs (on the title-page, half-title-page, or any other part of the book) in many languages, that in the favoured language of the library, and if it does not occur, that in the language which occurs and is the earliest in the scale of languages of the library is to be chosen.

Ccc's prescription does not make it necessary to go outside the document catalogued and outside the scale of languages main-tained in the library. This gives satisfaction to the Canon of

Ascertainability and the Canon of Consistency. On the other hand, *Rdc*, *Ala* and *Vat* make it necessary to go outside the library and find out what is current in the market as it were. This tradition was originated by *Rdc*. *Ala* and *Vat* perpetuate it. This perpetuation is due to their not having evolved the concept of "Scale of Languages" for each library. The failure to evolve the concept is also responsible for reducing *Rdc*, *Ala* and *Vat* to the status of national catalogue codes. The adoption of the concept by *Ccc*, on the other hand, has made it qualify to the status of an international catalogue code. At the same time, it satisfies the Principle of Local Variation. It can thus be used also as a national catalogue code by any country.

5451 EXCEPTION

Ala Rule 97 (para two). Local rotary clubs are entered according to the general Rule 91 under their own names.

Vat Rule 147 (para two). International societies which have an independent organisation in various countries are entered under the name that is in use in each of these.

Vat is more general than *Ala*. *Ccc* does not deal with this problem. Because, the Canon of Ascertainability decides the issue for it.

546 Label Entry

Ccc Rule 43. A Label Entry is to consist of the following sections in the order given :—

    1 Label Heading (Leading Section) ;
    2 The directing word " *see* " ; and
    3 The heading to which reference is made.

Rule 431. There is to be a Label Heading using each of the terms " University ", " College ", " School ", " Museum ", " Observatory ", " Laboratory ", " Library ", " Botanical Garden ", " Zoological Garden ", etc.

Rule 433. In the place of the Heading to which reference is made is to be written the name of the Institution as it is written in the related index entry.

Rule 4331. If there are alternative names of the same institution, there is to be a separate Label Entry using each such name in the place of the heading to which reference is made ; in such cases the two following additional sections are to be written in the order given :—

    1 the words " *indexed as* " ; and
    2 the actual form of the name of the institution, which is used as the Heading in the Book index entry.

Ex.—1 **University.** *See*
    University of Madras.

2 **University.** *See*
    Madras University, *indexed as* **University of Madras.**

Ccc provides this species of cross reference index entry to meet the very complicated, indefinite and impermanent nature of the way in which the name of an institution changes and alternates in the minds of readers and often in title-pages too. As a result of this provision, for example, each term used as heading for a university-author-entry will occur as a referred-to heading in a label entry with " University " as the referred-from heading. No doubt a reader will have to wade through a long list of headings to pick out the term into which the name of a particular university has been entered. Of course, whatever be the likely name he brings up, that can be spotted out in its proper alphabetical place under the label-entry. Moreover, the number of entries which will get accumulated under the label-heading " university " will be less than the number of entries which will have for the main heading the name of a place like London, Washington, Paris, England or United States, if both governments and institutions are to be rendered with the name of place as the main heading. Thus, there is nothing really gained, but there is something actually lost by deviating from the Canon of Ascertainability in the rendering of the name of an institution, and establishing a cataloguing convention that weakens the potency of the entry word for a governmental author heading, itself established by cataloguing convention.

547 Listless Variation

Change of name of a person is made consciously and deliberately. His life time is short. He does not change the name often. Moreover, he changes it himself. But, an institution is impersonal. It lives longer than a person. Unlike a person, an institution *qua* institution has no memory. Its name is put on the title-page of its document or of a document on it, by an officer of it or by somebody else. He is seldom as careful about its name as he is of his own name. He is liable to make minor changes in it unconsciously and listlessly. This change may occur quite often. Even the first substantive word in the name of the institution does not escape such a change. The other words too get changed. Above all, at least the sequence of the words in the name is changed quite

often. These changes are found scattered at random among the
documents with the name of an institution as author or as subject
of study. Is the Canon of Ascertainability to force all such listless
headings on to the rendering of heading in a catalogue entry ?
If it does, it will be like the old man who went to the market along
with his son to sell his ass. We have to find some method of escaping from the results of blindly applying the Canon of Ascertainability, so as to give weight even to such trivial unintended listless
variations. The method is that of Uniformisation. But the phenomenon is not peculiar to names of institutions only. This phenomenon of listless unintended variations in name is incident also
in the names of departments of government, conferences, classics,
and works of the main class literature. Therefore, we shall deal
with the problem of Uniformisation in section 591 at the end of
this chapter, so as to cover all cases.

548 Organ

Ccc Rule 123208. If the corporate author is not an institution as a whole
but an organ of it, subheadings are to be added on the analogy of rule 12311 to
12316 and their sub-divisions.

In the above rule, the word " organ " has been substituted
for the term " dependent body ", in accordance with the terminology arrived at in chapter 2.

An organ of an institution may be the author of a document
instead of the whole institution. But, the name of an organ of an
institution is mostly homonymous. To resolve the homonym,
the name of the organ has to be individualised by the addition of
the name of the parent body. As stated in section 5072, the individualising element should be made an anterior heading. Thus
the name of the parent body becomes the main heading. *Rdc*,
Ala, *Vat* and *Ccc* all agree on this. *Ccc* has implemented this idea
by its single Rule 123208. This is simple and elegant. But the
other codes have not given a similar rule. Therefore, they are
obliged to repeat the idea in every rule concerning an organ as
author. Moreover, *Ccc* has defined " organ " once for all in
category 4 of its Rule 1230. The other codes have not done so.
Therefore, they have to give several rules to prescribe when the
actual organ-author should contribute only to subheading. Over-
numerousness of rules, clumsiness and verbosity, therefore, charac-

terise the rules of *Rdc*, *Ala*, and *Vat*. Here are the rules that can be avoided by following the example of *Ccc* :—

5481 *Rdc*

The following are avoidable rules, with proper drafting :—

Rdc Rule 65C. (Federated society).
Rule 66. (College library).
Rule 67. (College society).
Rule 68. (University observatory).
Rule 90. (Committee).
Rule 91. (Conference of institution)

5483 *Ala*

The following are avoidable rules, with proper drafting :—

Ala Rule 99. (Federated society).
Rule 101A. (College or University society).
Rule 101B. (Alumni organisation).
Rule 102. (Integral part).
Rule 135A. (Conference of institution).
Rule 136B. (Exhibition).
Rule 138. (Festival).
Rule 139B. (Commission).
Rule 147. (Park).
Rule 149. (Botanical and zoological garden).

5484 *Vat*

The following are avoidable rules, with proper drafting :—

Vat Rule 128. (Integral part).
Rule 133*b* and *c*. (Observatory, botanical and zoological gardens).
Rule 134*b* and *d*. (Collections).
Rule 144. (Section).
Rule 149. (Branch).
Rule 151. (Committee).
Rule 163. (Conference of institution).

55 Conference

Rdc Rule 93. If they (conferences) have a definite name use that ; *Ex.* **National Quarantine and Sanitary Convention.** This holds even if only one convention is held.

Ala Rule 135A. Enter institutes, meetings, conferences, etc., under the name of the meeting, except when they are meetings of the members of a society or other body and have no distinct name of their own.

Rule 135B. If the institute or meeting is held at some institution (college, university, etc.) add the name of the institution to the heading.

Care should be taken not to confuse with such conferences, the " institutes " " workshop ", etc., which are departments or seminars in departments of academic institutions, and which are entered as such (*i.e.*, as organs).

Rule 135C. If the institute or meeting is associated with a particular city add the name of the city to the heading. If the meeting is held only once, or the heading relates only to one meeting, add the date also.

Vat Rule 162*a*. National congresses are entered under their official name in the vernacular followed by the name of the place in which they were held and the date.

Ccc Rule 1233. If the Corporate Author is a conference as a whole, the Name of the Conference is to be used as the Heading and it is to be individualised by the name of the place or places where it was held and its year. These two are to be deemed as separate sentences.

Vat and *Ccc* regard the name of a conference as likely to turn out to be a homonym. Therefore, in anticipation they prescribe place and year as individualising terms, to avoid homonyms arising in future. *Rdc* fails to prescribe them. *Ala* prescribes them, curiously, when there is only one meeting. But it adds both the individualising terms in the examples. The use of the name of host-body or sponsoring-body as the individualising term as prescribed in *Ala* Rule 135B, is a desirable alternative to the name of the place, in the cases covered by that Rule.

551 Periodical Conference

Vat Rule 162c. Proceedings of periodic national congresses that are published regularly under a uniform title are entered under the name of the congress, just like the proceedings of an academy, institute, etc., giving the title and imprint.

Ccc Rule 123301. If the Conference is periodically held, the number of the Conference is to be interpolated as a separate sentence in Arabic numerals between the name of the Conference and the name of the place. If the number of the Conference is not found in the book but is supplied by the cataloguer, it is to be enclosed in square brackets. In the case 'special sessions' not forming part of the regular series, the phrase " Special session" or some other appropriate term is to take the place of the serial number.

Rdc and *Ala* do not prescribe the interpolation of a numeral or its equivalent in this manner. But the examples given by them accept this prescription. In the card-technique of *Ccc*, as a consequence of the conference being periodical the information about number, place, and year will be given on the back of the main card in the sequence of the serial number. This is on the analogy of *Ccc* Rule 76 for a periodical. This should be explicitly stated as Rule 761 in edition 4 of *Ccc*. Curiously, *Ala* comes nearest to this rule in its own Rule 132B for international congresses which are irregular.

552 International Conference

Rdc Rule 63. Enter international meetings, conferences, congresses of private persons [*i.e.*, other than of nations (Rule 57) or of societies (Rule 93)] under their English names ;

    a but if no publications have appeared in English enter under the name in the language in which most of the publications have appeared ;

    b if publications have appeared successively in various foreign languages, but not in English, use the best-known name ;

    c if there is no difference in this regard, take the name used in the first publication.

Ala Rule 132. Same in substance as *Rdc* Rule 63.

Rule 133. Enter congresses of a group of states having similar language or culture (*e.g.*, the Scandinavian countries or countries of South America) under the language in which most of the publications have appeared. If this cannot be ascertained, enter under the language of the country inaugurating the series.

No definite decision as to the final best form of entry can be made until a considerable body of material has been assembled.

Vat Rule 164. Same in substance as *Rdc* Rule 63.

Ccc Rule 123302. In the case of an International Conference, the Heading is to give its name in the favoured language of the library provided its publication has appeared in it once at least or it is recognised as one of its official languages. In its absence that language which satisfies one of these conditions and occurs earliest in the scale of languages of the library is to be used.

Ccc is general and international in scope. At the same time it satisfies the Principle of Local Variation. *Rdc*, *Ala* and *Vat* are national in their prescriptions.

553 Diplomatic Congress

Rdc Rule 57. Enter congresses of several nations under the name of the place of meeting (as that usually gives them their name).

Ala Rule 131. Enter diplomatic congresses or conferences for the negotiation of a peace between belligerent powers, and all other official congresses or conferences commonly known by the name of the place of meeting, and non-continuing under the name of the place of meeting.

In more recent years many conferences and congresses have been called for the purpose of discussion, mutual understanding, and the promotion of international agreement ; some of them are consultative only ; others lead to international pacts and treaties. It is preferable to enter congresses of this nature under their names, as they frequently form a continuing sequence, held at intervals in different places.

Vat Rule 165 is in substance similar to *Rdc* Rule 57.

Ccc has failed to prescribe a rule for a diplomatic congress without a distinctive name. But it has no need to give a special rule for the case covered by the second paragraph of *Ala* Rule 131. Because the Canon of Ascertainability will take care of it. *Ala* Rule 131 is verbose. It is bad drafting. The first sentence can only go into a commentary.

554 Citizens' Meeting

Rdc Rule 91. Reports of " a committee of citizens " etc., not belonging to any named body, should be put under the name of the *place*.

    Ex.—**Boston. Citizens.**

Ala Rule 140 is in substance similar to *Rdc* Rule 91.

Vat and *Ccc* have not provided any rule to cover this class of corporate author-ship.

Is the use of the name of the territory as the main heading, as prescribed by *Rdc* and *Ala*, sound ? Does it not produce a homonym by coming into conflict with the prescription of the name of the territory for the main heading of governmental author ? Should not such a creation of homonym be avoided in an arti-ficial heading set up by a catalogue code ? Can not the conven-tional term " citizens " be made the heading ? In that case the name of the territory can be made merely an individualising term. It is not desirable to use the name of a place to denote any informal gathering of the citizens of the place. It should be used only to denote the government of the state or the local body of the place.

555 Redundant Rules

Ala Rule 134. Enter National Congresses under the vernacular form of the name.

There cannot be any need for saying this. Because the Name of the National Congress will normally be in the language of the nation. It may in certain cases be in a foreign language, as it was in India in the British period. In such a case there is no point in forcing the vernacular form of the name. Surely, this matter should be left to the care of the Canon of Ascertainability and the scale of languages of the library.

Rule 135B. If no name can be found for the meeting, enter it under the place and supply a name descriptive of the character of the meeting.

There is no need to make a special rule for this. *Ala* Rule 141 can be worded so as to cover this case also.

Vat Rule 166B. The various congresses held under the auspices of the League of Nations are entered under their own name, according to the ruling in the previous paragraph (International congresses) and not as a sub-division of the League of Nations.

This does not deserve a special rule. Only a commentary under *Vat* Rule 164 is called for.

556 Label Entry

Ccc would use terms such as " Conference ", " International Conference ", and " Diplomatic Congress " as label headings for label entries under its Rule 43 and its sub-divisions.

557 Unifomisation

Conferences held periodically are liable to make listless changes in their names. The question of using a uniform name, instead of the Canon of Ascertainability being made to take note of such unintended, insignificant listless changes, deserves to be considered.

558 Organ

Ccc Rule 123308. If the Corporate Author is not a conference as a whole but an Organ of it, sub-headings are to be added on the analogy of Rules 12311 to 12316 and their sub-divisions.

Rdc, *Ala*, and *Vat* have not provided for this contingency.

56 Title Heading

Pin has to face many more documents calling for title heading for main entry than the other codes. This is the penalty for its not recognising corporate authorship in spite of its accepting collaborator heading for an anonymous book. All the same, all the difficulties of rendering a title in the heading have to be faced by all the catalogue codes, though the number of occasions may be smaller. The other codes try to reduce the number of occasions for title heading by certain devices, in addition to the adoption of the concept of Corporate Authorship. *Rdc*, *Ala*, and *Vat* choose the heading not as for the book, but as for the work embodied in it. They prescribe bibliographical investigation to find the name of the author of the work, if possible. They minimise the number of title headings; they are prepared to violate the Canon of Ascertainability in this way. *Ccc* makes use of the device of making the heading of a main entry impotent. It takes freedom therefore to use the name of collaborator as the heading. It thus bypasses the difficulties. All the same, all the difficulties of a title heading have to be provided for by *Rdc*, *Ala* and *Vat* when the author of the work could not be found. Even the *Ccc* has to provide for these difficulties in rendering title heading for added entry.

5601 Uniformisation

In sections 261 of chapter 2, a sacred work, a classic, or a work of the main class Literature, has been described as a quasi-class or quasi-subject. Therefore, *Ccc* leaves to the classification scheme to choose a crisp traditional name for it. This is for added entries. For main entry, title-page should be followed. *Rdc*, *Pin*, *Ala* and *Vat* prescribe rules for the uniformisation of the title of such a work, for adoption as heading. This is quite independent of the title portion of the main entry having to follow the title page. The " Uniform title " is to be taken from tradition. Or, it is fixed by convention. *Ccc* expects the classification scheme to have done similarly. The following rules of *Pin* amount to prescription of uniformisation of titles :—

Pin Rule 181. The same work is always arranged under the same title, and the same words are always established in the same form.

Rule 182. The work is arranged under its original title if another has not supplanted it in use.

Ex.—**Code Napoleon** (the official title introduced in the year 1807 which has again gone out of use) under **Code Civil des Francis** (the original title).

These are the basic rules of *Pin* for title heading.

561 Sacred Work : Uniformisation

Most of the codes attempt to give exhaustive rules for choice of uniform title for every sacred work of every religion.

5611 HINDUISM (VEDIC)

The uniform title recommended is as follows :—

Rdc Rule 124. (Veda). *Ala* (Vedas : Brahmanas ; Aranyakas ; Upanishads).

5612 HINDUISM (POST-VEDIC)

The following uniform titles may be usefully prescribed :— Dharma Sastra ; Purana ; Samhita ; Agama ; Tantra.

5613 JAINISM

The following uniform titles may be usefully prescribed :— Anga ; Upanga ; Prakirna ; Chedasutra ; Nandi ; Anuyogadhvara ; Mulasutra.

5614 BUDDHISM

Ala Rule 35B. (Tripitaka ; Vinayapitaka ; Suttapitaka ; Abhidhamma ; Dhammapada ; Jataka).

The above is neither an exhaustive list nor a list of co-ordinate titles. Dhammapada and Jataka are subdivisions of Suttapitaka.

5615 JUDAISM

Rdc Rule 124. (Talmud) ; *Ala* Rule 35A. (Talmud ; Mishnah ; Tosefta). *Vat* Rule 215. (Talmud).

5616 CHRISTIANITY

Rdc Rule 123. (Bible). *Pin* Rule 224. (Title in the Vulgate). *Ala* Rule 34. (Bible). *Vat* Rule 200. (Biblia).

5617 ISLAM

Rdc Rule 124. (Koran) ; *Ala* Rule 35B. (Koran) ; *Vat* Rule 215. (Koran).

56182 CONFUCIANISM

The following uniform titles may be usefully prescribed :—
Yi Ching ; Shi Ching ; Shu Ching ; Li He ; Chun Chin ;
Analects.

56184 SIKHISM

Rdc Rule 124. (Adi Grant).

56185 ZOROASTRIANISM

Rdc Rule 124. (Avesta).

562 Classics. Uniformisation

It is obviously impossible to give an exhaustive list of the
uniform title of each classic in each language. It should be the
business of the National Catalogue Code of each country to give
such a list. *Rdc* and *Ala* give general rules on the subject. *Vat*
complicates matters.

Rdc Rule 124. National and popular anonymous epics should be treated
in the same way (entered under conventional title).

Ala Rule 33A. Enter editions of anonymous classics and their translations
under a uniform heading of the traditional or conventional title of the work in
the language of the original version when known.

Vat Rule 193. National epics, romances of chivalry, popular medieval
romances, sagas etc., are entered under their traditional titles in the original
language.

Rule 192. Anonymous Greek and Latin works are entered under the
traditional Latin title by which they are known in literary history.

Rule 194A. Translations are likewise entered under their original title.

Rule 194B. Retellings and adaptations of a poem or romance are entered
under their traditional title in the language of the adaptation.

Rule 195. Romances, stories and poems which appear in various forms in
European literatures are entered under their traditional Italian title.

Editions of little known anonymous works of foreign origin are entered under
their particular titles.

Rule 199A. Codes of ecclesiastical laws, of ancient and medieval laws as
well as digests and various compilations of laws of the Germanic and Scandinavian peoples are entered under traditional titles.

Vat is prescribing the language of the original in some cases
and Italian in other cases. Therefore it is obliged to give so many
rules.

5621 INITIAL HONORIFIC OR TITLE

Rdc Rule 125. Medieval romances whose title begins with Sir go under the
word following.

Ala Rule 33A (6). When the titles of anonymous classics involve personal names either real or fictitious, the uniform heading may be limited to the name involved, retaining titles of honour and address.

Rdc and *Ala* prescribe in different ways.

5622 ADAPTATION

Ala Rule 33D (1). Enter an adaptation which is more or less a free translation of the original text under the uniform heading of the original text.

Rule 32D (2). Enter adaptations or paraphrases which have become literary works in their own right, or which have been freely made from many texts, as in the case of many adaptations for the use of juvenile readers, under the author of the adaptation.

These rules are redundant. If at all, their substance may be given in a commentary on the basic rule 33A.

Rule 33B (2) (*a*). The versions of the King Arthur stories which bear Malory's name on the title page are always entered under Malory even though they are not always editions nor confined to adaptations of Malory's version of the tales of the cycle.

The example enters the *Story of Sir Galahad* retold from the *Le morte de' Arthur* of Sir Thomas Malory by Mary Blackwell Sterling, under **Malory**. Obviously, this is at variance with Rule 33D (2). If the word " Malory " had been omitted in the title-page, even under Rule 33D (2)*a* this book would have received the heading " Sterling " and not " Malory ".

563 Main Class " Literature "

Uniformisation of title becomes necessary in the main class " Literature ". There is a tendency, however, among modern men of letters to use short and crisp titles almost equivalent to proper names. But all do not do so. It was done by few in the past. So far as a work of the past is concerned, tradition would have already evolved a uniform title. " David Copperfield ", for example, is now the conventional short title for the " Life and adventures of David Copperfield " of Charles Dickens. In its modern editions, either the uniform title alone is printed in the title-page, or at least the uniform title is printed in a more dominant type face than the other words in the title. In a work of modern times also, such a typographical aid should be given to facilitate the choice of uniform title. Of course, this will not be necessary in the main entry, unless the work is anonymous. But even if the work is onymous, it will be necessary for title entry as added entry. For, a work in literature is a quasi-class. Therefore there is bound to be an added entry with the name of the work as heading.

Some works of Indian literature have the honorific term, "Sri" or "Srimad" prefixed to the title. At the same time, a rule for the omission of such a prefix in all titles may not be safe. For, in a work such as "Sri Bhashya", it is an intrinsic part of the title. Cataloguers not born and bred up in Indian culture should be helped in this matter by typographical aid in the title-page.

564 Uniform Name of Part

Rdc Rule 131. An anonymous work which forms a *part of* a *larger whole* is to be entered in the place where the whole would be.

Pin Rule 230. If the different titles occur in editions of the whole work and of individual parts, the title of the whole work is decisive for the arrangement. If, however, individual parts of a work form a separate entity with special well-established title, they are put under it.

Ala Rule 33B (1). Enter parts of a composite anonymous classic which forms an organised literary unit, so that the parts when issued separately are remembered in relation to the whole title, under the uniform heading for the classic as a whole.

Rule 33B (2). Enter parts of a composite anonymous classic, which is merely a collection, so that the parts when issued separately are remembered as independent title, under their own uniform headings.

These rules are helpful. But *Rdc, Ala* and *Vat* do not allow parts of sacred books with uniform conventional names, being given main entry under the name of the part as main heading. *Rdc* explains this differential treatment in the following commentary on its Rule 123 on "Bible" :—

This is the best handbag—in an English catalog for the Bible and for any of its parts in whatever language written and whatever title published. This is the British Museum rule. It is of a piece with putting all periodicals under the heading "Periodicals". It would be much more in accordance with dictionary principles, but much less convenient, to put the separate books of the Bible each under its own name as given in the Revised Version.

"Much less convenient" tells the tale. It is really capitulation to the urge for classified pockets, in an alphabetical catalogue. As it has been often reiterated, this dilemma is avoided by Classified Catalogue. Its classified part propitiates this urge for classified arrangement, by arranging the main entries of the cards in a classified sequence. For in any scheme of classification, parts of a sacred book or a classic are made sub-classes of the original. The alphabetical part is free to serve the cause of alphabetical approach fully and strictly.

565 Homonym

Homonym in title may arise in two ways :—

1 Two or more works may have the same name ; or

2 A work may have the same name as a person, or a place, or an institution or a subject.

In the first case, name of language, and/or form of exposition, and/or year of first publication, and/or name of author can be used as individualising term, to resolve the homonym. In the second case, if the name of the person has a secondary element, the homonym between title and person will be resolved ordinarily. But the name of a person may itself be the title of a book, or the secondary element may happen to be absent in the name of the person. One way of resolving the homonym in this and the other possibilities of the second type, will be to add an individualising term such as " Biography " or " Work " or " Poem " or etc. after the title. *Pin* and *Ala* prescribe something similar in the following Rules :—

Pin Rule 231. Like titles of different works are arranged chronologically according to the year of first publication and if that does not suffice, according to the place of publication.

Ala Rule 33A (1). To avoid confusion with entries of similar phraseology and to aid in identification, where necessary or helpful, a term denoting literary type may be added after the uniform heading.

The advantage of such a practice is especially obvious when the uniform heading resembles a personal name, whether real or fictitious.

For anonymous classics based on the lives of saints, other holy personages or holy things add the term " Legend " to the heading.

Ccc has not explicitly provided for the resolution of a homonym of this kind. This should be provided for in edition 4.

566 Over-Information

5661 CLASSIC

Ala Rule 33A (2). When the classic appears in many languages, either as direct translations or versions, add to the uniform heading the name of the language of the text of the translation or version.

Ccc will have no need for this rule, if the scheme of classification used, has a system of book numbers having language facet. In fact, if *Ccc* and Colon Classification are used together, there is no need for such a rule. For a classic is a quasi-class. It will have a class number of its own. The translations or versions of it in a specific language will be brought together by their respective

book numbers. This help comes in the classified part of the catalogue. In the alphabetical part, the entry with the name of the
classic as heading will be only a class index entry. Its business
will be merely to tell the reader the region in the classified part
where all the main entries of the classic lie.

In the Dictionary Catalogue, however, a classified pocket has
to be formed as prescribed in *Ala* Rule 33A (2) quoted above.

Ala Rule 34. Include as sub-heading of " Bible ," the language of the text,
the date of publication and, when known, the version.

Rule 34A. Enter Bibles containing the identical Biblical text in three or
more languages under the heading " Bible. Polyglot ".

Rule 33E (1). In order to distinguish readily one version from another,
add (if ascertainable) after the date in the heading, in English, the name of the
version or the translator ; or the name of the printer ; or the name of the place
and printer.

Rule 34F. The form divisions when required in a Bible heading follow
immediately after the language specification. These form divisions are :—

1 For the Blind	5 Manuscripts
2 Harmonies	6 Paraphrases
3 Lessons	7 Selections
4 Liturgical	8 Shorthand.

Ex.—**Bible. N T. Gospels. English. Hormonies. 1937. Moffatt.**

Vat Rules 203 to 211 give the substance of the above mentioned *Ala* rules.

Ccc, used along with a call number like that of Colon Classification has no need to load the heading ' Bible ' in such a heavy
way. The example given under *Ala* Rule 34F illustrates the extent to which loading can reach. The object of such a loading is
really to produce a systematically classified pocket in the Dictionary
Catalogue. Indeed the resulting heading ceases to be a true title
heading. It really becomes a subject heading. This is of course
on a par with a governmental author heading—rather, alleged
to be author heading—really becoming a subject heading in the
case of laws, for example. This is a recurring violation of the
Canon of Consistency and the Canon of Purity in *Ala* and *Vat*.
There is, no doubt, need for such a subject heading. But what is
described as " Rules for Author and Title Entry " should not
prescribe subject entries. This is avoided in a Classified Catalogue. Because, in its classified part, the form-of-exposition facet,
the language facet and the year facet of Book Number will take
care of the systematic arrangement intended to be secured by such

loaded headings in a Dictionary Catalogue. What cannot be done by the book number will be done by the secondary phase of the class number.

567 Pedestrian Book

Uniformised title is equivalent to quasi subject in most cases. Moreover, tradition gives us such titles in the case of sacred works, classics, and works in the main class 'Literature'. This help is not available in the case of pedestrian anonymous work. Elaborate rules are necessary to decide Entry Element in its title. A crisp title, more or less stable, and sticking to memory as a whole like a proper name gives no difficulty. Then its first word can be made the Entry Word in the full confidence that the reader will look it up naturally, that he will come across it in all references, and that he will take it into his memory in its entirety or at any rate make little mistake about the first word. On the other hand, a flabby title with near-puff words calls for rules. The chief elements in it for choice as Entry Word are :—

1 The catch word, *i.e.*, the word most likely to stick to the memory ;

2 The subject-word, *i.e.*, the word denoting the subject of the book ;

3 The first word other than an initial article or honorific ; and

4 The first noun, or word used substantively.

Pin introduces the fourth type of element for choice as entry word. This will be considered in section 568.

5671 CATCH-WORD

No code prescribes Catch-Word of title to be used as entry word in the heading of the main entry of an anonymous book. This is correctly so. For, it cannot be determined uniquely. All readers may not choose the same word as the Catch-Word.

5672 SUBJECT-WORD

Rdc Rule 121. For anonymous biographies, if the title mentions the subject of the life, omit the title entry, leaving only the subject entry. The word " subject " should be added to the heading to show why the entry is made under it.

Rdc is the only code prescribing the omission of title entry altogether in the case of one class of anonymous books. Indeed, it makes the subject entry the main entry. This emphasises the fact that a generic non-descript first word in a title is seldom re-membered. It is true. The majority do not remember it. If somebody remembers it, is he not to be helped ? Atleast an added title entry should be given.

Ala does not " except anonymous biographies form first word entry ". *Rdc* itself adds this information and comments upon it as follows :—

> Small catalogs have been in the habit of excepting " anonymous works relating to a person, city, or other subjects distinctly mentioned in the title, which are to be put under the name of the person, city, or subject." In the catalog of a larger library where more exactness ("red tape," "pedantry") is indispensable, biography should be the only exception, the place of entry under subjects and under large cities being too doubtful. And in planning a manuscript catalog, it should be remembered that a small library may grow into a large one, and that if the catalog is made in the best way at first there will be no need of alteration.

Incidentally, what a clear grasp, even in those far-off days, of the Fifth Law of Library Science, " Library is a growing orga-nism "! This proves that *Rdc* had been guided by some normative principles, unconscious and un-enunciated though.

5673 First Word

Rdc Rule 120. Make a *first word entry* for all anonymous works.
It must be noted that the rule mentions " work ", and not " book ".

Rule 136. When a title begins with an article, the heading of a first-word entry is the word following the article.

> This is the common rule. It is found to work badly to except the preposi-tion in the title of novels and plays, and it is awkward to omit or transpose it in any case. One reason for excepting the article—that there would be an immense accumulation of title under the unimportant words A, The, Le Der, Uno, etc.—is not so strong in the case of prepositions ; the other—that it is difficult to re-member with what article a given title begins hardly applies at all to prepositions. The preposition is as likely to fasten itself in the memory as the word that follows it. The strongest argument in favour of confining preposition-entry to fiction and the drame is that in other cases the word following the preposition will probably be a subject-word, so that one entry will do the work of two. This will occasionally be true, but not often enough, I think, to make much difference.

The second of the above paragraphs is only a commentary on Rule 136. It has been quoted in full to demonstrate how the unconscious part of the mind of this pioneer in cataloguing code had evidently seized even in those far off days, the Canon of Prepotence.

Rule 137. When a foreign phrase is used as English title (the initial article should be retained).

Rule 138. When a title begins with a word expressive of the number which the work holds in a series the first-word entry is to be made under the next word.

Rule 139. A motto beginning a title may be neglected and the entry made under the first word of the real title following.

Ala and *Vat* do not give any rule corresponding to the above-mentioned important Rules of *Rdc*.

Ccc Rule 128. The First Word of the title of a book, excluding an initial article or an initial honorific word, if any, is to be used as the heading, and to this is to be added the descriptive words " First Word '.

This is a cumbersome rendering. It will be simpler to put the whole title in the heading with first word alone as the Entry Element. The other words in the title are to be added thereafter as Secondary Element. This would mean that the two sections—Heading and Title-portion—get merged into a single section. This revised form of Rule 128 should be incorporated in edition 4 of *Ccc*.

5674 Grammatical Variant

Rdc Rule 140. When the first word of a title is spelled unusually, all the editions should be entered under the word spelled in the modern or correct way.

Rule 142. When the first word of a title is an oblique case, use the nominative as heading.

Pin Rule 207. Real entry words are established in the case in which they appear in the title.

Rule 210. Entry words are valid in the current usual spelling : in German particularly *k* and *z* are preferred to *c*, and *t* to *th* in varying uses. Expressions which are not treated as compound in the copy are nevertheless regarded as a compound word if this corresponds to present-day orthography.

Rule 211. Also in slight grammatical variations the different forms are united under the form most common at the present time.

Rule 212. If names of persons are used as real entry words, the form of the word under consideration remains unchanged, but it is established in the orthography, customary at the present time. Abbreviated or missing forenames are not completed.

Rule 213. Other abbreviated words are effective in their full forms.

Rule 214. Numbers and other signs as entry words are established in words, in the most usual form of the language of the title. In Germanic languages the numbers from 1,100 to 1,999 are established as hundreds.

Ala Rule 32E. If the first word of a title entry may be spelled in more than one way, follow the spelling of the title-page and refer from other forms.

When different spellings have been used in successive editions, follow the title-page in each case.

Alternative Rule of British Library Association : When the first word of the title of anonymous work is spelled in more than one way, choose one form of spelling.

Where different spellings have been used in successive editions enter the earliest form. In the case of obsolete or archaic forms of spelling enter under the modern form.

Vat Rule 185*a*. Anonymous works which have different spellings in the titles of various editions are entered according to the individual title-pages.

Rule 185*b*. Anonymous works which begin with archaic words or obsolete spellings are entered under the title as given on the title-page.

Rule 185*c*. If the variant spelling is an obvious error it may be corrected.

Ccc does not give any rule on grammatical variants of the first word of title in an anonymous book. For, it follows unerringly the Canon of Ascertainability. The contradictory prescriptions found in the other four codes show the wisdom of following the Canon of Ascertainability. If it is followed, all the above rules can be omitted. It must be remembered that all the codes prescribe the right of every rejected grammatical variant to a cross reference/index entry, the referred-to heading being the preferred variant.

5675 TRANSLATION

Rdc Rule 132. *Translations* of anonymous works should be entered under the same heading as the original, whether the library possesses the original or not.

Ex.—**Arabian Night Entertainments** would appear under **Alif Laila.**

Pin Rule 221. The original title serves as the main title.

Rule 222. ... even when the original title is not in the library.

Rule 223. If, however, the title is known mostly in a language other than the original, then the entry word is taken from that.

Ala Rule 32G. Enter a translation of an anonymous work under the translated title as it appears on the title-page.

Alternative Rule of British Library Association : Enter a translation of an anonymous work under the heading adopted for the original work.

Vat Rule 189. Translations of anonymous works are entered under their titles in various languages.

Ccc does not give any rule on the form of title to be chosen for a translation of an anonymous book. For, it follows unerringly the Canon of Ascertainability. The contradictory prescriptions in the other codes show the wisdom of following the Canon of Ascertainability. If it is followed, all the above rules can be omitted.

5676 MULTI-VOLUMED BOOK

Rdc Rule 147. Anonymous works that change their titles in *successive volumes* are to be entered under their first title, unless the greater part of the work has the latest title, or the whole is much better known by the later title, in which case the entry should be made under that.

Pin Rule 227. If different titles occur in works of more than one volume, the original title remains decisive.

Rule 228. If, however, the original title was changed shortly after the publication of the first part the latter title becomes decisive.

Ala Rule 32A. When the title-pages of an anonymous work in several volumes vary, catalogue from the title-page of the first volume unless a majority of the volumes are issued under a later title and the work for this or some other reason is decidedly better known by this title.

Vat Rule 187. Anonymous works that are issued in two or more volumes or are divided into several parts are entered under the title of the first volume or part, provided that the title of other volumes or parts is not better known.

Rule 188. Continuations, additions, and supplements to anonymous works are catalogued under the entry for the original work in the usual manner.

Ccc has no need for a separate rule to cover the case of a multi-volumed anonymous book, of which the different volumes have variant titles. For, its Rule 52 and its sub-divisions will take care of this case. One implication of these rules should be mentioned. The heading should be the title of the first-published volume of the set. This is indicated by the Canon of Permanence and the Law of Parsimony. This is implied in the rule. It is desirable to make it explicit in a commentary on the rule. This commentary should be added in edition 4 of *Ccc*.

The prescriptions of the other codes are not as precise as that of *Ccc*.

5677 PERIODICAL

It has been shown in section 496 and its sub-divisions that each volume of a periodical should be entered under its title as heading. *Rdc* and *Ccc* prescribe it. In implementing it, the card technique of *Ccc* is preferable to that of any other. *Ala* and *Vat* prescribe only the latest title. *Pin* prescribes the latest title in the majority of cases. However, it makes an exception in the following rules :—

Pin Rule 229. In periodicals if the variations of the later titles are considerable and at the same time a new numbering sets in with the change, each title is treated by itself. General indexes to several series are put in the last.

This is too vague. *Ccc* rules are precise and helpful.

5678 GOVERNMENTAL SERIAL. UNIFORMISATION

Governmental serials such as annual reports and administration reports, consular reports, and so on, vary the title of the successive volumes, listlessly and without purpose. It is desirable
that a uniform heading is used for all the volumes of such a serial.
Perhaps it is even better to have a uniform heading for all the
serials of the same species whatever be the government or the
department of government which issues it. For, the varying
first words used in their titles will not be significant in their variance,
nor will they stick to memory. Therefore, no purpose will be
served by overworking the Canon of Ascertainability and adding
a new section for each change of title, as prescribed for a periodical.
Of course these will have the name of governmental author as
heading. Even then, it is emphasised that it is not necessary to
add a new section for every change in title.

568 First Noun

Pin has prescribed more complicated rules for the rendering
of a title in the heading of a catalogue entry. The whole of Chapter
I of part III " Arrangement under Real Titles " is devoted to the
rendering of title. It comprises Rules 181 to 206 — 26 rules in all.

Pin Rule 2a. In the title are distinguished :—*Real title*, the name of the work
(and additions to it).

Rule 187. In titles in the usual form (*i.e.*, titles which express the content
of the work through a noun or a word used substantively with or without an
attribute), the first noun, not standing in attributive or in adverbial relationship,
or words used substantively (*Substantivum regens*), becomes the entry word, no
matter in what case it occurs.

Rule 188. The article is taken into account only when it is attached to the
noun, as in the Scandinavian and Rumanian languages.

Ex.—Archaeologische Zeitung *is rendered as*
  Zeitung archaeologishe.

The application of the above rules is not as simple as it looks.
Many of the succeeding rules in the chapter complicate the application of these rules.

5681 NOUN TO BE PASSED OVER

Pin Rule 189. If, however, the first noun not standing in an attributive
relationship designated only the extent of the work or its relationship to other
parts of the same work, such as *Volumen, Pars, Romus, Liber, Continuatio, Nachtrag,
Supplement, Register, Veiheft, Ergenzungsblaetter*, etc., the next noun dependent on
it becomes the entry word.

Ex.—Ergaenzungsblaetter zur allgemeinen literatur-zeitung is rendered as **Literatur-Zeitung** allgemeinen Ergaenzungsblaetter.

The following rule prescribes an exception to this exception :—

Rule 191. If, however, the expressions to be passed according to Rule 189 not only designate the extent etc., of the work, but belong inseparably to the title, or if they are number concepts in fixed substantival form such as biga, triga, quaternio, dutzend, etc., then they become the entry word.

Ex.—**Buch** der weisheit.

5682 NOUN IN APPOSITION

Pin Rule 193. Of two nouns standing in apposition to each other, not forming a compound the second becomes the entry word.

Ex.—Stadt Berlin *is rendered as* **Berlin** Stadt.

5683 COMPOUND NOUN

Pin Rule 194. Compounds (with or without a hyphen) are taken as one word. However, an adjective added to the final noun disrupts the composition. If several proper nouns are connected, a compound is admitted only when a unitary concept is expressed through the combination ; otherwise the individual names—in spite of hyphens—are taken as independent.

> *Ex.*—**Chaucer Society. Leisure Hour Library, Madras Presidency**
> but, Nozze Centazzo-Tamassia *is to be rendered as* **Centazzo-Tamassia.**

Rule 195. The following are also taken as forming compounds :—

1 Forenames and titles. *Ex.*—**Johns Hopkins University Studies.**

2 Adverbs and prepositions. *Ex.*—**Pro Memoria.**

3 The prefix *Sankt, Saint, San*, etc., in place names and appellatives.

4 Attributes which are blended with their noun in a unitary concept.
> *Ex.*—**Comptes-Rendus. Great Britain. Cataloguing Rule.**

5 With adjectives, such adverbs as modify the concept of the adjective.
> *Ex.*—**Christlich-Sozial.**

6 In English, adjectives which belong to the following nouns in such a way that only together with it do they form the determining word of the compound.
> *Ex.*—**Natural History Review. Foreign Office List.**

The yearly Supreme Court practice *is to be rendered as*
> **Supreme Court Practice** yearly.

5684 CONTRACTED COMPOUND NOUN

Pin Rule 196. Contracted compounds are resolved.

Ex.—Danger, Distress and storm signal codes *is rendered as* **Danger Signal Codes,** distress signal codes and storm signal codes.

Rule 197. Contractions of works of which only one is a compound or which have only one element of word formation in common are treated similarly.

5685 SECONDARY ELEMENT

Pin Rule 198. The further arrangement of titles whose entry word is determined according to Rules 187-97 is regulated by the other essential words and of course, these are effective in the sequence given in the title. Mere letters with which a person is designated are not passed over in this, but are taken into account in the given sequence.

> *Ex.*—Rheinisches Museum for Philologie *is rendered as* **Museum** Rheinisches Philologie.

Rule 199. Grammatically dependent which precede their *regens* are effective only after it.

> *Ex.*—J W Goethes Herman *is rendered as* **Herman** Goethes J W.

Rule 200. Forenames and substantival appositions are also taken as grammatically dependent.

Rule 201. If preceding words depends at the same time on several subsequent ones then only the first of these serve as the *regens*.

> *Ex.*—Theologische studien und kritiken *is rendered as* **Studien** theologische kritiken.

Rule 202. The following are disregarded :—

1 The expressions that are equivalent to prepositions and other combining expressions (mostly participial and relative).

> *Ex.*—Pieces pour servir a l'histoire du 19 siecle *is rendered as* **Pieces** histoire siecle 19.

2 Indefinite numerals which are not used substantively and ordinal numbers which give only the sequence of the publication.

> *Ex.*—First Annual report of the Board of Regents of the Smithsonian Institution *is rendered as* **Report** annual Board Regents Smithsonian Institution.

3 Appositional titles of honour, designations of office and rank, so far as they precede the name ; likewise adjectives and adverbs derived from titles of honour if a pertinent territorial adjective follows.

> *Ex.*—Furst Bismark in Deutschen Liede *is rendered as* **Bismark** Liede Deutschen.

4 Dates in laws, transactions and the like, in case the law, transaction, etc., is defined not only by the date but also more closely by a positive statement.

> *Ex.*—Gesetz vom 28 Juli 1906 Betreffend die unterhaltung der offentlichen volksschulen *is rendered as*
> **Gesetz** Unterhaltung volksschulen.

Rule 203. Parts passed over come into consideration for the first time when there is complete identity of the entry words.

5686 TITLE IN SENTENCE FORM

Pin Rule 204. If the title has the form of a sentence (complete or elliptical) the first word not an article becomes the entry word. The successive words are decisive for the further arrangement, precisely in the given sequence.

> *Ex.*—**Mehr** licht.

Rule 206. If a title in the usual form turns into a sentence title, then each part of the title is treated according to its rules. The procedure is the same when an expression stands in apposition to the whole sentence.

> *Ex.*—Mais und wo er waechst *is rendered as*
> **Mais** wo er waechst.

5687 CASE FORM

Pin Rule 207.   Real entry words are established in the case in which they appear in the title.

Rule 208.   If, however, the case in point is dependent on one of the sentences or words which according to Rules 185, 189 and 190 do not come under consideration for the arrangement, then instead of it the nominative becomes the entry word.

Rule 209.   For the further arrangement the case endings added to the nominative form in German nouns are disregarded and are omitted in setting out the entry word.

This series of prescriptions is too difficult for readers to follow. But it is claimed that German readers feel at home with them.   The difficulty will be even greater with a non-inflectional language.

57 Connecting or Descriptive Word

Ccc Rule 122.   If the title-page contains the names of two ... authors both the names are to be used as the heading with the conjunction " and " connecting them.

The other codes have no need to a rule of this kind.   Because, they prescribe the name of the first author alone to be put in the heading in the case of joint authorship.

Rule 126.   (When the name of collaborator is used as heading) a descriptive word is to be added thereafter indicating the role of the person.   The descriptive word so added is to be regarded as a separate sentence.

The other codes, except *Ala*, do not prescribe explicitly the addition of such a descriptive word.   However, they use it in the examples given by them.

58 Punctuation Mark

Ccc prescribes that the following should be deemed to be separate sentences :—

1 Name of author and descriptive word ;
2 Name of parent body and organ ;
3 Any main heading and a sub-heading ; and
4 Heading and individualising term.

This prescription implies insertion of a fullstop.   This leads to awkwardness when such a heading has to be reproduced in the second section of an added entry.   For example, Rules 3224, 3226, and 3227 have to prescribe that

If a name is in two or more sentences, the fullstops in it are to be replaced by commas.

There is no reason why this awkwardness should be continued.

227

The following alternative rules in relation to punctuation mark may be considered in the edition 4 of *Ccc*.

Ccc Rule 0373. Individualising or descriptive term should be preceded by a comma.

Rule 0374. Sub-heading is to be preceded by a semicolon.

The other codes do not give a definite rule on the subject. But their examples imply some rule.

591 Uniformisation

In several sections of this chapter, we had to deal with certain names which undergo change in course of time.   This is particularly so in the case of entities which have long bibliographical persistence. This is very pronounced in the case of virtually immortal entities, such as,

1 Governmental organ ;

2 Institution ;

3 Sacred book ;

4 Classic ;

5 Work in the main class " Literature " ; and

6 Administration report and any similar serial of a corporate body.

The names of such entities are multi-worded. Hardly any word in these names has the status and stability or enduring quality of a proper name. A person too may change his name. But he does it deliberately and consciously. Moreover, he has his memory to help him to stick on to the preferred name, until he changes it again for definite reasons. But a corporate body has no such compelling internal memory. Almost from year to year, and even from one publication to another, a governmental organ changes its name unconsciously and listlessly. Slight changes in the words or in their sequence are frequent. Even more serious changes occur not infrequently. There is purposeless and unmeant drift in this matter. In the case of institutions too, the cumulative result of unmeant changes becomes serious in course of time. The names of classics and other titles mentioned above are similarly changed either by pruning or by inversion or by addition, either by successive editors or in the mouth of the common folk. The cataloguer can have no control over this. Perhaps, the adoption of an international standard practice for title-page may minimise the trouble. But even then it may not be possible to eliminate it altogether.

This problem creates a serious situation in the application of the Canon of Ascertainability. The reader too will not have memory for the exact name of the title-page. Most of the words in the names are too flabby and have far too little of crispness to stick to memory. To meet this difficult situation, it is worth considering whether the Principle of Uniformisation may not be used instead of the Canon of Ascertainability, in the case of flabby, impermanent and listlessly shifting names. The Principle of Uniformisation may prescribe for the choice of entry word in a heading or a sub-heading, that word or perhaps a couple of inseparable words in a name, which is relatively stable, sticks to memory, and is sought element among readers, because it either denotes the subject or area or other field of jurisdiction as in the case of names of organs of governments and of other institutions, or because it has nearly gained the status of a proper name as in the case of classics, or because it can be arbitrarily fixed as in reports of corporate bodies.

But the jurisdiction of the Principle of Uniformisation should be carefully defined and limited in precise terms. Otherwise, the flood gates of confusion will be thrown open. All the good service of the sheet anchor of the Canon of Ascertainability will be nullified. Of course, in a Classified Catalogue Code, the drafting of the formula for the jurisdiction of the Principle of Uniformisation might be easy to evolve. However, this is a problem for the future.

CHAPTER 6
ADDED ENTRY

Added entry may be a Book Entry—*i.e.*, it may belong to one and only book. It will specify that book by the title alone or by author and title. Of course, it will also give its call number. Added entries may also be General Entry—*i.e.*, it may not belong to any book in particular. In Classified Catalogue, Class Index Entry and Cross Reference Index Entry are General Added Entries. The former has subject heading. It is not so with the latter. In Dictionary Catalogue, *see also* Subject Entry and Cross Reference Index Entry are general added entries. The former has subject-heading. The latter has the name of some other entity in its heading. Among added book entries, cross reference entry in Classified Catalogue has class number in its leading section ; and specific subject entry in Dictionary Catalogue has subject-heading. The term " Book Index Entry " may be used to denote added book entry not having subject heading or class number in the leading section.

61 Book Index Entry

The *rendering of heading* in a Book Index Entry is just similar to the rendering of heading in name entry. One chief difference is the addition of a descriptive term in the case of joint author or a collaborator. Another difference may be the prefixing to a series heading, the name of sponsoring body, when the name of the series is not distinctive and is liable to create homonym. The only problem for which rules should be provided is the *choice of heading* in the case of Book Index Entry.

611 *Rdc*

Rdc Rule 110 makes a list of all the rules prescribing " reference ". But neither in this rule nor in the respective rules listed, indication is given as to which is to be a book index entry and which a general index entry. Moreover, it spoils the unity of the rules on the choice of heading for main entry, by mentioning referred-from headings in them.

612 *Pin*

Pin uses " Particular Reference " in the sense of " Book Index Entry ". *Pin* Rule 20 gives a summary account of the choice of heading for book index entry. Here it refers to the body of the Rules beginning with Rule 30, where the respective headings for book index entries are prescribed. *Pin* also violates the Principle of Unity in Rules 30 onwards.

613 *Ala*

Ala Rule 157A-C indicates, in general terms, the choice of heading for added entry. *Ala* uses " added entry " in the sense of " Book Index Entry ".

Ala Rule 157A. Make added entries, for joint authors collaborators, editors, compilers, translators, illustrators, (if the illustrations form an important feature of the work)—in short, for any person or corporate body other than chosen for the main entry that has a significant part in or responsibility for the production of the work.

Rule 157B. Make added entries for the purpose of assembling closely related matter, *e.g.*, an added entry under the original author of a work when a free adaptation of it has been entered under the adapter ; or an added entry under a uniform heading for the various versions of an anonymous classic whose main entries are under their own titles.

Rule 157C. Make added entries for titles also ; in general, whenever an entry under the title will ensure the ready finding of the book, in particular :

1 For all single works of the imagination such as novels, plays, poems, and other literary forms ;
2 For all works entered under an author which were published anonymously ;
3 For composite works and collections where main entry is not under title ;
4 For works (except reports, transactions, proceedings, etc.) the author entries for which are corporate names ; and
5 For all works of any character bearing distinctive or striking title : make partial title entry in cases where a subtitle, alternative title, or some striking part of the title (catch-word title), is likely to be remembered, but prefer a subject heading or a reference to a subject heading where the title added entry would be substantially the same.

These rules are not precise enough for a code. Nor do they mention that the heading should be drawn only from terms found in the main entry.

6131 REDUNDANCE

The heading for added entry is specified in each rule, all along the rules preceding Rule 157, whenever it is indicated by the general principles laid down in Rule 157. This is redundant. A more economical drafting will be to make the wording of Rule 157 precise, and comprehensive, and to omit all reference to added entries in each of the earlier rules. This will add to elegance without any loss of helpfulness. As it is, however, unity is taken away from most of the rules prior to Rule 157.

6132 Doubtful Value

Ala Rule 157A (last sentence). These designations (*Ed, Comp, Tr, Illus, Joint Author,* etc.) are used with personal, never with corporate names.

This prohibitive sentence gives a wrong direction. For there are documents with a corporate body as joint author or editor, or joint editor.

614 *Vat*

Vat destroys the unity of most of its rules in the same way as *Ala*. It prescribes book index entries, arising out of the preference of a particular form of heading for a document in its several rules. It does not make a general review or give some general rules for the choice of heading of book index entries, as *Ala* does.

615 *Ccc*

Ccc Rule 321. A Book Index Entry is to be given using as Heading each of such of the following as the book admits of :—

1 The Heading of the Main Entry, provided it is not, as such, eligible to be used as the Heading of a Class Index Entry appropriate to the Book ;

2 The Name of the Second Author, or Collaborator, in case the Heading of the above-mentioned first kind consists of the names of joint authors or joint collaborators ;

3 The Name of each Collaborator mentioned in the second part of the Title-Portion of the Main Entry ;

4 The Name of the Series occurring in each Independent Series Note of the Main Entry ;

5 The Name of each of the Series occurring in the Interdependent Series Notes of the Main Entry ;

6 The Heading of the Work mentioned in the Related Book Note (" Extract Note " has been changed to " Related Book Note ") ;

7 The title of the book, if it is Fanciful, *i.e.*, not descriptive of the subject matter dealt with in the book, provided it is not eligible to be used as the Heading of a Class Index Entry appropriate to the Book or the Heading of the Main Entry is not the Title (" First Word of Title " has been changed into " Title ") ; and

8 Category (1) once again if the Book has appeared with other Titles, for each of them.

Ccc gives the clearest prescription for Book Index Entry, as compared to the other codes. It is in general terms, no doubt. But it is exhaustive. It also preserves the unity of the rules prescribing the heading for main entry. This is also easy to apply. Such a clear, simple, and exhaustive single prescription is equally possible for a Dictionary Catalogue. In fact, the *Dictionary catalogue code*, a twin of *Ccc*, has done so in its Rule 31.

616 Ordinary Composite Book

Ccc Rule 613. In the case of an Ordinary Composite Book other than encyclopaedias and memorial volumes, Index Entries are to be given also for each of the contributions contained in it.

Rule 613201. For convenience of reference, a Book Index Entry of a contribution in an Ordinary Composite Book is to be called a " Contribution Index Entry ".

Rule 61321. The Heading is to be that of the contribution as determined by Rule 321 and its sub-divisions.

This prescription brings the Laws of Library Science into conflict with the Law of Parsimony. *Rdc* supports the demand of the Laws of Library Science :

Rdc Rule 193. Enter in full every work, forming part of a set which fills the whole volume or several volumes.

Rule 194C. Enter analytically, *i.e.*, without imprint—under *author* every separate article or treatise over (this limit must be determined by each library to itself, with the understanding that there may be occasional exceptions) in length.

Pin is not so precise.

Pin Rule 64. For a collection, the bibliographically independent parts which are named in the collective title receive a reference.

The Law of Parsimony may well lose its breath at this wholesale capitulation to the Laws of Library Science. It may well say that the Laws of Library Science remind of Caliban, " Oh Ho, O Ho ! Would't had been done ! Thou didst prevent me ; I had peopled else, this isle with Calibans ". The Fifth Law of Library Science would join the Law of Parsimony. Therefore, a compromise is adopted : " Contribution Index Entry is not to be given for an ordinary composite book covered by a national or a linguistic or an international bibliography, such as *Essay and literature index* ". The Fourth Law of Library Science, which is as anxious to save the time of the staff as that of the reader, in order to spare as much staff as possible for reference service to readers, is

233

15

glad in the shifting of the burden of Contribution Index Entries from individual libraries to national or international organisations.

617 Artificial Composite Book

Rdc Rule 194.   Enter analytically, *i.e.*, without imprint—

   a Every work, forming part of a set, which has a separate title-page and paging, but forms only part of a volume of the set.

Pin Rule 66.   A collection of individual works, without a collective title, is put under the title of the first work, with reference from others.

Ala Rule 54(2) is in substance the same as *Pin* Rule 66.

Ccc Rule 623.   All the Index Entries appropriate to each Constituent Work in accordance with Rule 3 and its subdivisions are to be given.

The Law of Parsimony cannot raise any objection to this. For it is only fortuitously that several works happen to be sharing the same cover. If it objects to separate entries for these, a library will have to resort to the even more expensive method of rebinding the constituent works into independent books.

62 Cross Reference Index Entry

There is no difference between Classified Catalogue and Dictionary Catalogue in the choice or rendering of heading for cross reference index entry.

621 *Rdc*

Rdc Rule 110 makes a list of all the rules prescribing cross reference index entry. But neither here nor in the respective rules, indication is given as to which is to be a book index entry and which a general index entry.

622 *Pin*

Pin uses the term " general references " in the sense of " cross reference index entry ".

Pin rule 20 gives a summary account of the choice of heading for " reference ". But it does not state which is to be used for " particular reference " and which for " general reference ". Nor is this made clear in the body of the rules beginning from its Rule 30 and marked as part 2, to which reference is made for fuller indication.

623 *Ala*

Ala uses " reference " in the sense of "cross reference index entry ".

Ala Rule 158. The function of a reference is to direct the user of a Catalogue from one of several headings under which an entry might be looked for to the one adopted. The following rules deal with the most frequently recurring instances in author and title entries where references are required. Other specific cases where references are necessary are noted throughout the rules. A reference may always be made wherever good judgment and experience agree upon its usefulness. Whenever a heading, whether for main or added entry, is chosen from two or more possible forms, make references freely from the alternative forms to the form of heading chosen, *e.g.*,

A From full name to short form used by author and adopted as heading.

B From original name to name adopted in civil or religious life.

C Conversely, refer from name in religion to real name, if the latter is chosen as heading.

D From parts of a compound name to the part selected as entry word.

E From the part of a prefix name following the prefix if entry is under prefix, and conversely from family name to title when entry is under title, and conversely.

F From family name to title when entry is under title, and conversely.

G Enter from maiden name to married name, when entry is under the latter, and conversely if both names have been used by the author.

H From pseudonym to real name when entry is under real name, and conversely.

J When an author's work may appear in the catalogue under his personal name and also under official heading connect the different headings by references.

K General references should be made between variant spellings of the same name.

L Corporate bodies entered under name require references from place of head quarters, while those entered under place must have reference from name of body. Change of name or variation in the form used necessitates reference from any name by which a body has been or is known to the one adopted as heading. Reference should also be made from an inverted form of name if the distinctive word is not the first word of the corporate name, unless the use of a subject heading or a subject reference obviates such a necessity.

M In national or local official documents where the entry word is a geographical name used as *author* rather than *location*, reference from the office is not ordinarily necessary unless it is popularly referred to by its name. Individual libraries will naturally be guided by local considerations.

N Refer from a larger body subdivided by a smaller division, bureau, etc., if entry is directly under the smaller body, and, conversely, refer from a subordinate entity to the large body of which it is a part if entry is under the latter.

O Refer from any name which a periodical has borne to the name under which it is entered in the catalogue.

P Refer variant names by which an anonymous classic is known to the form chosen as uniform heading for it.

The drafting of this rule is bad. For example, two sections B and C are devoted to converses. In all other cases, the converses are put in one section. Further, this rule is essentially a policy-statement in general terms, with some specific types given as examples. These types are not exhaustive. There is therefore a direction to look up " throughout the rules ". This is bad drafting. There is redundance of rules. The unity of the earlier rules need not have been nullified by mentioning the headings for cross reference index entries in each of them. Rule 158 should have been made exhaustive. This will add to elegance without any loss of helpfulness. This is demonstrated by *Ccc* Rule 4 and its sub-division.

624 *Vat*

The remarks on *Vat* are similar to those on *Ala* in section 623, except that *Vat* does not make a general policy statement as *Ala* does in its Rule 158.

625 *Ccc*

Ccc gives rules for choice and rendering of cross reference index entry, in chapter 4. Some faults in drafting have been discovered in the course of writing this book. The relevant rules are given here in an amended form. These should be incorporated in edition 4 of *Ccc*. Consequential alterations should also be made in the other rules and the examples contained in that chapter.

    Ccc Rule 4.   A Cross Reference Index Entry is to be one of five types, *viz.* :
1 Alternative Name Entry ;
2 Alternative Title Entry ;
3 Variant Grammatical Form of Word(s) Entry ; or Variant Entry, in short ;
4 Editor of Series Entry ; and,
5 Label Entry.

6251 ALTERNATIVE NAME ENTRY

    Rule 411.   There is to be Alternative Name Entry, using as Heading each of all the possible Alternative Names by which any person or corporate body, or place, or series whose name has been used as the Heading for any Entry, is known, or likely to be known.

It is difficult to make an exhaustive list of all types of alternative names. The name of a person may change for various reasons :—Marriage, peerage, change of religion, change of religious status, adoption of pseudonym, legal obligation and even a fanciful desire for change. Names of places are changed for political and other causes. Some places are also given familiar names different from real names. In the case of a corporate body, in addition to regular change of name, there may be need to permute the sequence of the words in the name so as to bring a certain significant word to the beginning, as the body may be remembered by the public under that word. The correct statutory name of certain institutions may be either too long or unfamiliar. In such cases, it would be convenient to use such an unused statutory name as the Heading of a Cross Reference Index Entry, referring from it to the form of the name which actually occurs on the title-page of documents published by them. There are also some series which have alternative name.

It may then be generally remarked that the causes giving rise to Cross Reference Index Entry are many. Further, new causes may appear at any time in future. The choice of Alternative Names to be used as Headings of Cross Reference Index Entries is to be regulated to a large extent by the selective instinct of the cataloguer for what is paying. It is this flair that distinguishes an efficient cataloguer from an unimaginative one.

6252 ALTERNATIVE TITLE ENTRY

Rule 421. There is to be an Alternative Title Entry using as Heading each of all the possible Alternative Titles by which any document—book or periodical—whose name has been used as Heading for an Entry, is known or likely to be known.

Occasionally, the title of a book is changed. It also happens that the same book is published in different countries with different titles. Apart from these regular changes of titles, Citation-Title is often made shorter than the real title. We have already seen that it is desirable to use a uniform Citation-Title for anonymous works, and particularly for sacred books, classics and works of the main class literature. Here again, the choice of alternative titles to be used as headings for Cross Reference Index Entries is to be left to the judgment of the cataloguer.

6253 VARIANT ENTRY

Rule 431. There is to be a Variant Entry using as Heading each of all possible Variant Forms in which the name of a person or a place is known, or occurs, or is likely to occur.

Variant forms may be due to transliteration from one script into another, difference in usage in regard to archaic or modern forms of spelling, preferences of singular or other numeral forms, masculine or feminine forms and other inflectional forms. These have been discussed and illustrated in detail in chapter 12 of *Theory*.

Apart from these casual changes, several alternative spellings are current at the same time for one and the same word, such as, Braune and Browne for Brown. These too should be tied up by cross reference index entries.

6254 EDITOR OF SERIES ENTRY

Rule 441. There is to be an Editor of Series Entry using as Heading the name of the Editor or the names of Joint Editors, as the case may be, that may occur in the Series Note in any of the Main Entries of the Catalogue.

Chapter 21 of *Theory* entitled "Series *versus* Editor" shows how the use of the name of Editor of Series as heading of cross reference index entry instead of a book index entry is arrived at as a compromise between the Laws of Library Science and the Law of Parsimony.

6255 LABEL ENTRY

Rule 451. There is to be Label Heading using each of the terms " University ", " College ", " School ", " Museum ", " Observatory ", " Laboratory ", " Library ", " Botanical garden ", " Zoological garden ", etc.

The value of Label entry has been brought out in section 546 of chapter 5 of this book.

Rule 74. A Periodical Publication is to be given Cross Reference Index Entries of the fifth kind, *viz.*, Label Index Entries.

Rule 743. The Label Headings to be used are " Periodical ", and " Serial ".

Rule 7431. Notwithstanding the provision in rule 75, when " Periodical " or " Serial " forms the Heading of an Entry, the Class Number of the publication is to be entered in the place and in the style prescribed for Index Number in a Class Index Entry.

While preparing the alphabetical index of the *Union catalogue of learned periodical publications in South Asia* (1953), it was realised that this label entry is redundant in a Classified Catalogue, if the scheme of classification used admits of a distinctive digit to denote a periodical or any kind of serial, as the case may be. For, the chain procedure gives rise to a class index entry with the heading 'Periodical' or 'Year-Book', or 'Report', etc., as the case may be. Evidently it is this that should have been responsible for *Ccc* inserting its Rule 7431. Now it is clear that Rule 74 and its subdivision should be deleted from edition 4 of *Ccc*. However, in a Dictionary Catalogue, Label Index Entry of the kind mentioned will be necessary for periodical publications. In other words, the corresponding rules of the *Dictionary catalogue code* are not redundant.

626 STEP-OFF FROM TITLE PAGE

Any catalogue code will have to deviate to some extent from the Canon of Ascertainability, in the choice of heading for cross reference index entry. This is done in obedience to the Second Law of Library Science.—Every Reader His Book. A reader may approach the catalogue from various alternative names. Here, the Second Law over-rules the Canon of Ascertainability on the one side. On the other side, as a compromise with the Law of Parsimony it has accepted a general added entry instead of an added book entry. However, with the cooperation of the publishing world and authors, the number of occasions for stepping off from the title-page and violating the Canon of Ascertainability can be largely eliminated if the standard practice suggested in section 714 and its sub-divisions and section 727 of chapter 7 are adhered to.

63 Specific Subject Heading

Subject heading is not dealt with in *Pin* and *Ala*.

Rdc Rules 162 to 175 and 191 to 194 are devoted to the rendering of subject heading—eighteen rules in all. They raise issues such as

- (*a*) Choice between general and specific, (Rule 161) ;
- (*b*) Choice between person and country (Rule 162) ;
- (*c*) Choice between event and country (Rule 163) ;
- (*d*) Choice between subject (or form) and country (Rules 164 and 165) ;
- (*e*) Choice between subjects that overlap (Rule 166) ;
- (*f*) Language (Rule 167) ;
- (*g*) Synonyms (Rules 168-171) ;
- (*h*) Subject-word and subject (Rule 172) ;
- (*i*) Homonyms (Rule 173) ;
- (*j*) Compound subject names (Rules 174 and 175) ; and
- (*k*) Form entry (Rule 189 to 192).

Vat Rules 369 to 450 form a hotch-potch of rules on the choice and rendering of subject heading.

631 DUPLICATION OF WORK

In its part 1, chapters 11 to 13, *Theory* has discussed fully the whole subject of Specific Subject Heading. It has shown the duplication of work involved in the cataloguer's determining the specific subject of a document *ab initio*, quite independently of the classifier. It has emphasised the economy in man-power that will flow by determining the Specific Subject Heading machanically with the aid of the Class Number. It has also pointed out the greater consistency that can be got thereby both in the choice and in the rendering of Specific Subject Heading.

632 CHAIN PROCEDURE

To mechanise the choice and rendering of Specific Subject Heading, including the sequence of sub-headings with the aid of Class Number, *Theory* devised Chain Procedure. This has been since improved upon in the successive editions of *Ccc* and *Dictionary catalogue code*. The experience of the *British national bibliography* confirms the certitude *cum* comfort and convenience afforded by Chain Procedure, even when classification is by Decimal Classification, which is a rigid, enumerative, non-individualising scheme. The gain will be much more if an individualising or co-extensive, expressive, non-enumerative, and analytico-synthetic scheme, such as Colon Classification is used.

633 *Ccc*

6331 CHAIN PROCEDURE

Ccc Rule 310. The following Chain Procedure will be of help in the choice and rendering of Headings of Class Index Entries.

Rule 3100. The Class Number is to be represented in the form of a Chain of Classes,

1 making

11 the first Link out of the first digit :

12 the second Link out of the first two digits : and

13 the third Link out of the first three digits,

and so on upto the last Link which is to be made of all the digits ;

2 writing the Links one below the other in succession ;

31 writing the translation of each link into natural language—*i.e.*, the name of the class of which the Link is the Class Number against the Link ;

32 Connecting each Link with its translation by an ' equal to sign ' : and

4 Joining the ' equal to sign' of each Link with that of the next succeeding Link by a downward arrow.

Rule 3101. A link is deemed to be a False Link if

1 it is not class number—*i.e.*, is not a concatenation of symbols intelligible according to the rules of classification ; or

2 the focus in its last facet is name-less—*i.e.*, does not have a name in common usage in natural language.

Rule 3102. A link is deemed to an Unsought Link if

1 it ends with a part of a focus in a facet or a part of a phase ; and

2 it represents a specific subject on which reading material is not likely to be produced or sought or not likely to be looked for by a reader seeking materials on the specific subject equal to the last Link of the Original Class Number.

Rule 3103. A link is said to be a Significant Link if it is neither false nor unsought.

6332 CHOICE

Ccc Rule 311. A Class Index Entry is to be given using as Heading the term represented by the last digit of each of the Significant Links of the chain representing the Class Number of each Main Entry and Cross Reference Entry.

6333 HOMONYM

Ccc Rule 3111. If the term derived for the Heading by Rule 311 does not by itself individualise it, it is to be taken as the Main Heading. To secure individualisation the aid of the Canon of Context (enunciated and explained in the *Prolegomena to library classification* of Ranganathan) is to be sought and an additional term(s) is (are) to be derived from the last digit of one (or more) of the preceding links. The smaller the number of such links used the better. Each additional term is to be regarded as a sub-heading.

6334 PROPER NAME OR SINGLE WORD

Ccc Rule 3112. If it happens that the whole Class Number or a part of it represents a proper name or can be translated into a single word in popular usage, it is to be used as the Heading.

6335 RENDERING

Ccc Rule 3114. The terms used as Heading are to be the standard ones given in the Classification Scheme in use.

Rule 31141. If the term used as Heading is the name of a person or corporate body, it is to be written on the analogy of Rule 121 and 123 of Chapter 1 and their sub-divisions.

Rule 31142. If the term used as Heading consists of more than one word and Rule 31141 is not applicable, the words in each sentence of the term are to be written in their natural sequence.

Rule 3115. If the Class Number has two or more phases, the terms of the different phases should, wherever necessary, be linked up by appropriate connecting words like ' influencing ', ' biasing ', ' compared with ', etc., which are the standard equivalents of the Phase-Relation Symbols as given in the Classification Scheme in use.

Rule 31151. If the part of the Heading corresponding with any of the phases, linked up by connecting words, is in more than one sentence, all the fullstops in it are to be replaced by commas.

3116. The terms used as Headings are to be watched and as they become obsolete, fresh entries are to be made with their current equivalents in the headings, and the old ones removed.

It can be seen from the above rules that

1 the choice of subject heading can be brought within the purview of the Canon of Ascertainability if the Call Number of the document is printed on the back of the title-page and it is expressive of and co-extensive with the specific subject of the document ; and

2 the term to be used in the heading is outside the purview of the Canon of Ascertainability and has to depend upon the Classification Schedule and popular usage.

634 DICTIONARY CATALOGUE

The *Dictionary catalogue code* has prescribed exactly parallel rules—Rule 21 and its sub-divisions—for establishing specific subject heading in Dictionary Catalogue. Messrs. A. J. Wells and E. J. Coates of the British National Bibliography brought to my notice, during my visit to London in June 1954 that the current rules of chain procedure do not always yield subject headings commonly sought by users of Dictionary Catalogue. The difficulties that come up have been explained briefly in the article, *Chain procedure and dictionary catalogue* by Ranganathan, published in *Annals of library science*, 1, 1954, 216-221. A large scale application of Chain Procedure began in 1951. This was in *British national bibliography*. It is a Classified Catalogue. In his paper, *Our Debt to India* published in *Library science in India* (1953) ed by K Chandrasekharan, pages 57-63, Wells writes:

"I have decided to introduce three techniques into the BNB...detailed featuring, chain indexing and the imposition of the facet formula on the DC schedules. It was soon realised that the chain procedure is not helpful unless the Class Number is co-extensive with the subject of a book. DC notation fails in this respect. BNB developed its " (1) " symbol and its system of verbal extention of class number to make the latter fit for use in chain procedure."

Generally speaking the rules of chain procedure yield helpful, sought, class index headings for a classified catalogue. However, there has been no large scale application of chain procedure to a dictionary catalogue. No concrete experiment has been made. However, intellectual experiment can be made. Moreover, the advent of documentation work calls for an investigation of this problem.

64 *See also* **Subject Heading**

The choice of *see also* subject heading in a Dictionary Catalogue can also be mechanised by chain procedure. In Classified Catalogue, the corresponding problem is the choice of Headings for Class Index Entries corresponding to the Sought Links other than the last one. There is no need for guess work in these matters. Nor is it necessary to pre-determine *ex-cathedra* and print them as *List of subject headings*.

Rdc Rule 187. Make references from general subjects to their various subordinate subjects and also to co-ordinate and illustrative subjects.

Rule 188. Make references occasionally from specific to general subjects.

Vat Rule 451. The *see also* references suggest related and subordinated subjects which in various ways may throw light on the topic.

It should be particularly noted that references are necessary from the inverted form of a compound expression.

Rule 452. *See also* references are made from the general to the specific subjects which are subordinate to them ; as, for instance, from the name of a science to the particular discipline which it comprises, and from the names of the disciplines to the specific topics with which they deal.

In actual application, these rules will have to depend upon guess work. Inconsistency will result. The chain procedure prescribed by *Ccc* will eliminate all guess work.

Ccc, in its Rule 311 has prescribed that, not only the last significant link, but each one of the upper significant links should contribute to a Class Index Entry. Correspondingly, each upper link will give also a *see also* subject entry in the Dictionary Catalogue.

65 **Alternative Names**

Theory, in its chapter 12, has discussed in detail the problem of establishing " *See* reference entries ", corresponding to alternative names of a subject whose name has been used as heading in a specific subject entry. These are, of course, general added entries.

651 SYNONYMOUS WORD

Ccc has definitely prescribed in its Rule 3114 that only the word used in the Classification Scheme should be used in Subject Heading. This of course presumes that the terminology used in the classification scheme has been chosen with care and circumspection. Indeed, the symbiosis between classification and cataloguing is a true symbiosis. It is not parasitism. Not only the

Class Number throws forth a tow in the form of Chain Procedure to reach at the correct subject headings ; but also its obligation to catalogue alerts classification scheme to be careful and circum-spective about the terminology in its schedules. There should indeed be a holistic co-operation between classification and cataloguing. If there is, there will be no need to give a " *See* reference entry," with the preferred name of a subject as the referred-to heading, and a synonym of it, as the referred-from heading. Surely, the catalogue should not be expected to re-produce sections of a dictionary and give ' *See* subject references " from the synonyms of the standard word chosen.

652 PERMUTATION

Another way, in which synonyms of a heading are got, is by a permutation of a multi-worded term or a multiple subject heading. The chain procedure makes this unnecessary. The sequence into which the sub-headings are thrown by the chain procedure is believed to be one that is usually sought. This problem has been fully discussed in chapter 14 of *Theory*. Further a formula has been arrived at for the number of alternative subject headings that may have to be coined to correspond to any preferred subject heading. This is given in chapter 12 of *Theory* as follows :—

$$n\,!\,(p_1\,p_2\,p_3\,...\,p_n + q_1\,q_2\,q_3\,...\,q_n + r_1\,r_2\,r_3\,...\,r_n + ...)$$ where

$n =$ the number of words in the name of a subject ;

$p_1 =$ the number of synonyms of the first word ;

$p_2 =$ the number of synonyms of the second word ;

    ...   .

$q_1 =$ the number of synonyms of the first word in an alternative name of the subject ;

$q_2 =$ the number of synonyms of the second word in that alternative name ;

    ...   .

$r_1 =$ the number of synonyms of the first word in an another alternative name of the subject ;

$r_2 =$ the number of synonyms of the second word in that alternative name ;

    ...   .

    ...   .

66 Periodical Publication

Change in name of a periodical publication or of its sponsor needs special attention. In addition, a periodical publication is also prone to several idiosyncrasies causing difficulties in cataloguing. Eighteen of them have been isolated in chapter 8 of *Ccc*. The rules in chapters 7 and 8 of *Ccc* prescribe Class Index Entries in a very detailed manner.

Ccc Rule 731. In the case of a periodical publication, not covered by Rules 7301 and 7302 (Annual or Periodic reports of a corporate body) a Class Index Entry is to be given using each of the following as heading, so far as they are applicable :

1 The heading of the main entry (each one of the changed headings used in succession) ;

2 Alternative names, if any, by which the name used as the heading of the first kind is familiarly known ;

3 The name of the sponsoring body (including each one of the changed sponsoring bodies) ; and

4 Alternative names, if any, by which the name used as the heading of the third kind is familiarly known.

Rule 7323. If the Heading is of the Third or the Fourth kind, the second section of the book-index entry is to consist of the title of the periodical publication also and not merely of the Class Number of the publication.

The above rules are in the modified form arrived at while preparing the *Union Catalogue of learned periodical publications of South Asia*.

Chapter 8 of *Ccc* gives compact rules on the lay-out of an abstracting periodical and on the Subject and Author Analyticals for the articles in a periodical and sections of books embodied in it.

CHAPTER 7

TITLE-PAGE

We have made a survey of the rules of the five catalogue codes. Heading has been seen to form the very essence of an entry in a library catalogue. We have also seen that the heading, of any entry except a cross reference index entry, has to be forged on the anvil of the title-leaf.

701 Choice of heading

We have seen the advantage of being guided by the Canon of Ascertainability in the choice of heading. In its present stage of evolution, the title-page and its back, or its equivalent, of a document form in the material plane a good ally of the Canon of Ascertainability which belongs to the plane of principles. It is proving to be a never-failing ally in the choice of heading for the Main Entry. This is its direct contribution. Indirectly also, it helps in the choice of heading for every Book Index Entry. If the back of the title-page gives the call number of the document, it will also provide unerringly and without any waste of time on the part of the cataloguer, the call number to be inserted in the main entry. If the classification scheme is capable of giving an expressive and co-extensive class number, it will also help the choice of the heading for every Class Index Entry in the Classified Catalogue, and for every Subject Entry in Dictionary Catalogue. To get every possible benefit fully out of the Canon of Ascertainability, a standard practice for title-page and its back should prescribe for their containing author statement, title and call number. So much about the choice of heading for Book Entries. But to choose the heading for a cross reference index entry, the cataloguer will have to go outside the title-page. The Canon of Ascertainability cannot always give much help in this matter. It can do so to some extent, however, if a supplement to author statement is given on back of title-page mentioning all the alternative names of persons, places, institutions and books.

702 Rendering of Heading

The title-page or its back, as it is to-day, is unable to give the necessary help in rendering heading for the main entry or for any book index entry. The title page has not brought itself within the purview of the Canon of Ascertainability in this matter. We have shown in several sections in the last three chapters that it is possible to establish such a standard practice for title-page and its back, as will let in the helpful sway of the Canon of Ascertainability in the rendering of heading also.

7021 PERSONAL HEADING

The name of personal author or collaborator usually consists of many words. The function, the position and the potency of each of the words vary from one cultural group to another. Even in the same cultural group, they vary with time. Therefore, a cataloguer is now and again obliged to make some research into the cultural practices of different groups in the formation and structure of personal names. Much judgment has to be exercised in finding out in each name the Entry Element, the Secondary Element, the Irremovable Impotent Attachment to entry element, and the removable impotent words. We have seen in section 51 and its sub-divisions how tangled this problem is, and what a great risk there is in cataloguer striving to do the rendering of a name of foreign culture. The plea now is that this is all avoidable waste and risk. No body knows the various elements in the name of an author more accurately than the author himself. National economy points to the value and the practicability of the author and the publisher making the various elements in the name easily distinguishable, in the way in which the words in the name are printed in the supplement to author statement on the back of the title-page.

7022 GOVERNMENTAL HEADING

In a document of governmental authorship, it will be of help if the name of the government is given in the title-page invariably, with the name, of its territory printed prominently. Very often, the corporate author happens to be a specific organ of a government instead of the whole government. The name of that specific organ also should be clearly stated in a conventional page on the title-page. The name of an organ of less remove than the specific one should be given only if the name of the latter is homonymous. Even then, only the names of the minimum number of such extra organs should be mentioned, in order to remove the homonym. It will be of further help if the word denoting the territorial or the subject jurisdiction of the organ and the other generic and common words in its name are printed so as to be easily distinguishable. Conformity to a standard in the printing of a governmental name in the author statement on the title-page should be even more practicable than in the case of a document of private authorship. For the government is a well-organised author as well as publisher of its own documents.

7023 Institution Heading

The name of an institution is often long. Moreover, it is often abbreviated for purposes of citation. In printing the name of the institutional author on the title-page it will be a help to cataloguing work, if the words intended to be used as its citation-name are made easily distinguishable from the other words in its name. All the remarks about organ mentioned in sections 7022 are applicable to institution also.

7024 Conference Heading

Similar help can be given in the title-page of a document of a conference also.

703 Change of Name

The standard practice for supplement to author-statement, to be given on the back of title-page, can helpfully extend the sway of the Canon of Ascertainability to the choice and rendering of the heading for a cross reference index entry also. The name of a person changes occasionally. He writes documents in several of his different names. Viewed from the angle of cataloguing work, Pseudonym also is only an alternative name. The catalogue has to show together all the documents, having one and the same person associated with it as author or collaborator. This is a demand of the Laws of Library Science. Much man-hour is now being spent in collecting information about alternative names. It always looks like the play of hide and seek. What is the advantage of this game in cataloguing work? The author knows all the alternative names under which he has written. Without any effort, he can give the publisher a list of all the alternative names used by him as author or collaborator. If the publisher can insert this list in a standard place on the back of the title-page, it will result in national and international economy. It is equally true about the change of name of corporate body or any of its organs.

7031 Title

Books require title-entry if they are anonymous or if they have a title not disclosing the subject of the document or a title which is nearly a proper name. Again, some titles are a yard long. They are flabby. Such titles get usually contracted, in the minds of readers, into a few crisp words. This is particularly true of sacred books, classics and works in the main class " Literature ". The standard practice for title-page may also include the printing of the citation-title of such books in such a way as to distinguish it from the other words in the title. The back of the title-page should also give all the alternative titles with which a document might have been published.

704 Periodical

Similarly, each volume of a periodical should give a history of the periodical—*i.e.*, changes in its own name and in the name of its sponsoring body, its amalgamation with another periodical when it occurs, the names of the periodicals it has amalgamated, its having been split into others, or from others, and, in a word, any of the eighteen possible changes listed in section 81 of chapter 8 of *Ccc*. The proper place for this is the back of the title-page and its overflow.

705 Year of Publication

Both for classification and cataloguing the year of publication of a document is found to be necessary. The years of earlier editions too are helpful. The year of commencement of a periodical publication is also necessary.

706 Standard

It will be a help if publishers could give all this information in a conventional place on the back of the title-page and its overflow if necessary. To begin with, all this means that there should be an international standard on all the above-mentioned features of a document. It also means that there should be an international standard for the lay-out of the title-page and its back. In fact, it is desirable that a bunch of standards is established for the lay-out and contents of all the preliminary pages of a document.

707 Periodical Publication

ISO/TC46 has already seized the standard for the lay-out of a periodical publication in general and of its preliminary pages in particular. The draft standard has been under consideration for several years. It has been experimented upon in several countries. Some periodical publications have also adopted it. The first official text of the standard in its full form will soon be on the field.

708 Book

The appeal is now to the same international body and the corresponding national bodies to lay down a similar comprehensive standard for the preliminary pages of documents other than periodical publications. In the succeeding sections of this chapter, draft standards are provided for author statement, to provoke thought and to provide a starting point for the investigation of the problem. This is commended to the attention of the IFLA, ISO/TC46, International Publisher's Association, the corresponding National Bodies, UNESCO, and the Governments of the different countries. The Documentation Committee of the Indian Standards Institution is just now circulating a draft standard on the subject.

71 Standard Practice for Author-Statement (Personal)

710 Sections

710 The personal author-statement shall consist of
1 author-section, followed by
2 collaborator-section, if there be collaborator(s) ; and
3 supplementary section.

7101 The author-section and the collaborator-section shall be printed on the title-page.

7102 The supplementary section shall be printed on the back of the title-page.

711 Author-Section

711 The author-section shall comprise one block of line(s) for each author.

7111 The name of each author shall appear in the nominative form.

7112 No word, such as " by ", shall be used to introduce the author-section.

7113 The words in the name of an author shall appear in the sequence in which they are habitually mentioned by him, or are current in public usage.

7114 Words, if any, in any block of the author-section, describing the position of the author or his relation to any other book, person or corporate body shall be printed in a line different from that of the name and in a type face less dominant than that of the the name.

712 COLLABORATOR-SECTION

712 The collaborator-section shall comprise one block of line(s) for each collaborator such as commentator, translator, editor, foreword-writer, illustrator.

7121 The name of each collaborator shall appear in the nominative form.

7122 The name of each collaborator shall be introduced by a term describing his role, printed in a separate line.

7123 and 7124 similar to 7113 and 7114.

713 DOMINANCE OF TYPE FACE

713 It is desirable to have a gradation in the dominance of type faces in the author and collaborator-sections.

7131 The dominance of type face shall be the same in each author-block.

7132 The dominance of type face in each collaborator-block of the same species shall be the same.

7133 Wherever necessary and possible, the dominance of type face in the following species of collaborator-blocks may be in descending order :—

1 commentator ;
2 translator ;
3 editor ;
4 foreword-writer ; and
5 illustrator.

7134 The dominance of type face in an author-block shall be greater than that of type face among the entry elements in the collaborator-block(s).

7135 The dominance of type face of word(s) connecting the names of authors or author-blocks or collaborator-blocks of the same species, or introducing collaborator-blocks shall be suitably small.

714 SUPPLEMENTARY SECTION

714 The supplementary section on the back of the title-page

shall be given in the upper half or the lower half of the page according to exigency.

7141 The supplementary section shall comprise one block for each person—author or collaborator.

7142 Each block of the supplmentary section shall give each of the alternative name(s), including pseudonym(s), under which books have appeared with him as author or collaborator, provided it is not imperative to hide the identity of the person.

7143 Each block of the supplementary section shall give the year of birth of the person in Arabic numerals and according to Christian Era and also the year of death in the case of a deceased person.

7144 The words in the name of a person shall be printed, in a block of the supplementary section, in the sequence in which they occur on the title-page.

7145 The removable attachment, if any, to the name of a person, indicating his privileged position such as honorific word(s) or word(s) of endearment, representing civil or military or academic title(s), or word(s) indicating civil or religious status, shall be omitted.

7146 The word(s) in the name proper of a person, including irremovable attachment(s) such as word(s) indicating community, or religious denomination, or patronymic office or status, shall appear in a single line wherever possible.

7147 The name proper shall appear in two different type faces, one for the entry element (*i.e.*, the word(s) in the name by which the person is to be listed in catalogues and documentation lists), and the other for the secondary element (*i.e.*, the remaining word(s) in the name, added after the entry element in cataloguing practice).

7148 The type face for the entry element in the name of a person shall be more dominant than that for the secondary element.

715 Over-Flow Page

715 Whenever necessary, the supplementary statement may be printed in succeeding page(s) forming over-flow of back of title-page.

72 Standard Practice for Author-Statement (Corporate)

720 Sections

720 A corporate body may be an author or a collaborator of a book.

7201 Change may occur in the name of a corporate body.

7202 The succeeding rules deal with the printing of the name of a corporate body in the author-section, collaborator-section, or supplementary section, as the case may be.

721 Government

721 If the book is of government authorship, the name of the government, which should include the name of the country, shall be printed either in the usual place for the name of personal author, or in a separate block near the top.

7211 The crest or the coat-of-arms of the government shall be printed either along with the name of the government or in some other consistent place on the title-page.

722 Institution. Conference

722 If the book is of institutional authorship or conference authorship, the name of the corporate body shall be printed in the usual place for the name of personal author.

7221 The words in the name of a corporate body shall be printed in the sequence in which they are habitually used by that body, or are mentioned in its constitution, if any, or are current in public usage.

7222 If the name of corporate body is long, or contains words admitting of omission without loss of identity, the words deemed sufficient for citation shall be printed in a more dominant type face than the other words ; or these other words may be omitted.

723 Organ

723 If the author is not the whole corporate body but an organ of it, created for a specific purpose such as deliberation, execution, administration or investigation—be it temporary or permanent— the name of the specific organ shall be printed above or below the name of the parent body according to grammatical or other exigency.

7231 Notwithstanding 723, if the parent body is printed near the top of the title-page, the name of the organ shall be printed in the usual place for the name of personal author.

7232 If the name of the specific organ, which is the author, is too general such as Bureau of Statistics, Division of Public Relation, Publication Department—and does not individualise it unless taken along with the name of a larger organ having it as a part, the name of the larger organ shall be printed above or below the name of the specific organ according to grammatical or other exigency.

7233 If necessary for individualisation, the names of a chain of such organisations may have to be printed.

724 PURVIEW

724 The word(s) in the name of an organ of a corporate body, denoting the subject or the area or the field of its jurisdiction or purview or pursuit, shall be printed so as to be readily distinguishable from the other words in the name.

725 OFFICER'S NAME

725 The name of no officer should be printed in the author-statement of a document of corporate authorship *per se*—*i.e.*, if the document is within the purview of deliberation, execution, administration or investigation of the corporate body, and is not one embodying original thought of the officer in his personal capacity involving and extension or deepening of a region of knowledge.

7251 If the name of the officer has to be printed for any reason in the title-page of a document described in 5, it should be printed in a separate block with type face less dominant than that of any word in the name of the corporate body or its organ.

726 PERSONAL CAPACITY

726 In the case of a book by an employee of a corporate body or by a non-employee but sponsored by the corporate body, if it is not within the description given in 725, but embodies original thought of the person in his personal capacity and involves extension or deepening of a region of knowledge, the author-statement should mention only the name of the personal author, though the book is written in office-time or as part of the duty of the officer, as in the case of a professor or a research officer.

7261 In the case in which 726 is applicable, the name of the corporate body may be mentioned only outside the author-statement.

727 OTHER DETAILS

727 All other details shall be on the analogy of the standard practices for Author-Statement (personal).

CHAPTER 8

CATALOGUE CODE

Library Catalogue is an ancient library tool. But catalogue code of a rigorous kind is of recent origin. It first attained rigour in stray local codes—*i.e.*, in individual libraries. Now it is attaining rigour in national codes. An international code is yet to be established. The five codes studied in this book are largely national. *Ccc* has, however, some features of an international code.

81 Norm for Drafting

811 NORMATIVE PRINCIPLES

The five codes do not stem from the same fundamental basis in certain aspects. The differences can be eliminated. This requires some mental and emotional adjustment. The votaries of each national code should shed all sense of prestige. They should be prepared to sit at a round table with others. They should leave behind all vestiges of political superiority or inferiority. They should adopt a scientific attitude. Inheritance from the past may make it difficult. But, they should work for the present. They should also look into the future. They should no doubt have a glance at the past. But it must merely be to accept practices of permanent value. They should reject the encrustations of the out-moded past. In other words, they should on no account tie their ideas down to the past in all entirety. Even the fear of re-cataloguing miles of old books in depository libraries should not hamper their march forward. This has been fully dealt with in section 3475 of chapter 3 of this book. A practical, scientific, go-ahead attitude will make the Principle of Osmesis acceptable. Let us assume then that, all the cultural groups of the world put up, for the Round-Table, persons of high intellectual calibre, proper physical stamina, and necessary freedom from lower emotions, such as decadent imperialism, inhibiting camp-bearerism, prejudice of colour, east-west or realistic-practical, and every other kind of slogan-phobia. As a meeting of intellectual peers with concentration on the essential common elements in all human beings and cultural groups, with due respect for one another's culture, capacity and acumen, and brought together to find what is best and true, the Round-Table should first determine the normative principles to guide their further work.

812 STYLE

The second point to decide is the style of the rules of catalogue code. In the five codes studied, there is almost a tidal difference in style. A catalogue code is like a legal text. Each rule should be precise. It should be terse. It should satisfy the Principle of Unity to the fullest degree. No two rules, however allied, should be coalesced into a single rule. No two ideas, capable of standing each by itself, should be put into the same rule. No rule should carry in it any word or idea which can be managed by a commentary or an illustration. The body of the rules taken as a whole should be free from tautology of any kind. It should form a verbally consistent whole. No homonym should be allowed. No synonym should be allowed either. The ideal is to avoid sentences other than simple ones—viewed from the angle of the ideal plane or the verbal plane. Each natural language may not be able to attain such an ideal in style. But the draftsmen of legal text in each language are taking it up towards the ideal. It is easier for a catalogue code to attain it. Because, there will be less of human emotion or vested interests involved in a catalogue code. It is not like the text of a treaty between war-minded nations. It does not have these handicaps even as much as municipal law. *Vat* is furtherst away from this ideal in style. *Ala* comes only next to *Vat*. *Pin* makes a better attempt. The English translation used in this book prevents a more definite statement. *Rdc* has made a close approximation to this ideal. It is remarkable for a veteran of the earlier generation of codes to have done it. Among recent codes, *Ccc* makes an even closer approximation. English not being the mother tongue, it could not have taken a greater liberty with the language. Nor did the example of English legal texts give much encouragement to go further in that direction. But, the Sanskrit version, *Anuvarga-suchi-kalpa* (1953), demonstrates the closeness of approximation possible. For it has adopted the *Sutra* (aphorism) style usually employed for the drafting of a code. *Ccc* has come out really well in that style in Sanskrit. There are some difficulties still. These are largely due to the *Samasa* (Coalesced word). The next attempt in drafting should be to eliminate it.

813 WHY ALL THIS ?

The need for the preliminary settling of principles and style will be realised by remembering that any document embodying any recorded socialised thought produced in any spot on earth is needed for consumption in every other spot. Without the aid of catalogue, documents cannot be located. Unlike classification, catalogue cannot use a purely artificial international symbolic language. It has to be expressed in the words of a natural language. Of natural languages, there will always be many. This linguistic hurdle obstructs international exchange of thought. But the language of the headings in catalogue entries can be made to shed most of its hurdles, though the script, the nouns used, and just a handful of the auxiliary words needed, are preserved in the natural language itself. This is not yet fully realised. At any rate, it has not yet been fully exploited. By agreeing on normative principles and on the ideal to be reached in regard to the drafting of the rule, it can be exploited. The result will take us close to the ideal in making socialised documents circulate effectively among all possible readers in spite of the basic words in the Heading belonging to an alien language. An additional help of great potency will be the classified form of catalogue using a good scheme of classification. Obviously, none of these can overcome a political barrier obstructing the flow of documents *qua* physical materials. But the extent to which political curtains allow their free flow, the various national catalogues will admit of easily being pooled and used together. This will further facilitate circulation. On this assumption, let us plan a lay-out for catalogue code as the basis for further discussion.

82 Lay-out

Each catalogue code—whether international, national, regional, local, or bibliophilic—should have a similar lay-out. This is the next point to be agreed upon at the Round-Table.

821 TERMINOLOGY

A code should begin with a chapter on terminology. Terminology of a discipline is different from the natural language used as meta-language to build up the technical language. Natural language grows in the lips of the man in the street. In spite of the severest control and taboo, by even the most influential academy with the least possible territory of sway, natural language cannot be tied down without growth. Therefore to frame a code of rules entirely in a natural language is to court trouble sooner or later. But the use of a natural language as a meta-language to establish the terminology of a discipline will not lead to much harm. The terminology can grow or change only in the hands of the small specialist class establishing it. Further, this class is presumed to be trained in scientific method and in terminology. This does not mean that cataloguing-terminology can be made once for all. It too must change. But it will be changed with notice, circumspection, and conformity to the Canons of Terminology. These canons themselves are the product of severe scientific method.

8211 EXPECTATION OF LIFE

Convenience requires a fairly long expectation of life in a catalogue code. Changes in it should be few and far between. In this, a catalogue code is comparable to the enacted constitution of a country. The amendments should be even fewer and only after long stretches of time. Agreement on normative principles, pure style without roughage words, and properly defined exclusive terminology, can secure this quality in a catalogue code. The expectation of life of a catalogue code without need for amendments can be increased thereby.

8212 BASIC WORD

The basic word used in the terminology of a catalogue code will have to be naturally different in different natural languages. But the meaning of the corresponding terms in different languages can be and should be made to be strictly alike. The number of technical terms needed in cataloguing-terminology are very few. Moreover, cataloguing terms denote comparatively concrete concepts. Therefore, their meanings can be made precisely alike, with the aid of suitable examples.

8213 MULTI-LINGUAL GLOSSARY

It should be quite possible to have a multi-lingual glossary for the few scores of cataloguing terms. This has been demonstrated splendidly by *Vat* in a separate appendix. The Italians and the Americans sat together to agree on the terminology in their respective languages. And this has had some success. The idea is that one should look up the examples in the text for clarification and concreteness. Therefore, *Vat*'s glossary can serve as a model. This is a fit field for ISO/TC 46. It should promote standard terms for cataloguing. The Ifla should co-operate with it in this matter. But unfortunately, the glossary of library terms recently sponsored by Unesco are nearly anti-model. It is not even complete to any degree. The Kiplingian heresy of East and West never meeting seems to have been its motto. It could have been made useful if :—

1 it had been equally representative of usage in all the areas of the world ;
2 a comparative evaluation of the corresponding terms had been made ;
3 reconciliation had been first made in the ideal plane ;
4 the shades of difference had been brought out ; and then,
5 an attempt had been made to arrive at their reconciliation in the verbal plane.

Perhaps, it may be claimed that the intention was not to cover items 2 to 5. But it could not have been the intention to neglect whole-sale, published glossaries emanating from outside the chosen half of the world.

8214 Guinea Pig

The correct procedure for the Round-Table should be :—

1 To start with, some consistently and organically worked-out terminology in any one natural language ;
2 To find out equivalent terms in other natural languages;
3 To examine their shades of difference in the natural languages, as shown in illustrations ;
4 To see how best terms of precisely the same meaning can be got out of them, either by modification or by official re-definition ; and
5 To see that the resultant terminology in natural language is an organic whole, internally consistent and free from flaws of synonym and homonym.

Some languages, such as English, spoken in distant lands, naturally reflect a tendency to put forth autonomous sub-languages. Here the Round-Table for each linguistic group will have to do some preliminary work to arrive at an agreed common terminology. The terminology built up in chapters 2 and 3 of this book is a sample.

Through a long series of articles and books, and on the basis of teaching the subject for more than a quarter of a century, an endeavour has been made to establish a self-consistent, precise, organic terminology. The one given in chapter 2 is not a copy of what is found in earlier writings. The very process of this comparative study disclosed a few weak points in the terminology in use hitherto. These have now been removed. A long-filtered and progressively rigged-up terminology, like this sample, can be the guinea pig, with which the Round-Table can start with advantage. The main point here is that each catalogue code should have a chapter on self-consistent and fairly exhaustive terminology.

822 NORMATIVE PRINCIPLES

Then should follow a chapter on normative principles. *Rdc* is the only code of the earlier generation, showing evidence of having been guided by some such principles. Of course, these are not stated in one place. With all the flash of a genius, the drafting of the code had been done without explicit enunciation or examination of these principles. But, their unexpressed presence in some level of consciousness is disclosed by the sparkling sentences and phrases scattered throughout its commentaries. *Pin*, *Ala*, and *Vat* have not done so. *Ccc* was guided even at its first draft by a few normative principles at least. But, later intellectual examination of the rules, teaching of them and a comparative study of a few codes, have led to the enunciation of the additional normative principles set down in chapter 3 of this book. This can form the basis of discussion for the Round-Table. A critical study by several competent persons may prove helpful. For example, there is a feeling that the essential Laws of Interpretation, likely to be of value in applying the rules of a catalogue code, should be added. The main point here is that each code should add a chapter on normative principles.

823 MAIN ENTRY—HEADING

Next should come a chapter on Main Entry. Even so, it should be confined to the choice of its heading. *Rdc*, *Ala* and *Vat* have begun that way. But they have spoiled the unity of the rules in the chapter by adding everywhere whole sentences or parts of them on added entries. *Ccc* has avoided this error. But it has-

slipped into another. It has mixed in one chapter rules on choice
as well as rendering. These two are different mental processes.
That these have not been mixed up in one and the same rule, is no
doubt good. But it will be better for the two sets of rules to be put
in different chapters. This will facilitate continuity of thought
on choice. It will be equally so in regard to rendering. This
will also be a help in using the rules in the choice between compet-
ing claimants to the status of heading.

8231 KINDS OF DOCUMENT

This chapter under consideration should deal with the choice
of heading for main entry of every kind of document—simple,
multi-volumed, ordinary composite, artificial composite, periodical
and serial.

8232 KINDS OF CATALOGUE

This chapter should also indicate any difference necessary
in the practice of Classified Catalogue and that of Dictionary
Catalogue.

8233 TO BE AVOIDED

The determination of who the author of a document is, should
not be left to the rules of this chapter. This question should be
settled fully in the sections on author and collaborator in the
chapter on Terminology. Not a little of the inelegance, redundance, and occasionally even fault in *Ala* and *Vat* is traceable to
failure in this respect.

824 RENDERING OF HEADING

The next chapter should be on the rendering of Heading.
Its rules will be applicable to all kinds of entries. It should settle
the question of multi-worded names of different kinds,— of persons,
places, corporate bodies, or their organs, or titles of documents.
These rules should clearly lay down by rules, backed by enumerated
schedules wherever necessary, the method of spotting out the
entry word, entry element, secondary element, impotent but
irremovable element, impotent and removable element, main
heading, and successive sub-headings. These rules will vary with
language and cultural group. The main point here is that each
code should have a chapter on this subject.

825 MAIN ENTRY—SECTIONS OTHER THAN HEADING

The succeeding chapter should give rules for the choice,

rendering and sequence of the sections—other than heading—
that may have to appear in main entry. It should have special
sections of rules on the different kinds of documents mentioned in
section 8231. The number and the nature of these sections will
vary with the nature of the catalogue, the material, and the library.
The main point here is that each code should have a chapter on this
subject.

826 Non-Subject Book Index Entry

The next chapter should be on the choice and rendering of
book index entries other than subject entries of Dictionary Catalogue and cross reference entries of Classified Catalogue. Its
rules should mention the descriptive words to be added to the
heading. If unit card system is not followed, it should also
give rules on other sections. The number and kinds of added
entries to be given will depend on the nature of the library and
the available national and international bibliographies listing
micro thought. The main point here is that each code should
have a chapter on non-subject book index entry.

827 Subject Entry

There should be a chapter on subject entry. In Classified
Catalogue, this would mean " cross reference entry "—*i.e.*, " subject analytical "—and " class index entry." In Dictionary
Catalogue, it would mean " specific subject entry "—or " subject analytical "—and " *see also* subject entry." This is the most
imprecise, inconsistent, and unsatisfactory chapter in the codes
giving them. The *Ccc* and its twin *Dictionary catalogue code* have
tried to bring in some consistency, precision and mechanisation
in this matter, by chain procedure. How far this can be adapted
to documentation work on micro-thought is yet to be seen. The
main point here is that each code should have a chapter on the
choice and rendering of subject heading.

828 Cross Reference Index Entry

There should be a chapter on cross reference index entry.
It should collect together all the rules on this class of entries.
They should not be scattered in the chapters on heading or rendering
of names. This spoils the unity in rules and also irritates or
produces a cloudy sense. No code except *Ccc* has strictly followed

this prescription. Every code will gain in value by following it with equal strictness.

8291 PERIODICAL PUBLICATION

Periodical publication should have an extra chapter. This chapter should deal with the way of handling all the 18 idiosyncrasies to which it is prone.

8292 STYLE OF WRITING

There should also be a chapter on the style of writing, or typing, or printing entries. No doubt, this will depend on the favoured script of the library. The main point here is that there should be a chapter on the style of writing.

8293 ODDS AND ENDS

There should also be chapters on other odds and ends, such as contraction, punctuation mark, capitalisation, arrangement of entries, individualising term and descriptive term. These chapters will also depend on the nature of the catalogue, and the favoured languages of the library. The main point here is that there should be chapters on such odds and ends.

8294 STANDARD PRACTICE

The standard practice for the lay-out of a catalogue code is a fit subject to be taken up by ISO/TC 46 and the corresponding national bodies. The Ifla and the national library associations should work with the standard bodies in this matter. The Documentation Committee of the Indian Standards Institution is taking up this subject.

83 International Catalogue Code

The preceding sections of this chapter show that an international catalogue code cannot give definitive rules in some of its chapters. It may have to give only a blue-print as it were without too many details. Perhaps, it may give some directives in a few cases. It may even give samples. There are, however, some chapters where it can be complete. Such chapters can be incorporated by any other kind of code, in its own favoured language. The others can only be adapted in them.

831 BODILY ADOPTION

The chapters on normative principles, choice of heading for main entry, book index entry, subject entry, cross reference index entry, and periodical publication can be bodily adopted by other codes, from the international code with perhaps omission of a few rules. These chapters should be common in all catalogue codes.

832 DIRECTIVE

The chapters of an international code on rendering of names and style of writing can only be taken as directives by any other code.

833 ADAPTATION

The chapters, on terminology, sections of main entry, other than heading, should be suitably adapted by the other kinds of codes.

84 National Catalogue Code

Language is the very essence of communication. Catalogue is a means of communication. It should therefore be in the language of the nation if it is mono-lingual. The distinctive function of a national catalogue code will therefore be to give precise rules on the style of writing. Again, the structure and the sequence of words in names will be generally a distinguishing feature of a nation with a strictly homogeneous cultural group. Therefore, another distinctive function of a national catalogue code will be to give precise rules on the rendering of names. These rules will have to be backed by the necessary number of schedules of removable impotent elements, irremovable impotent elements, and of other multi-worded entry names. It should also give some fool-proof device for the entry element and the secondary element being distinguished from each other by a foreign cataloguer. The chapters on terminology and odds and ends may have to be adapted by it from those in the international catalogue code. But it will adopt bodily all the other chapters, including the one on sections of main entry other than heading. It is by the effective carrying out of the directives of the international code that a national catalogue code can make itself as useful to outsiders as to its own people. Further, the adaptation of the terminology in full conformity to the explanations and the examples of the international code will help the building up of multi-lingual glossaries of cataloguing terms.

85 Regional Catalogue Code

Some countries consist of cultural sub-groups and linguistic sub-groups. There should be several regional catalogue codes in such a country. In their case, a national catalogue code cannot go far beyond an international catalogue code. Therefore, all the remarks of section 84 will be applicable to them. India, Russia, Switzerland, Yugoslavia and Czechoslovakia are examples of such countries. Reciprocally, there are two or more countries more or less of the same culture and language. It will be a help if they agree to have a common regional catalogue code. Great Britain, Australia and United States can have a single regional catalogue code.

86 Local Catalogue Code

The main function of a local catalogue code—say, the catalogue code of a particular library—will be to adapt the rules of the national or the regional catalogue code so as to suit the Principle of Local Variation. There may not therefore be a need to have a full-fledged local catalogue code. A supplement to the national or regional catalogue code, showing the policy of economy adopted by the library will be sufficient. But it is necessary. For cataloguers may come and cataloguers may go ; but the catalogue will go on for ever. Even in the lifetime of the same cataloguer, it is difficult for him—to be consistent without the aid of a recorded supplement. Otherwise, the library catalogue will soon become a hotch-potch. Moreover, the Canon of Currency and the Fifth Law of Library Science are not unmindful of the library catalogue. Even before the published national or regional catalogue code comes out in a new edition incorporating the latest alterations, the supplement of a local library catalogue should provisionally make all such alterations in its supplement, as and when they become necessary. A periodical revision of the catalogue code, at the national, regional, and/or international levels will have to be fed realistically by such tentative alterations introduced in local catalogue codes, along with samples of the documents necessitating them.

87 Bibliophilic Catalogue Code

In the case of a bibliographical descriptive catalogue, whether of incunabula or even later documents, a special bibliophilic catalogue code will be necessary. It will have to add many more rules to those of an international code. In this respect they are different from the other kinds of codes. There are already many such codes in different countries. They are promoted by bibliographical societies.

88 With Standard for Title-Page

The rules on rendering of names and on cross reference index entries will be simplified beyond measure, after the adoption of an international standard for author-statement on the title-page and its supplement on its back, described in chapter 7 of this book.

CHAPTER 9

EPILOGUE

A wish cherished through twenty years is now fulfilled by the Grace of God. The Unesco projects on the Rendering of Asian Names and of the Union Catalogue of Learned Periodical Publications in South Asia led to a tight grip with the tangled problems of personal and corporate authorship. Prayerful thanks to Providence for arranging this experience. The pressure of this experience gave an insight into the present book. This makes a closer approximation than the *Theory*. Even that first approximation of eighteen years ago owed itself to the unsolicited advice of two spiritual friends and the unexpected contact with a colleague in the profession living at the antipodes, though then unknown to me. Thus, we are but channels. We should be participating channels. True way is the way of Acceptance.

90 Introduction

Library organisation in the world calls for considerable rationalisation. Rationalisation calls for the formulation and adoption of international standard and simplification of library practices. These should cover the information to be carried by the title-page and its over-flow, catalogue code, and scheme of classification. The amenability of these to international standardisation is perhaps in decreasing order. But the adoption of international standard in these will, without doubt, lead to economy. It will lead to a better utilisation of library man-power in local, national and international levels. This will release more library man-power for the essential and culminating phase of library service—reference service to give intimate personal help to every reader. This will mean better fulfilment of the Laws of Library Science. This will increase the socialisation and circulation of thought, created in every country, throughout the world at large. This in its turn will increase the social benefits of library service.

91 Local Economy

In a library accessioning 5,000 books in a year, there will be a saving of about one thousand dollars a year by the adoption of an international standard for the title-page and its over-flow. These figures are based on the staff-formula given in the *Library manual* (1953) of Ranganathan. There should be standards for the following :—

1 Indication by typographical variation, of the Entry Element, the Entry Word, the Secondary Element, and the removable Puff Element in the name(s) of author(s) and collaborator(s), to help in rendering of heading of entry.

2 Statement of the year of birth of author(s) and of collaborator(s) (and also year of death in the case of deceased persons), to help in resolution of homonyms in personal headings.

3 Indication of corporate authorship—government, institution or conference—to help in choice of corporate author heading.

4 Indication, wherever necessary, of the specific organ of the corporate body, which is the specific author, for choice and rendering of subheading(s) in corporate author heading.

5 Statement of each alternative name(s) of author(s) and collaborator(s)—including real name and pseudonym—used in other books, to help in disclosing all the books by a person.

92 National Organisation

Library development plan (1950) and *Library legislation* (1953) of Ranganathan developed the theme of National Library System. According to it, the libraries in a country should be linked as in a grid, with one another, with the NCL (= National Central Library) as the central station, and each of the other libraries as a substation for local service. The idea ' grid ' covers not only book selection, book service and library personnel, but also TW (= Technical Work = Clssification and Cataloguing)—group 1— and preparation of general bibliographies and documentation lists featuring micro thought embodied in articles, in periodicals and portions of books—group 2. The former group should admit of interchange ; and for this purpose it should conform to a national standard stated in broad terms. However all the items in that group have essentially a personal or local element in them ; they should all therefore be decentralised ; they should be left to the care of each local library. On the other hand, most of the items in the second group have hardly any personal element ; they are mostly impersonal ; they admit of centralisation.   Much of TW definitely admits of centralisation without any reservation.

921 CENTRALISED TECHNICAL WORK

Tradition makes each library do all the TW—from beginning to end, completely—with its own technical staff.   As a result, hundreds of copies of the same book are perused, classified and catalogued independently by the technical staff of each library. But a more rational practice in a national library system is to centralise in the NCL the non-local part of TW.   The separation of TW into local and non-local parts will become clear in sections 923 and 924.   Such a centralisation had been conceived by Jewett more than a centuy ago, as indicated in chapter 62 of the *Theory*. But it took nearly a century for the old tradition to be broken at least in some countries ; indeed such is the tenacity of tradition in any sphere of human life.

922 NATIONAL CENTRALISATION

The first stage in national centralisation of cataloguing was brought into vogue in the United States in 1901.   From then, the Library of Congress prints the catalogue card of each book. Copies of this card are available for sale.   I saw such a system in vogue in Denmark also during my tour in 1948.   The Bibliographical Institute was in charge of the work.   Since 1950, the *British national bibliography* is unobtrusively and obliquely influencing the British libraries to accept centralised TW.   It does not yet print cards.   But it will eventually do so.   This quiet and slow transformation is a characteristic of the British genius.

923 PRE-NATAL TECHNICAL WORK

While addressing a gathering of librarians in the Whittal Pavilion of the Library of Congress in August 1948, I happened to coin the terms Pre-natal Classification and Pre-natal Cataloguing. Full-fledged Pre-natal TW means the following items :—

1 Each publisher sends to the NCL a copy of the forme proof of each book.

2 The technical staff of the NCL completes the TW on each book before its release by the publisher.

3 The NCL gives a Finding Number for each book.   It consists of the three facets :—

    (1) Country   Number ;   (2) Year   Number   and

(3) Serial Number. For example 44,1955,2349 will be the Finding Number of the 2349th book published in 1955 in India—rather on which the NCL of India completed the TW.

4 The NCL inserts the finding number in the right hand top corner of the catalogue card of the book.

5 The publisher gets the finding number printed in a conventional place on the back of the title page of the book.

6 The publisher gives the NCL a proof copy of the Prels (= Preliminary Pages) of the book and also the correct details of the format and collation of the book simultaneously with the last forme being put to bed in the press.

7 NCL prepares the master stencil of the catalogue card of the book before its release by the publisher.

8 The NCL publishes, on a daily or weekly or any other suitable periodical basis, the primary instalment of the national bibliography.

9 The national bibliography as well as each trade list, published by any publisher or bookseller, or collectively by publishers' and booksellers' organisation, gives the finding number of each title.

10 The master stencils of catalogue.cards are kept by the NCL filed by their finding numbers.

11 It is sufficient for a library to mention merely the finding number in any book order.

12 Each library sends to the NCL a copy of each of its book orders.

13 The NCL sends to the library, copies of the catalogue card of each finding number in the order, in quantity sufficient for use as main card, added book entry cards, and shelf register card.

14 Each library returns to the NCL the catalogue cards of a book not procurable.

15 The NCL marks in the union catalogue of national books, maintained by it, the name of the library against each book on a report from the library concerned or on the basis of the cards of the unprocurable books returned by it.

924 RESIDUAL WORK

Pre-natal TW will leave only the following residual work to be done by each local or service library :—

1 Conversion of each of the catalogue cards of a book into the respective main, book index and shelf regtister cards by inserting in their respective leading sections the call number or the heading as the case may be, and the sequence symbol.

2 Whenever necessary, inserting the copy number in the book number in each of the cards.

3 Checking up the catalogue file of the library to find out if any additional general index card is necessary for a book—such as *See also* subject card if a dictionary catalogue, class index card if a classified catalogue, and cross reference index cards in both cases.

4 Preparation of the general index card found necessary.

5 Filing the catalogue cards.

93 National Economy

To get a concrete picture of the national economy resulting from pre-natal TW, we shall take a typical national library system and assume the following data :—

1 Number of publications in the country in a year,—10,000.

2 Number of local or service libraries in the country,—1,000.

3 Average number of annual accessions of books published in the country, in each local or service library,—5,000.

4 Number of technical persons required for TW if there is no centralisation—1 for every 1,000 books accessioned in a year.

5 Number of technical persons required for the residual work described in section 24,—1 for every 5,000 books accessioned in a year.

6 Number of persons required in the NCL for the sending of catalogue cards to the other libraries,—1 for every 100,000 books, to be attended to in a year.

7 Annual average gross emolument of a technical person,— Rs. 4,000 = 1,000 dollars = £300.

Without Centralised Pre-Natal Technical Work

Staff required :—NCL : 10 ; All the other libraries taken together : 5,000 ; Total : 5,010.

With Centralised Pre-Natal Technical Work

Staff required :—NCL : 60 ; All the other libraries taken together : 1,000 ; Total : 1,060.

Saving in staff : 3,950.

Annual saving in staff emoluments, in round figures : 3,950,000 dollars.

931 Formula for National Saving on Home-Produced Books

The annual national saving in the TW on books produced within the country, resulting from centralised pre-natal TW, may be expressed by the following formula :—

$$\frac{79 \, a \, L \, p}{100,000}, \text{ where}$$

a = annual accession of home-produced books in a local or service library

L = number of local or service libraries in the country

p = annual average gross emolument of a member of the technical staff.

932 National Saving on Home-Produced Books as a Percentage

Expressed in percentage, the national saving will be $\dfrac{79 \, a \, L}{a \, L + n}$, where n = number of home-produced books in a year.

As $a \, L$ will be large when compared with n, the saving may be taken to be approximately 79%.

933 Further National Saving

There is another step possible in national economy. A local or service library need not have its own file of catalogue cards for public use. This would mean the following items in organisation, work and service :—

The NCL publishes not only the primary instalment of national bibliography mentioned in category 8 of section 923, but also cumulations of it at intervals such as week, month, three months six months as may be found necessary, and also a cumulated annual national bibliography, a cumulated quinquennial national bibliography, and if found worthwhile, a decennial national bibliography.

3 Each local library buys a few copies of the primary instalment of the national bibliography and marks its own holdings in them for public use.

4 Each local library buys copies of the necessary cumulations, to be marked for its own holdings and put up for public use.

5 Each local library maintains three sets of catalogue cards for its books. These cards are bought from the NCL. One set is arranged parallel to the location of the books on the shelves in the main and branch libraries, for use as shelf register. The second set is arranged by the finding numbers, to enable the staff to know if a particular book is in its holdings or not. The third set also is arranged by finding number, to enable the public to know if a particular book, whose finding number they pick up in the printed national bibliography, is in the library or not ; this is an additional help even if the printed catalogue is marked. Each card in each set will of course have the location symbol for the book marked on it.

6 Perhaps each local library may also buy the national bibliography in bulk for distribution to the public gratis or on a nominal price. It may be sufficient if this is done for the weekly or monthly editions. I saw it being done in Danish libraries. This will make book selection get closely correlated to the needs of the clientale of the library. It will also widen the reading interests of the public. Incidentally such bulk purchase by local libraries will bring down the cost of production and the net cost per copy.

7 In one official copy of the quinquennial (and decennial) cumulations, the holdings of the library may perhaps be marked. This is however of doubtful value. Its cost implications should be worked out.

A book loses most of its potency and demand within ten years. If it has still value, there is every chance for a new edition to come out. There will not therefore be need to have cumulative editions of the national catalogue covering longer intervals. The few readers wanting older books may help themselves by looking through successive quinquennials (or decennials).

This further measure of national economy needs investigation. It may even prove to be of doubtful value. This idea suggested itself to me when I visited the Middlesex Library System in 1948, where the branch libraries were run without catalogues for their collections, if my memory is right.

94 International Organisation

Books of one country are taken in another country. Can

there be any economy possible by a world-centralisation of the impersonal TW on books ? The answer is " No ". Pre-natal TW in a World Central Library with world copyright is even more remote in realisation than pre-natal TW within one country. Secondly a monolithic world bibliography, on the lines of a monolithic national bibliography, is impracticable. Language and script will stand in its way. Distance will cause time-lag thwarting prompt production. There will not be adequate return on the man-power and money to be invested on it. The number of users interested in seeing an exhaustive catalogue of the books in all languages will not justify it. A practicable and sufficient approximation to a world bibliography is a collection of the national bibliographies of all the countries. This does not mean that no international organisation of the production of library catalogues can produce any economy whatever. An organisation, on co-operative lines can lead to considerable economy. This is shown in the succeeding sections.

941 INTERNATIONAL CO-OPERATION

International co-operation along economic lines is possible in the field of TW. In describing it, the following symbols will be a convenience :—

    1   D = Foreign Country whose language is different from that of the home country.

    2   F = Foreign country.

    3   H = Home country.

    4   S = Foreign country whose language is the same as that of the home country.

International co-operation implies several items as shown in the succeeding sub-sections.

9411 General

1 The NCL of each country does centralised pre-natal TW, as described in section 92 and its sub-divisions.

2 The NCL of each country has an International Exchange Bureau as the promoter and channel for all international exchange of books.

3 There is prompt exchange of all the instalments of national bibliographies between the NCLs of all the countries.

4 Any order even for a foreign book is made only by finding number.

9412 Foreign Book of S Country

1 Each S country, while sending a book on exchange or as gift to the NCL or any local or service library of H, sends, with the copy of the book, copies of its catalogue cards, sufficient in number for use as main card, added book entry cards, shelf register card and a card for the Union Catalogue of Foreign Books, maintained at the NCL of H.

2 A copy of the order for a book of S, emanating from any library—NCL or local library—of H, is sent to the NCL of the S concerned.

3 The bookseller or publisher in S handling the order collects from the NCL of S the necessary number of the catalogue cards of the book, as indicated in category 1 mentioned above, and sends them along with the book.

4 Each local library in H sends to the NCL in H a copy of the catalogue card for use in the Union Catalogue of Foreign Books, after marking on it the Library Number assigned to it by the NCL.

9413 Foreign Book of D Country

1 Each D country, while sending a book on exchange or as gift to any library in H, sends to the NCL of H one copy of the catalogue card of the book. It may be sufficient if it does so when the first copy of the book is sent to some library or other in H.

2 Guided by the catalogue card received from the NCL of D, the NCL of H prepares the stencil for its catalogue card in the language and script of H. This stencil mentions also the finding number of the book, already given to it by D.

3 While sending the exchange copy to the local library concerned, the NCL of H sends also the necessary number of its catalogue cards in the language and script of H.

4 A copy of the order for any book of a D country, emanating from any local library in H, is sent to the NCL of H.

5 If the NCL of H has a stencil for its catalogue card, it sends to the local library concerned the necessary number of catalogue cards.

6 If the NCL of H has not got the stencil for the book ordered, it gets a catalogue card for the book from the NCL of the D concerned, prepares the stencil in the language and script of H and sends the catalogue cards to the local library concerned.

7 For a book ordered by the NCL of H from a D country, procedure analogous to that described in 5 and 6 above is followed.

9414 Work at NCL of H on Union Catalogue of Foreign Books

1 From sections 9412 and 9413, it follows that the NCL of H has information of all foreign books coming into any library of H. It has also got stencil for the catalogue card of each D book.

2 It maintains a Union Catalogue of Foreign Books with the cards arranged by their finding numbers.

3 Behind the card of each book in the Union Catalogue of Foreign Books, it inserts a holdings card, indicating all the local libraries in H by their respective Library Numbers. A convenient system of Library Numbers, built on the Principle of Geographical Contiguity and helpful in advising local libraries of the nearest library for inter-library loan, has been described and used in the *Union catalogue of learned periodicals in South-East Asia* of Ranganathan. It indicates the library holding of the book by putting a mark on its library number in the holdings card of the book.

4 It publishes a Union Catalogue of Foreign Books at intervals and in cumulations, to be determined from experience about its use and the cost involved.

942 RESIDUAL WORK

By the international co-operation described in section 941 and its subdivisions, much of the TW on books coming into the country from F countries is saved in the NCL. It is saved even more in a local library. There will however be some residual work to be done in each library.

9421 NCL. Book from S

The residual work to be done at the NCL on a book from S is

1 similar to that described in section 924, for a book added to itself; and

2 marking in the holdings card of the book in the Union Catalogue of Foreign Books, whether the book is an addition to its own stock or to that of a local library.

9422 NCL. Book from D

The residual work to be done at the NCL on a book from D is

1 preparing a stencil for its catalogue card ;

2 same as in 1 of section 9421 ; and

3 same as in 2 in section 9421.

9423 Local Library

The residual work to be done by a local library on any foreign book is similar to that described in section 924.

95 International Economy

To get a concrete picture of the international economy, likely to result from international co-operation in TW, we shall first calculate the saving in a single national library system. In doing so, we shall make the following assumptions in addition to those mentioned in section 3 :—

8 Number of annual accessions of S books in NCL,—10,000.

9 Number of annual accessions of D books in NCL,—80,000.

10 Number of annual accessions of S books in a local library, —3,000.

11 Number of annual accessions of D books in a local library, —2,000.

12 Number of annual accessions, in all the local libraries taken together, of distinct D books, different from those accessioned in the NCL,—40,000.

13 Number of technical staff required for the residual work in the NCL, mentioned as category 1 in section 9422, on a D book, —1 for every 4,000 books to be attended to in a year.

Without International Co-operation

Staff required :—NCL : 90 ; All the local libraries taken together : 5,000 ; and Total : 5,090.

With International Co-operation

Staff required :—NCL : 82 ; All the local libraries taken together : 1,000 ; Total : 1,082.

Saving in staff :—4,008.

Annual savings in staff emoluments :—4,008,000 dollars in round figures.

951 FORMULA FOR
NATIONAL SAVING ON FOREIGN BOOKS

The annual national saving in the TW on the foreign books

coming into the country, obtainable from international co-operation, may be expressed by the following formula :—

$$\frac{160 \ S + 125 \ D + 158 \ (T + E) \ L}{200,000} \ p, \ \text{where},$$

D = Number of books from D countries, accessioned in the NCL in a year.

E = Number of books from D countries, accessioned in a local library in a year.

L = Number of local libraries.

p = Annual average gross emolument of a member of the technical staff.

S = Number of books from S countries, accessioned in the NCL in a year.

T = Number of books from S countries, accessioned in a local library in a year.

It is assumed that the number of distinct books from D countries, accessioned in all the local libraries taken together but not accessioned in the NCL, is $\dfrac{D}{2}$.

952 NATIONAL SAVING ON FOREIGN BOOKS AS A PERCENTAGE

Expressed in percentage, the national saving on foreign books will be

$$\frac{160 \ S + 125 \ D + 158 \ (T + E) \ L}{2 \ \{ S + D + (T + E) \ L \}}$$

As $(T + E) \ L$ will be so dominant that $S + D$ and $160S + 125D$ may be ignored, the saving may be taken to be approximately 79%.

96 Pre-Requisite

The pre-requisites for effecting local, national and international economy in the organisation of library system, in the measure indicated by the above-mentioned formulae, are :

1 Establishment and adoption of an international standard for the author-statement and other details in the title-page and its back ;

2 Framing and adoption of an international catalogue code ;

3 Framing and adoption of a national catalogue code in each country, using the international catalogue code as its core

278

and adding its own supplementary rules for the style of printing and for spotting out entry element, entry word, secondary element, irremovable impotent element and removable puff element in rendering the name of personal author, as current in the culture of the country ;

4 Adoption of an expressive, individualising, analytico-synthetic scheme of classification. This will be a convenience and not a necessity ; and

5 Prevalence of peaceful intercourse between nations (at least in regard to library co-operation).

97 Benefit

Manifold benefits will flow from rationalisation of library organisation in general and of technical work on books in particular, on national and international basis. A useful by-product will be a stimulus to circulation of the profound and perennial thought of the past and of the nascent and productive thought of the present, within a nation as well as across national barriers. International standards in classification and cataloguing will facilitate the production and use of secondary appetising reference materials, such as indexing and abstracting periodicals, designed to bring micro thought to the notice of all likely consumers scattered all through the world. This will add its own quota to economy in the organisation of the service of published thought. The general social benefit of the rationalisation suggested will fall into two categories—immediate and ultimate.

971 IMMEDIATE SOCIAL BENEFIT

The immediate social benefit will result from the release of four out of every five technical personnel in every local service library from impersonal work on books behind the screen, to personal service to readers, outside the screen in the stack room. At present, the maximum benefit is not drawn for the community, from the socialised knowledge stored in library in the form of reading materials. This failure is due to causes of commission and omission. A book is an artificial entity ; a higher order of artificiality becomes inevitable in the organisation of a large collection. The urge for knowledge or information often evaporates in reader, before the right book is got ; for, intellectual urge is fleeting ; it is not compelling as physical or emotional urge. Social

economy and well-being depend, however, on the harnessing of
intellectual urge in as many persons as possible. No technique,
no gadget, and no publicity can retain customers to intellectual
service, all by themselves. No doubt they are all necessary ; but
they are not sufficient. To produce the maximum result, these
mechanical devices should be dowered by the personality of reference librarians. There should be a sufficient number of reference
librarians to take each reader in hand, to help him through the
multitude of mute books and across the inevitable barrier of
library conventions in shelf-arrangement and cataloguing, to parti-
cipate with him in sharpening the enunciation of his needs and in
finding, without loss of time, all the necessary reading materials
relevant to his pursuit at the moment, and to be of aid in arranging
them in a decreasing order of pertinence. This is the paramount
social purpose of library as a social institution. Work and money
spent in selecting, acquiring, and organising reading materials will
become a waste in the measure of the inadequacy of the reference
librarians provided in library. Minimising of technical man-power
on impersonal technical work on books and maximising it on direct,
personal service to readers are therefore necessary. This is secured
by the rationalisation implied in the standardisation of title-page
and its back and the national centralisation and international co-
operation in the technical work on books. The immediate social
benefit will be a better cultiavation and utilisation of the mental
resources of a nation to improve social well-being.

972 ULTIMATE SOCIAL BENEFIT

The transfer of about 80% of the technical man-power of a
library system from desk-work to floor-service, will lead to a better
fulfilment of the Laws of Library Science. It will make people
better informed and more enlightened. This will gradually step
up their material sufficiency and happiness, and their intellectual
awareness, creativeness and joy. As these increase, they will
increase the chance for emotional sublimation and spiritual delight.
Further, international co-operation in library technique will gradually lead to an intensification of the spirit of co-operative sharing
of all the best thought created from time to time among the people
of the world, whatever be the differences in cultural heritage.
This may lead to the minimising of some of the miseries of the

humans inhabiting the earth.   One of the causes of misery is mutual violence meant or practised by the groups encircled by national boundaries.   Part of the violence is born of mutual fear.   Part of the fear is born of mutual suspicion.   Suspicion is born of ignorance of the true mind of one another.   Library socialises thought. International library co-operation will socialise the thought of every national group among every other national group.   It will internationalise thought.   Bad thought laid bare to the world-community will get sterilised.   Good thought circulated among the world-community will lead to the creation of better thought. Libraries will thus become messengers of light.   Light will remove mutual ignorance of true thought, among the national groups. Removal of ignorance will lead to the subsidence of mutual suspicion.   Subsidence of suspicion will lead to abandonment of mutual fear.   Abandonment of fear will lead to the outlawing of violence between national groups.   Non-violence will ultimately characterise world-order.   This is about one cause of violence. Another cause of violence among national groups is due to inequality in population pressure and economic resources.   The pervasion of the spirit of non-violence made possible by the removal of the first cause of violence will arouse willingness to prevent the co-existence of economic insufficiency in some countries and economic hoarding or even destruction in others.   This may make nations accede to an equitable distribution of the economic resources of the world as a whole.   As a result of such re-inforcement of the spirit of non-violence and mutual love among nations, the effects of the still-surviving lust in an individual for spontaneous cruelty will be localised ; it will be quenched before it swells to national or international dimensions.   Thus by the promotion of international co-operation in library service, the library profession will make its own contribution to the ultimate benefit of

    1 the development of each of the nations of the world towards its own fulness at its own speed and along its own lines ;

    2 the development of an atmosphere of peaceful co-existence among nations ; and

    3 the evolution of One-World.

      May Every Human Group Become Happy !

        लोका : समस्था : सुखिनो भवन्तु ।

INDEX

Geographical (*Contd.*)
   i r t (*Contd.*)
      rendering 52
  species 5253
  versus
     personal name 5254
     work name 5254
German woman's name 5143
Gild 2288
Given name
  as entry word in
     Burmese name 5123
     Viet-Namese name 5124
  in
     Europe 51102
     India 5130
     South India 51306
  split in
     Bengal 51303
     South India 514
     Uttar Pradesh 51304
Gjelsness *r i r t*
  genesis of catalogue code 11
  Theory of library catalogue 186
Glossary of cataloguing terms 8213
Gothra name 5130
Government
  def 2281
  i r t
    heading 53
    standard practice for prel. pages
                    708
  vs institution 2285
Governmental
  heading 7022
  serial 5678
  series 3328
Grammatical variant
  entry 6253
  i r t title 5674
Grid 92
Growth 32
Gross name 502
Guinea pig 8214
Gujarati
  double family name 514
  name 51302

Half title page 3311
Hanson 16
Head of government 531
Heading 4
  def 281
  i r t
    claimants 3332
    genesis 11
    lay-out of catalogue code 824
    Theory of library catalogue 187

Heading and canons 187
Hindi name 51304
Hindu name 5135
Hinduism
  Post-Vedic 5612
  Vedic 5611
Historical information 5262
Homonym, Artificial *see*
  Artificial homonym
Homonym
  def 283
  i r t
    administrative organ 5345
    catalogue code 812
    conference 55
    geographical name 525
      heading 2831
    individualising element 507
    institution 541
    judiciary 5352
    personal name 518
    place heading 54051
    title 565
Honorific
  i r t
    Burmese name 5123
    Indonesian name 5126
    South Indian name 5135
    Thai name 5125
  Scheduling of 51931
Hospital 2288
Human ecology 06
Hungarian double name 5142
Husband-wife double name 5143
Hyphenation in Viet-Namese name
                  5124

Imitation 2274
Imperial Edict 5122
Impotent attachment 504
Imprint 2305
Inconsistent rule 5622
Incorporated society 5435
Incunabula 3341
Index 2274
Indian
  Library Association 343
  name 513
  National Commission for Co-opera-
    tion with Unesco 343
  prefixed name 5155
Individualising element
  def 284
  i r t
    Head of government 5313
    lay-out of catalogue code 8293
    rendering 5071
Indonesian name 5126

BOOKS
by or edited by
Dr S R Ranganathan

(Continued from back of half title page)

17 Classification and communication, 1951.

18 Classified catalogue code, 1934, 1945, 1951.

19 Colon classification, 1933, 1939, 1950, 1952.

20 Dictionary catalogue code, 1945, 1952.

21 Education for leisure, 1946, 1949, 1954.

22 Elements of library classification, 1945.

23 Library catalogue : Fundamentals and procedure, 1950.

24 Library development plan, with draft library bills for Union Government and the Constituent States, 1950.

25 Library legislation : Handbook to Madras Library Act, 1953.

26 Literature for neo-literates, 1953.

27 Philosophy of library classification, 1951.

28 Preface to library science, 1949.

29 Rural adult education, 1949.

30 School and college libraries, 1942.

31 Social bibliography : Physical bibliography for librarians, authors and publishers, 1952.

32 Social education literature, 1952.

(Continued on page 300)

Copies available with :—

1 S. Viswanathan, 11 McNichol Road, Madras-31.

2 G. Blunt and Sons, 100 Great Russell Street, London-W.C. 1.

BOOKS
by or edited by
Dr S R Ranganathan

(*Continued from page* 299)

33 Bibliography of reference books and bibliographies, 1941.

34 Classification and international documentation, 1948.

35 Classification, coding and machinery for search, 1950.

36 Classification of Marathi Literature, 1945.

37 Classification of Telugu Literature, 1947.

38 Indian library directory, 1951.

39 Library administration, 1935.

40 Library development plan for the University of Allahabad, 1947. (reprinted as part of Mootham Report on Allahabad University, 1953).

41 Library development plan with a draft library bill for Bombay, 1947.

42 Library development plan for the United Provinces, 1949.

43 Model library act, 1931.

44 Model public library bill, 1941.

45 National library system : a plan for India, 1946.

46 Papers offered to the Library Service Section of the All Asia Education Conference (2 V) 1930-31.

47 Postwar reconstruction of libraries in India, 1944.

48 University reform in contemporary India, 1952.

Note :—The above books are out of print.